Principles and practices in
arithmetic teaching

Principles and practices in arithmetic teaching

Innovative approaches for the primary classroom

edited by
Julia Anghileri

Open University Press
Buckingham · Philadelphia

Open University Press
Celtic Court
22 Ballmoor
Buckingham
MK18 1XW

email: enquiries@openup.co.uk
world wide web: www.openup.co.uk

and
325 Chestnut Street
Philadelphia, PA 19106, USA

First Published 2001

A catalogue record of this book is available from the British Library

ISBN   0 335 20633 6 (pb)   0 335 20634 4 (hb)

Library of Congress Cataloging-in-Publication Data
Principles and practices in arithmetic teaching: innovative approaches for the primary classroom/[edited by] Julia Anghileri.
    p.   cm.
    Includes bibliographical references and index.
    ISBN 0-335-20633-6 (pbk.) – ISBN 0-335-20634-4 (hc.)
    1. Arithmetic–Study and teaching (Primary)   I. Anghileri, Julia.

QA135.5.P732 2000
372.7'2044–dc21   00-023299

Typeset by Type Study, Scarborough
Printed in Great Britain by St Edmundsbury Press, Bury St Edmunds, Suffolk

With thanks to my colleagues at Homerton,
to Meindert, and most especially to Bob.

Contents

List of tables

List of figures

List of contributors

Julia Anghileri (editor), Homerton College, University of Cambridge, England

Mike Askew, King's College, University of London, England

Meindert Beishuizen, University of Leiden, the Netherlands

Margaret Brown, King's College, University of London, England

Kees Buys, Bekadidact/SLO, the Netherlands

Koeno Gravemeijer, Freudenthal Institute, University of Utrecht, the Netherlands and Vanderbilt University, Nashville, Tennessee, USA

Julie Menne, Freudenthal Institute, University of Utrecht, the Netherlands

Kenneth Ruthven, University of Cambridge School of Education, England

Ian Thompson, University of Newcastle upon Tyne, England

Marja van den Heuvel-Panhuizen, Freudenthal Institute, University of Utrecht, the Netherlands

Erna Yackel, Purdue University Calumet, Hammond, Indiana, USA

Preface

International comparisons have revealed differences in pupils' performances on arithmetic tests and this has generated considerable interest among mathematics educators and the general population because all agree that competence with numbers should be a fundamental outcome of school learning. The interest can be extended beyond the comparison of scores in pencil and paper tests, to share practices that exist in different countries in order to establish the characteristics of effective practice. It is this desire to become better informed about existing practices, and the manner in which they have been developed, that has led to the exchange of ideas contained in this book. The contributors are leading mathematics educators in England, the Netherlands and the USA, who have been directly involved in recent developments in their respective countries, and who are uniquely positioned to give insight into the reasoning behind the changes, explaining and challenging the directions arithmetic teaching is taking.

As near neighbours, the populations of England and Holland have many similarities and the exchange of ideas is facilitated by easy communication. Discussions between colleagues, and exchange visits, have led to a better understanding of the different views on teaching that are characteristic of the two countries. Both countries are experiencing curriculum changes in mathematics in primary schools: in England, through the implementation of a National Numeracy Strategy in every state primary school, and in the Netherlands through the Realistic Mathematics Education approach which is now used in almost 90 per cent of Dutch primary schools. This book attempts to identify some of the key issues that have arisen and invite reflection on the way practices may be developed to help both teachers and learners.

This book brings together the views and experiences of researchers and practitioners from England and the Netherlands who consider the evidence of research and challenge traditional approaches. An overview from a colleague in the USA extends the discussion to reflect issues not only common to the three nations represented by the authors, but that are of interest across the world. This book is intended to stimulate discussion and challenge practices with the anticipation of not only raising standards, but of improving teachers' and pupils' experiences in the classroom.

⊖ Part I

Setting the agenda for arithmetic teaching and learning

Many countries have recently proposed changes to their curriculum in mathematics for children in primary school with a view to raising the standards of achievement, particularly in number work. The motivation for this drive to raise standards stems partly from an acknowledgement of the increased needs in technological society for skills in mathematical problem solving, but also as a response to international comparisons that have been made in recent years. Such comparisons have given arithmetic a high profile in research and curriculum development, and have prompted mathematics educators to look beyond their national traditions to consider alternative approaches to teaching number.

It is agreed that traditional methods, involving all children learning and practising the same routine procedures, should be replaced by approaches that develop their ability to reason mathematically, and to transfer skills to new situations. Focus has shifted from teaching methods whereby skills were learned in a rote fashion, to teaching approaches that value the pupils' own thinking and encourage mental calculating strategies. The trends in arithmetic teaching that were reported in the 1980s showed similarities across different countries (Shuard 1986b). In her summary, Hilary Shuard outlined the developing objectives, noting that 'number work is no less important but more time is to be spent on helping children to acquire the really important number concepts and skills'. The common characteristics were reflected in those identified as central in the Primary Initiatives in Mathematics Education (PrIME) project, which included the aims to develop pupils':

- ability to translate from a real life situation to the needed number calculation; and to apply the answer back into the situation;
- understanding of how numbers work and a friendly feeling for numbers and their properties;
- ability to calculate in one's head, obtaining exact results with small numbers, and approximate answers with larger numbers;

- ability to make sensible use of calculators as a labour-saving device when mental calculation is too burdensome for the individual;
- ability to tackle a new problem with confidence and interest.

(Shuard 1986a: 2)

These goals have been the fundamental basis for many curriculum changes that have ensued. There is a consensus of agreement about most of these aims for arithmetic teaching across different countries, but there are differences in the routes to achieving them in terms of the priorities for the desired outcomes and the practical implications for the classroom. In this section Julia Anghileri and Erna Yackel introduce some of the more recent developments in arithmetic teaching and establish the way research has been influential.

Julia Anghileri is a principal lecturer and researcher in mathematics education at Homerton College, University of Cambridge, with experience as a consultant and advisor in curriculum reform. In Chapter 1, she identifies some of the key issues affecting arithmetic teaching, and discusses differences in the teaching methods that have been developed in England and in the Netherlands. By introducing some of the characteristics that are fundamental in different approaches to calculating, she alerts the reader to issues that are central in the subsequent chapters. Such issues are not confined to English and Dutch discussions but typify the research and analysis that is taking place across the world as schools implement changes in arithmetic teaching that will prepare their pupils appropriately for life in an everchanging society.

The roles of *counting* and *place value*, as the basis for developing calculating strategies, contrast the Dutch and English approaches, while the use of *textbooks* and *apparatus/manipulatives* show differences in classroom practice. Whole class interactive teaching is questioned only in the English approach where small group work and even individualized tasks have, in the past, been recommended. Other key issues introduced in this section include the role of calculators and their impact on learning.

Erna Yackel is a key researcher at Purdue University Calumet in the United States of America where her studies with colleagues in the USA and in Europe have been influential in curriculum development, and related research findings have been used to challenge and change established practices. In the second chapter of this section she highlights some perspectives on teaching arithmetic that have resulted from classroom-based research. Central to this chapter is the need to resolve the tension that can exist between computational proficiency and conceptual understanding as the focus of arithmetic instruction. While noting that in the USA, the focus in arithmetic teaching is typically on children's learning the standard algorithms and becoming proficient at applying them to all situations, Yackel describes research that does not focus on algorithm development per se, but on students' development of the concept of number by associating quantities with visual images. Yackel observes that classroom experiences involving instructional materials can orientate the children's thinking towards different strategies even when the materials are no longer present and questions which materials, in which sequence, should be encouraged. She identifies teaching approaches that encourage the development of thinking strategies, using instructional techniques that involve children in explaining and justifying their thinking, and through which the majority of children develop their own efficient algorithms.

⊖ 1

Contrasting approaches that challenge tradition

Julia Anghileri

Introduction

Existing practices in arithmetic teaching in England have recently been under review, with a government appointed Numeracy Task Force reporting on reform to be implemented through a National Numeracy Strategy (DfEE 1998a). This reform is guided by way of the *Framework for Teaching Mathematics from Reception to Year 6* (DfEE 1999a) that will be the basis for the National Curriculum (DfEE 1999b), the latest statutory requirements for teaching mathematics in England and Wales. The Framework contains a set of yearly teaching programmes that cover all aspects of the National Curriculum for mathematics in primary school, and also planning grids to show how mathematical topics can be grouped in units of work with a recommended number of lessons for each topic.

In the Netherlands, by contrast, reform has come about more through collaboration between curriculum developers and researchers. Reform began with the ideas of Freudenthal (1973) in the first *Wiskobas* project, which evolved through teaching experiments in schools into the wider theory of Realistic Mathematics Education (Streefland 1991). Applied research, resulting in curriculum materials and lesson designs, has exerted a strong influence on the development of textbook series (Gravemeijer 1994b). Guidance for teachers is elaborated in the *Tussendoelen Annex Leerlijnen* (Intermediate Objectives in Learning Strands) publications whose first focus has been the development of descriptions for longitudinal learning/teaching trajectories, starting with whole number (TAL Team 1998). These provide guidance for teachers and attempt to make clear how relevant skills and understanding in mathematics are built up in connection with each other.

Giving arithmetic teaching a high profile in educational discussion carries with it mixed blessings. It can provide the impetus for constructively engaging teachers in reflection on teaching practices, or it can invite criticism of existing practice, and present opportunities for negative opinions to be expressed that only serve to undermine the efforts of teachers in an aspect of their work that is acknowledged to be difficult. Reporting on an inquiry into teaching arithmetic in England and Wales, the Numeracy Task Force identified 'the need to build up teachers' confidence and competence as quickly as possible' (DfEE 1998a: 2), which perhaps reflects a growing deterioration in government confidence in teachers in England. At the same time, this high profile invites the identification of real issues in arithmetic teaching that can be addressed through debate and research.

Key issues for practices in teaching in England and the Netherlands

Despite many social and cultural similarities between the two countries that suggest a uniformity of approach to arithmetic teaching, fundamental differences have emerged. Recent debates in mathematics education in the two countries have brought to the forefront a number of issues relating to the primary classroom. While the curricula in England and the Netherlands show much common practice, this book addresses some fundamental differences in teaching approaches that relate to:

- the role of *counting* for developing calculating strategies;
- the importance of *place value* as an organizing principle for calculating;
- the development of *mental* strategies;
- the relevance of standard *algorithms*;
- the role of *textbooks* in the classroom;
- *calculators* and their impact on learning;
- the use of *apparatus/manipulatives* as calculating aids or for developing imagery; and
- *organization for teaching* (e.g. setting, whole class teaching and differentiation).

The role of *counting* for developing calculating strategies

In England counting has been seen as a mechanical and meaningless activity and its use for calculating as 'primitive' (Askew and Wiliam 1995: iii). In the Netherlands, meanwhile, counting is viewed as fundamental to calculating procedures. The Schools Curriculum and Assessment Authority (SCAA) for England and Wales suggest 'One reason that some pupils do not learn strategic methods for mental mathematics results from an over-reliance on counting procedures' (SCAA 1997c: 14). By contrast, the Dutch RME approach advocates that 'It is not the learning of [written] computation procedures based on place value, but the re-invention of informal *mental strategies* based on counting which is one of the "few big ideas" in the RME view of early number teaching' (Beishuizen and Anghileri 1998, original italics).

When children use counting as an informal strategy, then structuring knowledge comes as a natural characteristic through replay and repetition, and they spontaneously discover counting in patterns and jumps. With more experience and more instruction with contextual models this develops into 'guided reinvention': schematizing and formalizing in a process referred to as *'mathematizing'*.

(Treffers and Beishuizen 1999: 28)

These views will influence approaches to calculating as counting is encouraged and developed, or discouraged in favour of 'strategic methods' that partition numbers with the focus on place value.

The importance of *place value* as an organizing principle

In the English approach place value is stressed as an organizing mathematical principle upon which many mental and written methods (in particular, the so-called *standard* written methods) will be based. Among the key objectives for learning are explicit references to 'digits', with the terminology of 'tens' and 'units' evident throughout curriculum documents. SCAA advise that 'Progression in understanding about place value is required as a sound basis for efficient and correct mental and written calculation' (1997c: 4) and this is reinforced through the publications of 'key objectives', for example:

Key objective for Year 2: 'Count, read, write and order whole numbers to at least 100, *know what each digit represents (including 0 as a place holder)'*.
Key objective for Year 4: *'Use* known number facts and *place value to add or subtract mentally'*.

(QCA 1999b: 6–7, my italics)

Recognition of the complexity in appreciating that a 'ten' can, at the same time, be 'ten ones', and the difficulty of relating the manipulation of concrete materials to an abstract calculation procedure, have led to the introduction of materials that give imagery to mental procedures involving whole numbers.

In the Netherlands, on the other hand, there are no references to place value explicitly, and the Dutch promote a more holistic approach to number, with the development of written calculation strategies that retain the values of whole numbers throughout. During the process of mental calculation, whole numbers are partitioned into 'tens' and 'ones', but the emphasis is less on place value and more on the multi-unit concept that tens and ones are different unit categories where the ten can, at the same time, be ten ones.

The development of *mental* strategies

An explicit focus on teaching mental strategies for calculating is relatively new in England and questions have been asked about 'exactly which methods should be taught and in what order' (Straker 1996: 14). Indeed, there has been speculation:

> Assuming that pupils have been taught a sound understanding of the place value system, a further question is whether strategies for mental calculation can actively be taught to pupils, or whether pupils develop them for themselves as a result of either maturation or experience.
>
> (SCAA 1997a: 15)

Distinction is made between 'two aspects of mental mathematics – knowledge of number facts and strategic methods', and research (Askew *et al*. 1997a) shows that pupils can be 'helped to move on from inefficient techniques to using known and derived facts by careful intervention, modelling of strategies by teachers, and working jointly on strategies' (SCAA 1997b: 15). There has been recognition that changes are needed in teaching approaches and a booklet has been published which offers 'guidance to teachers on teaching effective mental strategies for calculation' making clear the 'expectations for each year' in school (QCA 1999a: 3). Approaches to be encouraged include, for example, 'counting forwards and backwards', 'doubling and halving' and 'using "near" doubles'. Pupils are also encouraged to use written recording relating to their mental working in 'jottings' and 'part-written' calculations.

In the Netherlands, the teaching of mental strategies is longer established and the arithmetic curriculum is founded on the development of 'pupils' own informal strategies' with 'didactic *context situations* . . . deliberately designed and sequenced to invite specific strategies and to stimulate abbreviation towards higher-level strategies' (Beishuizen and Anghileri 1998: 525, original italics). Learning strands incorporating mental and written methods are identified that are 'stretched out over the long term and which move at various levels of abstraction' with 'the learning process . . . promoted through reflection . . . by considering [their] own thought process [and] that of others' (Treffers 1991b: 24–5). Mental and written methods are related and combined with the emphasis on mental strategies that will be developed into written approaches, inefficient at first, but later gaining in efficiency through curtailment that may be encouraged through specific contextual details. Unlike the English approach where mental strategies are seen as distinct from the standard written methods, and teacher guidance comes in a publication (QCA 1999b) independently of the Framework (1999a), in the Netherlands written methods are specific developments of the mental strategies that children have learned and are seen in the textbooks as a continuous progression within a learning strand.

The relevance of standard *algorithms*

The National Numeracy Strategy now recognizes the importance of avoiding premature introduction of formal written procedures but continues to focus on the requirement that 'for each operation at least one standard written method of calculation should be taught in primary schools' (DfEE 1998a: 520). In the Framework (DfEE 1999a), development is evident from informal mental strategies, through part-written methods, to 'standard' written methods but the progression is not altogether clear. The exemplification of standards for Year 5, for example, shows a variety of written methods illustrating that different methods are acceptable when working towards a standard method of long multiplication (QCA 1999b). The emphasis, however, remains on standardization with the recommendation that 'within a school, teachers choose one general method for, say, subtraction and aim for all children to use it' and 'variety in written formats is not the goal' (Straker 1999b).

Debate will continue about the meaning of 'standard', which has long been associated with 'traditional' in terms of the written methods that have been established in schools for many decades. A battle has, however, been won in terms of the statutory requirements for England and Wales because the achievement of level 4 (the level to be achieved by the large majority of 11-year-olds) has been changed from 'standard written methods' to 'efficient written methods'.

The Dutch approach to written calculations is to think more in terms of different *levels* of strategy ranging from 'informal context bound' methods through a progressive development to 'high-level abbreviated' strategies with acknowledgement that some pupils will not reach the highest level of formal written algorithm. Emphasis is placed on *progressive* development with 'curtailment' introduced according to the capabilities of individual pupils. Progression is carefully developed from mental strategies, and variety in the levels of efficiency in written methods is promoted with 'more emphasis on global arithmetic and on sensible estimation' than on standardization (Treffers and Beishuizen 1999). The holistic approach to numbers means that the abbreviated forms of traditional algorithms, that are based on the manipulation of digits, are not introduced in primary school. It is notable that there have been calls for such an approach in England for many years (Plunkett 1979; Thompson 1997b; Anghileri and Beishuizen 1998), and that the so-called 'math wars' in the USA, referred to by Yackel in the following chapter take this as one of the central issues.

The role of *textbooks* in the classroom

The appreciation of textbooks in English primary schools has deteriorated in recent years as the individualized learning that had become established in some classrooms has been blamed for lack of teacher involvement in children's learning. Harries and Sutherland (1999: 51) write: 'the dominant view is that [primary mathematics textbooks] provoke a routine approach to teaching and learning and are likely to be used by teachers to abdicate their responsibility to prepare and teach lessons'. 'There were cases where the teacher simply supervised groups rather than engaging in the direct teaching of mathematics' (Ofsted 1998). In addition to textbook use, 'teachers are often expected to assemble their own teaching material on the basis of . . . a Scheme of Work' developed for their own school which has been described as a 'burden . . . not placed on Continental schools and teachers' who follow textbooks 'considerably more closely than their English colleagues' (Bierhoff 1996: 3–4).

It is not the books themselves that incorporate difficulties, but the way they had come to be used, and due credit is not always given to their importance as a resource for teachers. Many schemes have, in recent years, provided valuable sources for investigative approaches to mathematics teaching and learning as they have addressed the 'using and applying' attainment target that has been aimed at developing mathematical thinking and communication. Textbook publishers have struggled to keep up with the rapid curriculum changes introduced by the government and the development time needed has not always been available.

In the Netherlands, textbooks have been central to curriculum development and Gravemeijer refers to 'reform via the textbooks' (1994b: 138). In contrast to the scepticism relating to the English textbooks, he speaks of a 'receptive climate . . . even though the reform of mathematics education on the primary school must, for the time being, be put into practice via the textbooks'. Textbooks in the Netherlands have been 'developed under the umbrella of a counselling agency' to help translate research ideas into feasible practice and all assume 'interactive instruction'. Fundamental to the Dutch textbooks is a carefully researched progression within topics with 'more attention [paid] to the intertwining of the various learning strands' (Treffers and Beishuizen 1999).

Calculators and their impact on learning

Extreme views are expressed about the role of calculators in children's learning and assumptions are often based on poorly informed prejudice rather than the findings of research. Bierhoff (1996: 37) claims that, 'In view of the priority given to mental calculation on the Continent, it is not surprising to find that the use of calculators is a relatively minor feature in the teaching of arithmetic . . . calculators . . . are hardly seen at all in primary schools'. This assumes that calculators have no benefits for the development of mental calculation skills, while research suggests that 'calculators can improve both performance and attitude' (Askew and Wiliam 1995; Ruthven 1998).

Although calculators have been 'blamed' for England's poor performances in international studies, a comparison of the profiles for 'Calculator use and mathematics achievement at age 13, in 1995' (TIMSS 1996) show that England (low scoring) most closely resembles Singapore (high scoring) and Canada (middle scoring), countries where calculator use is commonplace (SCAA 1997a).

Based in Cambridge, the Calculator-Aware Number (CAN) curriculum project generated innovative approaches in arithmetic teaching, with its emphasis on investigative and problem-solving tasks, and reported favourable findings in terms of the attitude and performance of participating pupils (Shuard *et al.* 1991). More recent research in the Calculator as a Cognitive Tool

(CCT) project shows that in post-CAN schools using calculator activities, 'a higher proportion of pupils . . . expressed positive attitudes to calculating mentally' and 'pupils were more liable to compute mentally, and to adopt powerful mental strategies' (Ruthven 1999a: 198). Calculators provide an important cognitive tool if they are used to provoke thinking in ways that Ruthven refers to as reflection in an 'observe–predict–surpass' or in a 'diagnose–explain–reinforce' sequence. This view is supported in teacher guidance for developing mental strategies which identifies classroom activities for promoting calculator use (QCA 1999a: 61).

Although the Dutch key goals of primary school mathematics include 'insightful use of calculators' this has not yet been reflected in the textbooks or implemented generally in present classroom practice.

The use of *apparatus/manipulatives* as calculating aids or for developing imagery

Traditionally children in English classrooms have used cubes (e.g. Unifix or Multilink) that can be structured into sticks of 10 and individual cubes to illustrate the place value nature of numbers. For more advanced calculating, Dienes apparatus of 'hundreds' (flat blocks), 'tens' (rods) and 'units' (individual cubes) have been used to 'model' the procedures, such as 'decomposition' and 'carrying', that are involved in traditional calculations. The 'hundred square' and, more recently, the 'Gattegno chart' provide further visual imagery together with individual number cards, and number arrows, for constructing and disaggregating numbers. There is considerable emphasis on developing understanding of place value for reasons that are discussed above.

During the 1960s and 1970s Unifix and Dienes apparatus were widely used in the Netherlands also, but criticism of their use as being 'helpful for the representation of abstract number structure, but . . . weak in the representation of number operations when they become more complicated' (Beishuizen 1999; in England too there have been critics, see Hart 1989) has led to the use of bead frame and bead strings that relate more closely to images of a counting strategy. This develops to the use of 'gold pieces' and a 'gold board' which continue with the emphasis on counting but introduce 'chunking' to make this more efficient.

A recent innovation in the Netherlands has been the 'empty number line' (ENL) which supports the development of mental strategies. As a response to teachers' complaints 'about children hanging on too long to these materials (cubes, blocks and numbered lines) and passively reading off answers from the blocks when doing sums', removing all calibration from the number line has enabled children to use it flexibly for 'jumps' of any size, in either direction, providing imagery to encourage and support mental strategies (Beishuizen 1999).

This empty number line has appeared in more recent publications in England, for example in teacher guidance on developing mental strategies, where it is suggested that 'the use of an ENL where the multiples of 10 are seen as "landmarks" is helpful and enables children to have an image of jumping forwards or backwards to these "landmarks"' (QCA 1999a: 28).

Organization for teaching

The best of Continental classroom practice has been identified with 'substantial proportions of lessons devoted to high-quality interaction between teacher and pupils, and on-task interaction among pupils in a whole-class setting' (Bierhoff 1996). There has been some suggestion that practices in England in the 1970s and 1980s, when individual and small group activities were a common feature, have contributed to the low achievement in arithmetic evident in some international tests. Although research evidence does not support this view (Brown *et al.* 1998), attention to classroom organization has been a feature of the National Numeracy Strategy, which recommends that 'a much higher proportion of time than was previously the case in mathematics lessons should be spent teaching the whole class together' (DfEE 1998a: 14). Recommendations note that

> it is particularly important for the class to be together at the beginning and end of the lesson, so that the objectives for the lesson can be made clear, and, at the end, the teacher and pupils can sum up together what has been learnt and correct any errors or misconceptions.
>
> (DfEE 1998a: 54)

Within this structure teachers are recommended to 'use their professional judgement to determine the activities, timing and organisation in each part of the lesson to suit their learning objectives' (DfEE 1998a: 19).

This perhaps reflects a major difference in practice in the Netherlands where teachers are guided by a textbook series which, to a large extent, determines the order and timing of topics to be taught, and introduces materials and problem contexts that will be used in common with other users of the same text. The Dutch approach revolves around the construction of carefully designed tasks that will be presented in a whole class setting, but which may be attempted using a variety of solving procedures on different levels with opportunities for students to make discoveries at their own level and to build on their own experiential knowledge and perform shortcuts at their own pace (Gravemeijer 1994b).

Other characteristics of organization for mathematics teaching in England and the Netherlands are notably different. In primary schools in England it is common to find classes of mixed ages, particularly with combined Year 3 and 4 classes, and Year 5 and 6 classes. These classes are often reorganized, according to ability for mathematics, to make the groups more homogeneous for teaching. This is one of the strategies for managing classes with a wide range of abilities including children with specific learning difficulties who are integrated in mainstream schools, sometimes with the support of a learning support assistant (LSA). In contrast, classes in the Netherlands are more nor-mally a single age group, with the exception of pupils who repeat a year in school to give them further opportunity to reach the attainment required, or pupils of high ability who are advanced early, and all lessons are taken by the class teacher. Dutch national policy means that pupils with special edu-cational needs will attend special schools, although this is beginning to change with the policy moving to one of integration. In the current situation, the spread of ages is greater in Dutch classes than in English classes, but the ability range is narrower.

Comparing and contrasting approaches

International comparisons of pupils' performances in arithmetic tests have generated questions about the teaching approaches used in different coun-tries. The discussion that has ensued has focused almost solely on practices in teaching arithmetic calculations, without addressing the role of arithmetic within the mathematics curriculum as a whole.

When the first National Curriculum for England and Wales was published in 1989 (DES 1989), 'number' was included in four out of 14 'attainment targets' (programmes of content) to be covered in the primary curriculum. Other attainment targets included 'data handling', 'probability' and 'using and apply-ing mathematics', with many mathematics educators suggesting that the last of these represented the most fundamental development in trying to introduce explicit teaching of mathematical thinking. Without changing the content, this National Curriculum was rapidly reorganized into five attainment targets: 'using and applying mathematics', 'number', 'algebra', 'shape and space' and 'handling data' (DES 1991). This move to broaden the curriculum and high-light a focus on 'using and applying mathematics' with the three strands: 'applications', 'mathematical communication' and 'reasoning, logic and proof', reinforced a trend recommended in the Cockcroft Report (DES 1982) towards applications of mathematics 'in practical tasks, in real-life problems and to investigate within mathematics itself' (DES 1991: 1). Textbooks and teaching schemes embraced this move towards more open-ended approaches to 'provide pupils with insights into the unique character of mathematics, the oppor-tunities it gives for intellectual excitement and an appreciation of the essential creativity of mathematics' (DES 1989: D4). These developments removed the emphasis from teaching arithmetic calculations and international comparisons suggest that with respect to data handling and problem-solving skills in math-ematics these targets have been effective in practice.

The Dutch curriculum, by contrast, has been influenced by research that has taken as a central issue the teaching of number, and textbook developers have, since the 1980s, used problems specifically designed to stimulate the progres-sive development of particular approaches (see Buys, this volume). Contexts have been chosen that are both meaningful for the children, and also capable of generating the 'progressive mathematization' that characterizes the Realistic

Mathematics Education approach that will be described in later chapters. Since the 1980s there has been a focus on the development of instructional programmes and curriculum materials for teaching arithmetic, with research to evaluate the effectiveness of innovative approaches. One example of such a teaching programme is that of Julie Menne, which is described later in this volume. That is not to say that mathematics teaching in the Netherlands has involved only arithmetic, but that number work has been central in the development of the Dutch curriculum.

Approaches that acknowledge the emphasis necessary in arithmetic teaching in order to address the changing needs of society today, particularly with fast developing technology, mark other differences in the practices in the two countries. Problem solving is central in both countries, but the English approach, intended to develop more autonomous thinking through investigative approaches, contrasts with the Dutch approach that guides pupils along a 'learning trajectory' (see van den Heuvel-Panhuizen and Gravemeijer, this volume). Open-ended questioning and tasks designed to initiate exploration are included in most English textbooks while the Dutch curriculum is less well developed in this aspect of mathematics teaching.

Unlike established Dutch practices, mental and written methods in the English curriculum sit forcibly alongside the recommendation for effective and appropriate use of the calculator. The Numeracy Task Force reports that 'it is very important for primary school children not only to use the calculator appropriately, but [teachers should] teach children the technical skills needed to use it constructively and efficiently' and children should 'be taught when it is, and is not, appropriate to use the calculator' (DfEE 1998a: 53). In the exemplification of standards for Year 6, for example, there is an illustration in which 'Rebecca used a calculator for larger numbers' – showing 8.27×3.91 initially estimated as 8×4, with the calculator used as a 'check' (QCA 1999b). This shows that, for such a calculation, it is important for pupils to recognize that the most appropriate choice involves the use of a calculator. Assessment practices reflect this need for pupils to make choices about the most effective solution strategies to use and Standard Assessment Tests (SATs) for England (and Wales) include items for solution with a calculator.

Although the comparisons in this chapter relate specifically to England and the Netherlands, the issues introduced are well known in mathematics education and apply equally well across the world. In the next chapter in this volume, Erna Yackel shows that the same questions engage researchers in the United States of America, and that collaboration across national boundaries can help to inform discussion and establish improved practices for pupils in all classrooms.

Note

Throughout this book, references to the stages in schooling will be made using the terminology associated with England and the Netherlands. A comparison of ages is given in Table 1.1.

Table 1.1   Ages of children in different classes

England	Netherlands	USA	Age on entry
Reception	Groep 1	K1	4
Year 1 (Y1)	Groep 2	K2	5
Year 2 (Y2)	Groep 3	Grade 1	6
Year 3 (Y3)	Groep 4	Grade 2	7
Year 4 (Y4)	Groep 5	Grade 3	8
Year 5 (Y5)	Groep 6	Grade 4	9
Year 6 (Y6)	Groep 7	Grade 5	10
	Groep 8	Grade 6	11

2

Perspectives on arithmetic from classroom-based research in the United States of America

Erna Yackel

Introduction

> The great generality and simplicity of its rules makes arithmetic accessible to the dullest mind. In fact, facility in reckoning is merely a matter of memory, and the lightning calculators are but human machines, whose advantage over the mechanical variety is greater portability.
>
> (Dantzig 1954: 36)

In setting out to write this book, the contributors have taken on the task not only of laying out the principles and practice of arithmetic, but of putting forth a perspective of what constitutes arithmetic. Historically, arithmetic developed out of number and operations with number. Historical accounts of arithmetic deal with the development of the numeration system and with various methods of calculating, especially adding, subtracting, multiplying, and dividing (Newman 1956). Societal needs, such as the need to engage in commerce and trade, and cultural developments, such as the development of paper and a means for a written record, influenced the way arithmetic developed. In her chapter in this volume on principles underlying the arithmetic curriculum in England, Brown explains how societal needs have influenced the instruction of arithmetic in schools as well. For example, Brown points out that in the nineteenth century societal needs driving the content of school arithmetic were the need for written calculations to be done neatly and accurately for commercial purposes. When used by the workforce, arithmetic was likely to be repetitive. By contrast, the increased availability of calculators and computers in society today is one of the driving forces behind the current calls for de-emphasizing speed, accuracy, and repetition of complex computations in favour of in-depth understanding of arithmetic processes. This emphasis on understanding is apparent in this volume. In particular, a number of the authors give considerable attention to the idiosyncratic methods developed by students to solve addition and subtraction problems.

The tension between skill development and understanding as the focus of arithmetic instruction has a long history. In a recounting of the history of arithmetic instruction in the United States, Lindquist (1997) points out that, as early as the middle of the nineteenth century, Colburn argued for an approach to arithmetic instruction based on understanding. His arithmetic textbook was based on the premise that mathematics should make sense to students. Colburn's claim, 'Almost all, who have ever fully understood arithmetic, have been obliged to learn it over again in their own way' (Colburn, as quoted in Lindquist 1997), stands in stark contrast to the quotation from Dantzig that opens this chapter. What lies at the heart of the difference between Colburn and Dantzig is their view of what constitutes arithmetic. For Dantzig arithmetic is a set of rules to be committed to memory. This view is compatible with the societal needs of commerce as described by Brown. From this perspective, the purpose of arithmetic is to produce an accurate result. For Colburn, arithmetic involves more than achieving correct results. It has to do with thinking and reasoning.

The debate about what constitutes arithmetic goes on today. There is currently much rhetoric in the media in the United States, especially in what has been called the 'math wars' in California, about what should constitute mathematics instruction. For the elementary grades, this debate is between proponents of basic skills and proponents of understanding. A frequent point of misunderstanding is that it may be thought that these two are mutually exclusive. There is a common misconception that an emphasis on understanding implies a laissez-faire attitude towards correct answers and development of efficient and conventional methods. As a number of the contributors of this volume demonstrate, this view is unfounded. The instructional sequences and curricula discussed in the following chapters are consistent with the perspective that my colleagues and I take, along with that of a number of mathematics educators in the United States and elsewhere (Hiebert *et al.* 1997), namely, that arithmetic instruction involves fostering students' developing understanding of number and the basic operations with number. The intention is that computational proficiency develops concurrently. To the extent that this is the case, these instructional approaches transcend the dichotomy between conceptual understanding and computational proficiency.

Why is an emphasis on conceptual understanding important?

In the above paragraphs I have pointed to historical development and societal needs as factors in determining what is taken as arithmetic and arithmetic instruction. In the following paragraphs, I discuss some influences of research in determining what my colleagues and I take as constituting arithmetic and arithmetic instruction. This work began in the mid-1980s when Cobb first conducted a number of individual interviews with American first and second grade pupils designed to gain an understanding of their concepts of number, including numerical operations. Subsequently, such interviews became an integral part of our classroom-based research and were conducted by various members of the research team.

One question that was posed in a number of interviews is the following: 'Do you have a way to figure out how much is 16 + 9?' The problem was presented in horizontal format using plastic numerals. Students used a variety of methods, including counting methods. No matter which method the students used, virtually all of them answered with 25. Later in the same interview the pupils were presented with what appeared to be a typical school workbook page. One item the pupils were asked to answer was 16 + 9, this time written in vertical format as shown in Figure 2.1.

Interestingly, for a number of pupils, the problem written in this format was a completely different task from the task they had completed earlier. This time a number of students attempted to use algorithmic procedures they had been taught in school. While some children obtained the correct answer of 25, other children answered with 15, still others with 115. What was most disturbing

Name _____

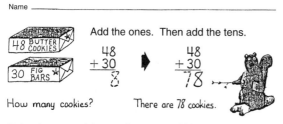

Add the ones. Then add the tens.

How many cookies?   There are 78 cookies.

Put a ring around the numbers you add first.
Add.

28	22	22	22	22
+ 41	+ 14	+ 15	+ 16	+ 17

22	81	16	28	37
+ 18	+ 12	+ 9	+ 13	+ 24

39	11	59	25	47
+ 53	+ 64	+ 30	+ 54	+ 12

82	43	78	32	11
+ 13	+ 46	+ 10	+ 17	+ 81

Figure 2.1   Copy of a typical workbook page used in the interviews

were the responses these children gave when asked about the discrepancy between these answers and their former answers of 25. For example, Cobb (1991) describes an episode with one girl who answered 15. He pointed out that she had obtained 25 when solving the problem presented in horizontal format. He asked her if both answers could be right and if one answer was better. She responded that, if you were counting cookies, 25 would be right but that in school 15 was always right.

There are several disquieting aspects to this episode. First, the fact that this pupil did not experience a conflict when her answer was less than one of the summands is troubling. Even more troubling is the fact that she gave priority to her 'school' answer over her 'real world' answer. That is, for her, computation in the real world makes sense but computation in school does not have to relate to reality. Similarly, the fact that students who answered 115 were not puzzled that their answer was so large is equally disturbing. As Cobb (1991) notes, these pupils' responses reveal their beliefs about school mathematics. For them, school mathematics (in this case, school arithmetic) does not need to make sense. It is not about thinking and reasoning. It is about following directions.

Sense making and reasoning

The issue raised by this and similar episodes is: what are children actually learning in school mathematics instruction? Is it mathematics (arithmetic) or is it something else? A conclusion that we came to was that it is important to teach arithmetic in such a way that students do not divorce their school experience from sense making, that they bring to bear the same type of thinking and reasoning in the school setting that they use in real world settings. This became an underlying principle in the work of our group. Arithmetic (mathematics) instruction is about sense making and reasoning. In this regard, we were taking the same perspective as Colburn took over a century ago, and others in this century, including Skemp. In his seminal article on relational and instrumental understanding, Skemp (1976) made the distinction between two different 'subjects', both of which are called mathematics. One is *instrumental* mathematics, consisting of rules and procedures, and the other is *relational* mathematics, consisting of relationships between ideas and concepts. Using Skemp's language, we would say that we took as an underlying principle that school arithmetic should be relational.

Our view of what constitutes arithmetic and arithmetic instruction was also profoundly influenced by the basic research of Steffe and colleagues (Steffe *et al.* 1983, 1988; Steffe 1994) that has resulted in models of children's mathematical conceptions, including children's concept of number, place value and multiplicative units. For more than two decades, Steffe has been researching children's development of concepts foundational to arithmetic. In doing so, he has brought attention to the distinction between a focus on conceptual underpinnings of arithmetic and a focus on computation per se. Steffe emphasizes what he calls 'children's mathematics' (Steffe and Kieren 1994). His goal is to understand the nature of the child's arithmetical activity. This is an important shift in focus. With this focus, arithmetic instruction is not about designing ways for students to develop facility in calculation, albeit meaningfully, it is about fostering students' underlying arithmetical conceptions, including their conception of number. This is, admittedly, a purely psychological approach that some would argue is too limited. Nevertheless, this research had a significant impact on our conceptualization of arithmetic instruction.

Examples of underlying conceptions

In the following paragraphs, I give several examples to illustrate this focus on underlying conceptions. Consider, for example, children's conceptions of number. A young child might count six beads by pointing to each, one at a time, while saying, 'One, two, three, four, five, six.' For this child, six might refer to the last bead counted. That is, for the child 'six' is a name associated with a particular bead. If one bead is removed, the child may need to count all of the beads again, starting from one. For another child, the six counted might refer to the entire collection of beads. When one bead is removed, this child may reason that there is one bead fewer and may count back one from six to get five.

Similar distinctions between students' concept of number can be made when a task such as the following is given. The task is to figure out how many are hidden when there are seven visible and 12 in all (see Figure 2.2). The child who needs to 'count all', and needs perceptual materials, is unable to solve this task as posed. Another child may be able to count on, saying, 'seven . . . eight, nine, ten, eleven, twelve', while putting up one finger with each number word beginning at eight. She may then notice that five fingers are up and report five as the answer. Another child may proceed in almost the same way but may need to count the fingers that are up to know that five have been counted. Yet another child may say, 'I know that 8 + 4 is 12 so 7 + 5 must be 12. So there are five hiding.' This child is using a thinking strategy approach (Cobb and Merkel 1989).

According to Steffe (1994), the distinctions between the children's solution methods in the above examples indicate differences in their concept of number. The child who is able to use a thinking strategy approach has a more sophisticated concept and has more efficient ways to solve problems. Whether or not these distinctions are characteristics of the children per se, or of their activity at the time is open to question. Steffe is careful to refer to these models as the researcher's constructs. They are the way the researcher makes sense of the children's activity. Nevertheless, the work of Steffe and others suggests that it is useful to be cognizant of differences in children's activity when thinking about their arithmetical learning. Instruction that takes this research seriously attempts to engage students in activities that have the potential to move all of the children forward in their thinking despite their conceptual differences. Such instruction abandons the traditional goal of having lesson objectives

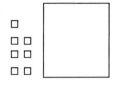

There are 12 in all. How many are hidden under the cover?

Figure 2.2   Missing-addend interview task

that purport to 'teach' all of the children the same thing in any given class session. Instead, instruction is now organized around broad goals of supporting conceptual development, in full acknowledgement of the fact that not everyone will come to the same understandings at the end of the class period. (This is not to say that there are no content goals. Such goals, however, are not thought of in individual terms, such as that everyone in the class will develop certain concepts. Rather, goals are thought of more in terms of big ideas that might arise for discussion. Through the discussion, some understandings may come to be 'taken-as-shared' by the class as a whole.) Another underlying principle for us was that arithmetic instruction has as its primary focus fostering children's conceptual development of number and related concepts, such as concept of ten, place value numeration, and multiplicative units. Having the children become skilful and efficient was a secondary goal. In our experience, skill and efficiency emerge as conceptual development progresses.

The classroom teaching experiment

In recent years in the United States, much of the research that has impacted arithmetic instruction has taken place in the form of classroom research. While classroom research can, in itself, take a variety of forms, one form that has been highly informative is the classroom teaching experiment. In this section of the chapter, I describe the type of teaching experiments that I have been involved with in second and third grade arithmetic and some of the lessons that we have learned about the teaching and learning of arithmetic (Yackel 1995b).

Originally, the intention of these teaching experiments was to use an approach similar to the one-on-one teaching experiment that characterizes the work of Steffe and colleagues, but to do so in the classroom setting. Our purpose in conducting these classroom teaching experiments was to investigate children's mathematical activity and learning in the classroom setting. (Not all of the mathematical activities were arithmetical in nature. Some were geometric. However, our focus was on arithmetic. Consequently, I will refer to arithmetical activity rather than mathematical activity in the remainder of this chapter.) Our purpose, therefore, was twofold. On the one hand, we attempted to facilitate the development of an instructional setting that promotes students' construction of increasingly sophisticated and powerful arithmetical concepts by designing appropriate instructional tasks and by assisting teachers with the use of an inquiry approach to instruction. On the other hand, we attempted to make sense of the students' and teacher's activity while they engaged in the aforementioned instructional situations. Note that the term 'inquiry instruction' is used here to mean instruction that is characterized by students' active involvement in mathematical activity, in which they develop personally meaningful solutions, explain and justify their thinking to others, and listen to and attempt to make sense of the thinking of others. The term 'inquiry' to describe this type of instruction is taken from Richards (1991) and is contrasted with 'school' mathematics instruction that is characterized by following rules and procedures (see also Cobb *et al.* 1992).

I have already indicated that, for us, an important aspect of developing instructional tasks and strategies was to base them on Steffe's detailed models of early number learning, rather than on the traditional arithmetical 'content'. This critical feature requires further explanation and elaboration. For example, in the United States the primary content of traditional second grade arithmetic instruction is two-digit addition and subtraction. The focus is typically on children's learning the standard algorithms and becoming proficient at applying them to all situations, including those that require trading. Students also are expected to 'know' the basic addition and subtraction facts. Rather than embracing these as instructional goals, our aims for second grade children were that they develop increasingly sophisticated concepts of number and develop their own efficient methods for adding and subtracting two-digit numbers. To that end, the beginning months of the school year were devoted to encouraging the development of thinking strategies and an abstract concept of number.

Developing thinking strategies

Interviews conducted prior to the beginning of the first teaching experiment indicated that some, but not all, children entering second grade have an abstract concept of number. A few of them will spontaneously use a plus one (or minus one) thinking strategy, making use of a known result to figure out one that is not known (e.g. a child figures out that 7 + 6 is 13 because she already knows that 6 + 6 is 12 and 7 is just one more than 6). Even fewer children spontaneously use the compensation strategy (e.g. where a child figures out that 7 + 5 is 12 by relating it to 6 + 6 is 12). Thus, a criterion for the instructional tasks we devised was that they could be completed in meaningful ways by children at vastly different conceptual levels. Critically, the instructional tasks that were developed encouraged the development of thinking strategies by providing opportunities for students to use them. Nevertheless, we were aware that not all of the children would do so. Some of the children with very primitive concepts of number might count on, or even count all, to solve the tasks, and view each task in isolation from the others.

A further consideration in our development of instructional tasks was that the tasks make it possible to sustain discussions about mathematics. In general, tasks that can be solved in a variety of different ways can lead to productive discussions as the children listen to and attempt to make sense of each other's solution methods. Such discussions create opportunities for problem solving of another type, as children compare and contrast different solution methods and make decisions about how to formulate and reformulate explanations of their thinking and how to pose questions and challenges to others (Yackel and Cobb 1996). In this sense, using instructional strategies that involve children in explaining and justifying their thinking, as well as in solving tasks, was a deliberate aspect of the instructional design.

The preceding discussion points to some of the critical aspects that we attended to in developing instructional tasks and strategies. However, it masks the dynamic nature of the development process. The cyclic process of developmental research, which characterizes Realistic Mathematics Education instructional theory and design (Gravemeijer 1994a and this volume), captures the approach we have used in our teaching experiments (Gregg 1992). According to Gravemeijer, this process begins with a thought experiment in which the developer/researcher tries to envision how the teaching–learning process will proceed. Children's activity in the classroom feeds back into new thought experiments leading to a cyclic process. In the teaching experiments described here, this cyclic process is ongoing and allows for daily adjustment and modification of the instructional tasks.

In subsequent teaching experiments, Cobb, Gravemeijer and others have given much more attention to instructional design aspects and have had the development of a learning trajectory as a specific goal. In doing so, they are using Simon's (1995) notion of a learning trajectory as a description of the possible route that students' learning might take. Accordingly, a learning trajectory is the result of developmental research. Researchers initially outline a hypothetical learning trajectory – a path that they conjecture students' learning might follow. To do so, they sketch out possible ending points, potentially productive starting points, and make preliminary conjectures about how the learning might progress. Throughout the teaching experiment, the hypothetical learning trajectory is continually revised, following the cyclic process of developmental research. After the teaching experiment is concluded, a retrospective analysis of the data results in the construction of a learning trajectory that describes how learning might progress in another classroom situation. In this use of the term, a learning trajectory is not an outline of instructional activities or a plan for instruction. Rather, it is a description of the ways students might act mathematically and how they might progress from one way of acting mathematically to another. Thus, a learning trajectory can be useful to another teacher in another classroom as a guide for thinking about how the students' conceptual development might progress but it is not the same as an outline of an instructional sequence.

Examples of students' arithmetical learning from second and third grade classroom teaching experiments

In this section, examples will be given from the first four teaching experiments that we conducted. These examples will then provide the basis for the next sections of the chapter. The first two of these teaching experiments were conducted in second grade and the next two in third grade. We chose second grade initially because, in the United States, a major focus of second grade arithmetic is addition and subtraction of two-digit numbers using the standard algorithms. The interviews described earlier in this chapter prompted this choice. We wanted to figure out ways that classroom instruction might support students' development of self-generated algorithms. However, to do so, we did not focus on algorithm development per se, but on students' development of the concept of number and of the concept of tens. In the process, the majority of the children developed their own efficient algorithms.

In one of the classes, the teacher used an instructional activity (that we called 'number sentence without counting') frequently throughout the second half of the school year. This teacher would write a number sentence on the chalkboard and allow several minutes for the students to figure out the result. The students had no paper or pencil; they did all of their work mentally. The following examples are illustrative of the types of problems the teacher posed and the types of solutions developed by the students.

Problem: 16 + 38 + 24 =

Mary: I took the 10 off of the 16 and the 30 off of the 38. That gave me 40. And the 20 from the 24 gave me 60. Six and 4 is 10 more, gives 70. And add the 8 from the 38, gives 78.

Charmaine: I added the 16 and the 24 to get 40. Then I added the 30 from the 38 to get 70 and the 8 makes 78.

Denzel: I added the 30 to the 16 to give 46. Then I added the 8. Four from the 8 makes it 50 and the other 4 makes it 54. Then I added the 24 to get 78.

Daria: I added the 6 and the 8 to get 14 and 4 more makes 18. Then I added the 10 and the 30 and the 20 to get 60. I took the 10 from the 18 and put it with the 60 to get 70. And there's 8 more left to give you 78.

Problem: 52 – 17 =

Lawrence: I took away 10 from 52 gives me 42. Then I took away 2 more gives me 40. I have 5 more to take away gives 35.

Latanya: I took 10 from the 52 to give me 42. Then I said, 41, 40, 39, 38, 37, 36, 35.

Denzel: First I took away the 2. Then I took away the 10. Then I took away the other 5. My answer is 35.

Lakisha: First I took away 20 and got 32. Then I put back 3 more and I got 35.

Dominique: First I take 10 from 50 to get 40. Then I take 2 from 7 to get 5. My answer is 45 [*sic*].

Counting-based and collections-based approaches

As we analysed the types of solutions students developed, it was apparent that we could distinguish between two different conceptions of number that underpinned these solutions. We call these *counting-based* (or *sequence-based*) and *collections-based* solutions. (In the remainder of this chapter, for simplicity, I will use the label *counting-based* conception of number to refer to what we have called *counting-based* or *sequence-based* conception of number. Compare this use of counting-based and collections-based conceptions of number, with the 'sequence' methods (N10) and 'split tens' methods (1010) identified by Beishuizen in Chapter 9 of this volume, and to Fuson's use of 'sequence tens and ones' and 'separate tens and ones'; Fuson *et al.* 1997.)

The solutions given by Mary and Daria for the addition task can be described as collections-based. In each case the child partitioned the numbers into tens and ones, combined the units of like type and finally combined those results. By contrast, the solutions that Charmaine and Denzel gave involved keeping one number intact and continuing on from there. Even though we have no evidence that either child counted, their solutions might be thought of as curtailments of counting on solutions. For this reason we refer to them as counting-based. For the subtraction problem, the solutions given by Lawrence, Latanya, Denzel and Lakisha all are grounded in counting-based conceptions. Dominique's solution is grounded in a collections-based conception.

In the initial teaching experiments we made no explicit effort to preference one of these conceptions over the other. Indeed, we were aware that having access to both conceptions provides much more flexibility for students. This is especially the case for subtraction where the common student error in problems that require trading is tied to a collections-based conception. (Refer to Dominique's solution for the subtraction problem.) Therefore, we became interested in attempting to foster the development of both conceptions.

The collections-based conception is closely tied to place value numeration. However, as I have indicated earlier, we took the position that the goal in teaching arithmetic is that students develop the conceptual underpinnings for arithmetic operations, not that they simply become proficient at completing computations. Here, our understanding of Steffe's work with models of children's number concepts is crucial. According to Steffe (1994), the conceptual operations that are central to making sense of place-value numeration are those that involve coordination of units of different rank. Hundreds, tens, and ones are units of different rank. The quantity 436 can be thought of as 4 hundreds, 3 tens, and 6 ones. It can also be thought of as 43 tens and 6 ones, or as 3 hundreds, 9 tens, and 46 ones. The ability to conceptualize the quantity 436 in these different ways, or in others, as the need arises, is what is called the ability to coordinate units of different rank.

Our goal in the teaching experiments for place value numeration, therefore, became fostering children's development of the ability to coordinate units of different rank. To do so we introduced a scenario of a candy factory in which 10 candies are packed in a roll, 10 rolls are packed in a box, 10 boxes are packed in a case, and so on. (In second grade classrooms, the focus is on two digits only and in this case we use a candy shop scenario that involves only rolls and pieces. In the third grade, the candy factory scenario is introduced to extend the quantities to three (and four) digits.) In this way questions about a quantity can be posed easily in terms of various units. For example, we might ask children to find different ways to make up the quantity of 358 candies using boxes, rolls, and individual pieces. At a simpler level, the task might be to find different ways to make up the quantity 43 candies using rolls and pieces. Specific quantities of certain units might be given and the children's task is to figure out the others. (See Figure 2.3 for an example.) Some children find these tasks very difficult, even with manipulative materials available. However, by attempting to solve tasks of this type, students' ability to coordinate units of different rank increases. That is, students learn through engagement in such tasks. (Our experience is that it is difficult to have sufficient materials for working with large quantities such as these. We have dealt with this issue in two ways. One is to include instructional activities that are posed in a money scenario. In this case, it is relatively easy to provide the children with enough play money to use when solving the problems. The second was to develop a candy factory computer microworld in which children can operate boxes, rolls and pieces; Bowers 1995.)

As these tasks illustrate, the instructional sequence designed to foster students' ability to coordinate units of different rank supports a collections-based view of number but not a counting-based view. After working within the candy shop/factory scenario, it is common that children subsequently figure out such sums as 16 + 38 + 24 by first partitioning each of the numbers into the tens component (rolls) and the units component (pieces). Then they combine the tens (rolls) and the units (pieces) to get the total. This approach is natural even though the problem is not cast in terms of the candy factory scenario. The point I wish to make here is that this scenario does not foster a counting-based view. While the scenario does not impose a specific type of solution, it orients the children's thinking even after the scenario is no longer present.

Developing a conceptual basis for a counting-based conception of number

As noted earlier, we felt it was important that children have both a collections-based conception and a counting-based conception of number. Once it became apparent that the candy shop/factory instructional sequence did not

358

Boxes	Rolls	Pieces
3	_____	_____
2	4	_____
_____	7	_____

Figure 2.3   Candy factory inventory form task

support children's development of a counting-based conception of number, the task became to figure out a way to do so. Cobb, Gravemeijer, and Stephan collaborated with a first grade teacher to conduct a classroom teaching experiment for this purpose. For details of the teaching experiment, see Stephan (1998) and Stephan *et al.* (1998). A brief sketch is provided in the following paragraphs.

The hypothesis on which the teaching experiment was founded was that a counting-based conception of number might be developed through measurement. Therefore, the teaching experiment sought to support children's developing conceptions of measurement. To this end, instructional activities were designed first to support children's development of the notion of measurement as the accumulation of distance. Subsequently, the children came to conceptualize space as something that could be quantified. For example, the space between the end of the cabinet and the wall could be thought of as a distance that one could figure out. Through a series of carefully structured instructional activities that were developed using the cyclic approach of developmental research, students gradually developed a need for a measuring device. They created and then used what they called a 'measurement strip'. The measurement strip is a strip of paper that is marked off into specified units. Consequently, it has many features of a standard ruler. The measurement strip was used in a variety of ways to support reasoning. For example, children were able to reason about the measure of an item that extended from, say, 5 to 18 on the measurement strip.

As the teaching experiment progressed, students' concepts of measuring and measurement evolved. The methods they used to figure out tasks posed to them suggest that this instructional sequence does, indeed, support a counting-based conception of number. However, the school year ended before this could be investigated further.

Earlier in this chapter, I emphasized the importance of focusing on the conceptual foundations for arithmetic and arithmetic operations. I have attempted to illustrate in some depth what might be meant by such a focus. Other issues that we found to be important and that are being given increasing attention in arithmetic instruction, at least in the United States, include the role of imagery, the role of tools, including notation and symbolizing, and social aspects of learning, including discourse and argumentation. The use of imagery, tools, and discourse might be seen as instructional means that are compatible with the principles of arithmetic instruction stated earlier in this chapter, namely that arithmetic should be seen as sense making and that arithmetic instruction should focus on the development of the conceptual underpinnings of arithmetic rather than on computation and calculation.

Role of imagery

It would be presumptuous to suggest that an adequate discussion of the role of imagery in arithmetic instruction might be included in a few short paragraphs. However, I would like to mention several aspects that are gaining increasing attention. First, carefully selected scenarios have the potential of forming an image basis for students' mathematical activity. This emphasis, which is derived largely from the Realistic Mathematics Education instructional design theory of the Freudenthal Institute (Gravemeijer 1994b), is gaining increasing prominence in the United States. For example, the candy factory scenario referred to earlier was highly productive in the teaching experiments we have conducted. There was considerable evidence that children used the imagery of the situation as they thought about how to solve problems. I have already illustrated how children used the imagery of the candy factory to solve problems posed in a purely symbolic form, such as 16 + 38 + 24. The difference between this scenario and the typical American textbook approach of using bundles of ten is subtle. However, the teachers with whom I work report that the differences in children's mathematical activity when using these two approaches is striking. It is important to note that, in line with the Realistic Mathematics Education instructional design theory, the scenarios that are selected are chosen because of their potential for supporting vertical mathematization (see van den Heuvel-Panhuizen, this volume). They are not selected primarily on the basis of being part of students' real world experience. In this sense their purpose is not the same as those situations that are typically called 'authentic' situations by American educators.

A second aspect relates more specifically to visual imagery. Considerable emphasis is being given in American arithmetic instruction to developing number concepts by associating quantities with visual images. For example, single and double ten frames are becoming increasingly common in American textbooks. Earlier in this chapter I referred to attempts to foster students' development of thinking-strategy approaches. An example of one approach that has proven highly effective, based on the double ten frame, is described below. In this approach the teacher plans a sequence of double-ten frame tasks to pose to the students by flashing the visual image on an overhead projector for a few seconds, turning it off, and then showing it again briefly one or two additional times. The purpose of the flashing approach is to encourage students to develop mental images of the quantities shown, using the ten frame to organize their thinking and reasoning. The students' task is to figure out how many were shown and to explain how they figured it out. The students solve the task mentally, without paper and pencil. For example, the teacher might flash the first task shown in Figure 2.4 and then conduct a whole-class discussion in which the children explain how they figured it out.

Subsequently, the teacher might flash the other tasks shown in Figure 2.4. The tasks have been carefully sequenced so that students might solve the tasks by relating them to each other. For example, a child might notice that in Task 2 there is one more dot in the second frame than in Task 1. So the answer has to be one more than it was in Task 1. Similarly, some child might relate Task 3 to Task 2 by noticing that if one dot from the first frame were moved to the second frame, the task would be the same as Task 2. So the result is the same. Another child might relate Task 3 to Task 1 by noticing that there is one more dot in the first frame than in the first frame of Task 1, so the answer has to be one more. Our experience is that the visual imagery of the dots on the ten frame provides support for students' use of thinking strategies in a way that posing the same tasks in purely symbolic notation, that is, as 8 + 4, 8 + 5, and 9 + 4, would not. The fact that students relate a task to a prior task, even though the earlier task is no longer visible, affords considerable evidence that the visual images provide a means of mentally organizing the quantities involved.

Role of tools

Several of the chapters in this volume make mention of tools, such as the empty number line and various means of notation, in the teaching of arithmetic. For example, Beishuizen (this volume) discusses how the empty number line might be used to support students' development of different calculating strategies. This explicit attention to tools and their use in arithmetic instruction is important for it causes us to reflect on our purpose in using the tools and our theories about how and why they might be useful. In the United States, virtually all teachers and educators now advocate 'hands-on' learning in mathematics. However, just what they mean by this phrase varies considerably. For many, it means that students are actively engaged in using materials (usually concrete) of some type as they solve problems. Motives range from making mathematics fun to supporting learning. Notating and

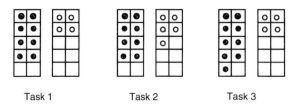

Task 1   Task 2   Task 3

Figure 2.4   Sequence of double-ten frame tasks

symbolizing have not yet gained the same prominence in American arithmetic instruction.

A comprehensive discussion of the role of tools in arithmetic instruction can be found in Gravemeijer *et al.* (in press). These authors provide a careful analysis of one instructional sequence that makes use of a device called the arithmetic frame (see Menne, this volume). The authors outline how students' development of number relationships, their arithmetical reasoning and their methods for calculating emerged from their activity with the arithmetic frame. It is important to note that students were not instructed in the use of the frame. Nor were they shown a variety of ways to use it. Instead, the children had the frame available to them as they attempted to solve a variety of problems. The ways in which the students made use of the frame reflected their individual conceptions of number. These ways became the focus of whole-class discussions. Differences in uses of the frame were highlighted and efficiency became an explicit part of the discussions. These discussions provided opportunities for the children to reflect on their activity and compare and contrast it with the activity of others. In the process, they advanced in their individual understandings and in their uses of the frame as a tool for reasoning. Thus, the arithmetic frame as a tool cannot be separated from the way in which it is used in the classroom or from the discourse that surrounds its use.

In making this statement, I am taking the position that a tool does not stand alone. In this sense, my position differs from that of Beishuizen (this volume) who takes the empty number line as 'a transparent model for children'. The position I am advocating is consistent with that of Holt (1982), Cobb (1991), and others who point to the fact that individuals bring their prior experiences to any situation and thus their interpretations are constrained by those experiences. Adults who already 'know' mathematical concepts interpret diagrams and models in ways that are consistent with their understandings. On the other hand, children who do not yet have those conceptual understandings do not 'see' the diagrams and models in the same way as the knowing adults. In other words, we see what we understand and not the other way around.

As tools, including materials, models, diagrams, notations, etc., become increasingly prominent in arithmetic instruction, it is imperative that we consider carefully what our intention is in using them. It is also imperative that we figure out what interpretations the students are making of these tools. Unless we do so, we are in danger of replacing verbal rules and procedures with rules and procedures for using tools.

Social aspects of learning arithmetic

Over the past several decades there has been increasing attention devoted to the social aspects of learning mathematics (Cobb and Bauersfeld 1995). In this volume, Gravemeijer's chapter gives considerable attention to the social aspects of learning arithmetic. One social aspect that I want to highlight here is that of argumentation. Increasing attention to discourse in mathematics classrooms (National Council of Teachers of Mathematics 1989, 1999; Ball 1991), even in the primary grades, has led to an increasing focus on the types of explanations students give and the argumentation that develops (Lampert 1990; Yackel 1992, 1995a, 1997; Krummheuer 1995). Here argumentation is seen as a collective activity that emerges as individuals attempt to explicate their thinking and reasoning and make sense of the reasoning and thinking of others.

One approach to analysing augmentation that has proven useful is to follow Toulmin's scheme, which has been elaborated for mathematics education by Krummheuer (1995). The scheme consists of *conclusion, data, warrant,* and *backing*. According to this scheme, the conclusion is a statement that is made as though it were certain. The support one might give for the conclusion is the data. A rationale that is given to explain why the data are considered to provide support for the conclusion is called a warrant. And further support for the warrant is called the backing. As I have argued elsewhere (Yackel 1997), this approach to argumentation is useful in thinking of arithmetic instruction for two reasons. One is that this approach helps to clarify the relationship between the individual and the collective, in this case between the explanations and justifications that individual children give in specific instances and the classroom mathematical practices that emerge. As classroom mathematical practices emerge, they become taken-as-shared, that is, they are beyond justification. Hence, what is required as warrant and backing evolve. Similarly, the types of rationales that are given as data, warrants and backing for explanations and justifications contribute to the development of what is taken-as-shared by the classroom community. Therefore, attempts to study arithmetic learning in the classroom can be informed by analysing the evolution of the rationales that are given by individual children and that are (implicitly or explicitly) required by the classroom community.

An immediate implication for the classroom is that our attempts to design arithmetic instruction cannot ignore the explanations and justifications the children give. If we wish to make decisions about which instructional activities to use and the order in which to use them, we must go beyond considering whether or not students are obtaining correct answers. We would be well advised to listen to what the students say as they explain their thinking and the types of statements they are questioning. What types of rationales are children providing? Are these rationales evolving over time? Is it the case that some statements that required supporting rationales at one time in the school year no longer require justification by the classroom community later on?

As Lampert (1990) and Ball (1991) have so eloquently pointed out, when explanation and justification are central components of arithmetic instruction, students learn far more than arithmetic. They learn what constitutes a mathematical argument and they learn to think and reason mathematically. In this sense, attention to argumentation in the arithmetic classroom expands the scope of the instruction from arithmetic to mathematics more generally. The study of arithmetic becomes much more than learning about number and numerical operations. Children are encountering the essence of mathematics, mathematical thinking and reasoning, even in their earliest learning experiences.

Concluding remarks

In this chapter, I have attempted to highlight some perspectives on arithmetic that have resulted from classroom-based research with which I have been involved, either directly or indirectly. Some of these perspectives have had considerable influence on arithmetic instruction in the United States and elsewhere (see, for example, the problem-solving approach to arithmetic advanced by Human, Murray, and Olivier in South Africa as described in Heibert *et al.* 1997). Others have influenced practitioners in localized settings. There are points of commonality and points of difference between these perspectives and those expressed in the chapters of this volume. My intention is to engage the reader in thinking about issues that might give him or her reason to pause and reflect while reading the other chapters in this book. Admittedly, the issues highlighted in this chapter are those that have been, or have become, important to me in my work in arithmetic in American classrooms. However, as the chapters in this volume make clear, apart from political and jurisdictional issues that may differ from one country to another, the overriding issues in the teaching and learning of arithmetic transcend national boundaries.

Acknowledgements

Over the past decade or more, the colleagues with whom I have worked, and whom I would like to thank have included Paul Cobb, Terry Wood, Grayson Wheatley, Koeno Gravemeijer, Diana Underwood, Jeff Gregg, and Nadine DiNuzzo. In addition, I have had numerous helpful conversations with Heinrich Bauersfeld, Gotz Krummheuer and Jorg Voigt.

⚊⚬⚊ Part II

The principles underpinning the arithmetic curriculum

The curriculum changes in arithmetic that are being implemented in many countries across the world may share many common characteristics but the routes to change can be starkly different. The following two chapters outline contrasting factors that have been influential in developing the primary mathematics curriculum in England and in the Netherlands, the principles that have been in operation and, to some extent, the mechanisms that have been used to bring about change. Both countries have arrived at a similar situation with a structured teaching programme, focusing initially on developing children's own mental calculation strategies, with introduction of standard written methods introduced later than has traditionally been the practice.

In the English case, the revised curriculum for primary mathematics has been implemented through the distribution to every primary school of a *Framework for Teaching Mathematics from Reception to Year 6* (DfEE 1999a) whose requirements are disseminated through National Numeracy Strategy 'consultants' and school mathematics coordinators, and supported by a training programme involving every school. These changes to both the content, and the teaching approaches, follow the report of a government-appointed Numeracy Task Force.

Margaret Brown is Professor of Mathematics Education at King's College in London and has been influential in national developments in mathematics teaching. Informed by her extensive experiences in mathematics education research, she has contributed to the most recent discussions through her membership of both the Numeracy Task Force, and the Advisory Group for the National Numeracy Strategy. In the first chapter she identifies how the latest changes follow the pattern of curriculum reform that has been established historically. She explains that a very 'English' approach is reflected in the way that 'precedence and evolution' are guiding principles, and uses *teaching methods, classroom organization* and *assessment* to characterize curriculum reform and to identify the position that exists today. Established practices are identified, such as, 'open problem-solving and investigation', to 'assist motivation, learning and application' and sociocultural language-based aspects of learning, such as 'classroom discussion, including pupils sharing their own ideas'. Difficulties are identified in reconciling some of the more recent developments with established educational principles and with the ideology of the individual teacher. The move towards more centralized directives in terms of curriculum content and teaching approaches is new in the English primary school and Margaret Brown identifies aspects that are central in the debate that must ensue.

In the Netherlands, in contrast, curriculum reform in mathematics has been generated more explicitly through research, with its foundations laid by Hans Freudenthal and his colleagues at the former IOWO (Institute for Development of Mathematics Education), a predecessor of the Freudenthal Institute. Although 'key goals' have been published by the Ministry of Education, there has been little government intervention and the reform in schools has been largely through the publication of textbooks with teachers' guides, based on the 'Realistic Mathematics Education' approach. Marja van den Heuvel-Panhuizen is a senior researcher at the Freudenthal Institute in Utrecht and has been influential in several government-funded research and curriculum development projects. In the second chapter of this section, she explains the way that research has been central in establishing the Realistic Mathematics Education approach, and discusses the impact this has on not only the content of the curriculum, but also the teaching approaches. Marja summarizes the main principles underpinning the teaching programmes that have become established and identifies how they are based on Freudenthal's principles of giving students the 'guided' opportunity to 'reinvent' mathematics by doing it within a process of 'progressive mathematization'. She outlines the way research is moving forward to identify 'student learning trajectories' that will form the basis for the further development of teaching programmes.

⊝ 3

Influences on the teaching of number in England

Margaret Brown

Introduction

The title 'Principles underpinning the arithmetic curriculum' is a formidable one for an English educator for two reasons of which the first is trivial:

> There has been for about 20 years a tacit agreement among educators to replace the word 'arithmetic' by 'number', since the meaning of arithmetic had over time become limited to performance in standard algorithms without any underlying understanding, and thus was associated with many people with anxiety.

The second, however, is more fundamental:

> To admit to having any principles is a most un-English thing to do.

I have therefore taken the liberty of translating from 'Principles for arithmetic teaching and learning' to a chapter title that is more English. (I should perhaps at this stage explain that I am using 'England' rather than 'Britain' or 'the UK', less because attitudes and practices are radically different in other parts of the United Kingdom than because there are some statutory curricular differences, reflecting minor historical differences in emphasis, in which I do not wish to get embroiled.)

One reason for the refusal to embrace 'principles' I believe arises from a tradition of English empiricism, preferring a pragmatic view dictated by 'common sense' or 'what works in practice', and highly suspicious of any Continental rationalist philosophy or 'fancy theory'. As an example of this, when the original National Curriculum Mathematics Working Group put forward a rationale for its proposals, it was dismissed by the Minister of Education as 'a load of jelly'; one of his successors spoke of teacher training as being dominated by 'barmy theory'. The 1989 National Curriculum for England and Wales was devoid of any aims and objectives, either in mathematics or more generally, except for a brief clause in the 1988 Act which referred, only rather vaguely, to the development of pupils and society, and preparation for adult life. Twelve years later we are still trying to develop, post hoc, a framework of aims; the latest version is a praiseworthy statement but unfortunately bears little relation to the new mathematics curriculum.

Precedence and evolution

This distrust of theory is reflected in the lack of any national written legal constitution and a reliance instead on case-law (precedence) and evolution. Loosely speaking I think this means that we go on doing what we have traditionally done until there is a feeling enunciated repeatedly by respected individuals or groups that this no longer represents a reasonable position, at which point a modification to the law is proposed and debated prior to acceptance. Alternatively, and more tacitly, new interpretations of existing law and/or changes of existing practice may simply evolve, spread through a variety of communication channels.

Alongside this evolution there has been historically a respect for individual and local freedom, applauded on occasion by Continental philosophers such as Voltaire; an argumentative parliament, representing the interests of both smaller landowners and commerce, and a constitutional monarchy, have on the whole acted to curb the desires of leaders to impose grand designs and centralized measures. The result has been devolved power built on a system of diverse checks and balances.

Thus to ask the question 'why' in England is to cause a deep sense of shock; the answer is always that a particular situation, which is rarely rational or tidy, has come about due to a variety of influences at different times in the past. The English have, on the whole, favoured an evolving diversity of practices rather than a nationally agreed set of principles from which standard national practice can be derived. Nevertheless on occasion, a national report has crystallized the current state of thinking, and provides some insight into principles that have achieved consensus.

This evolutionary process can be a strength, since we have avoided being swept headlong into a fashionable but ultimately unrewarding movement such as the wilder extremes of modern mathematics. It can also be a weakness as it reinforces conservatism and makes ultimately profitable change difficult to achieve on a wide front in a short time. It also means that it is difficult to understand the variety of principles that have contributed to current arithmetic teaching in England without some understanding of the historical development, that I feel I need to explain.

Historical background

In relation to primary education, the historical government predisposition to laissez-faire-ism has been upset twice in the more recent past by radical state intervention. Typically the argument in both cases was presented in terms of the perceived needs of industry and commerce, although some reformers were motivated by the grander and rather un-English principle of universal human rights to minimal education.

The first intervention was in the late nineteenth century, when the government belatedly imposed a universal primary education system. This was at a period when Continental countries, especially Germany which had inherited from Prussia an efficient universal education system, were overtaking our lead in industrial capacity and an obedient and minimally educated labour force was seen as essential to maintain our competitiveness. Curricular as well as some degree of institutional order was imposed on a diverse system by a framework of inspection and testing, but this was typically finally abandoned in the early years of the twentieth century, apparently less on principle (although authoritative voices certainly spoke against it) than because of the high costs of maintaining it.

The second occasion of state intervention once again took place against a background of argument in terms of human rights, specifically the entitlement of pupils in all schools to a broad and common curriculum. However, once again the lever that finally swung the government into action in 1987 was the drop in our economic competitiveness which was perceived to arise partly from an undereducated workforce:

> the Government believes that, not least in the light of what is being achieved in other countries, the standards now generally attained by our pupils are neither as good as they can be, nor as good as they need to be if young people are to be equipped for the world of the twenty-first century. By the time they leave school, pupils need to have acquired, far more than at present, the qualities and skills required for work in a technological age.
>
> (DES 1985: 9)

On both occasions of state intervention in the curriculum it is worth noting that the overriding respect for commercial freedom and the belief in the class system was enshrined in the fact that privately run schools catering for the more affluent classes were exempted from the national curriculum. The government only required control over the parts of the education system which it funded. Another reason for a lack of educational principles underlying the curriculum is related to these forces for change: the requirements were pragmatic and for skills that would be commercially useful, and were thought, by politicians at least, to be self-evident.

Nineteenth-century arithmetic

By 1858 only a minority of pupils then in elementary schools were being taught arithmetic. The working class, for whom the charitable schools were designed, were regarded as lacking in civilized Christian behaviour; there was indeed some fear of urban riot. The skills needed for personal control of money were thus introduced primarily as an aspect of moral education. Furthermore, in order to equip future shop assistants, bookkeepers, technicians and craftsmen, the requirement was for accurate calculation with numbers of items, money and common measures; a few would additionally need manual drawing skills for engineering. Good mental arithmetic, resting on a basis of addition and subtraction bonds and 'times tables', was needed for oral performance (e.g. in shops and workshops) and to underpin written sums, especially adding and multiplying numbers and again, money and measures. Written calculations had to be done neatly and accurately as they were likely to appear on written bills presented to the customer or to be entered in bookkeeping or other records. Like manual work, arithmetic for most workers was likely to be repetitive; anything that required real thought would be given to those in charge.

Thus the first national curriculum, the Revised Code of 1862, which was based on earlier curricula in charity schools, was mainly phrased in terms of types of sums, gradually increasing in their complexity from oral addition through written long division to calculations of ratio and proportion. The types of exercises were later known as 'mental', 'mechanical' (i.e. written sums out of context using numbers, money or measures) and 'problems'(word problems with a utilitarian context, e.g. the total price of 7 boxes of pins at 1s 5d per box and 3 yards, 2 feet, 5 inches of ribbon at 2s 4 3/4d per yard). Because the system of imperial measures used many different bases (e.g. 22 chains = 1 furlong; 5/32″ screws), complex conversions within the system of imperial units occupied much time. Also because of this, and a utilitarian emphasis on ratio and proportion (e.g. the cost of 5 hammers if 3 cost 7s 9d), fractions were emphasized rather than decimals.

Just as it seemed clear that manual skills such as sewing and woodwork were acquired by observation and practice, watching others more expert and repeating what they did until the standard attained was acceptable, arithmetical skills were assumed to be best taught by first copying, orally or in writing, and then by repetitive practice. 'Drill' in arithmetical 'exercises' was thought to be important for training the mind, just as drill in physical exercises was to keep the body fit. Presumably it was for this reason that the exercises were often more complex than could be in practice required in commerce and industry. If you couldn't do the exercise you had clearly forgotten how, and would have to be shown and to practice it again. Mnemonics could sometimes assist the memory. Neat presentation was all-important, for both moral and utilitarian reasons.

Teaching methods, organization and assessment

The curriculum was divided into 'standards' each defined by performance descriptions, and it was these rather than age that determined the organization of pupils. Thus in 1875, 11 per cent of pupils aged 10 were still in Standard 1 (McIntosh 1981). Accountability was maintained by a system of external tests conducted in the beginning by visiting inspectors who selected pupils at random for oral examination. The results of these would help to determine the school's grant. At a later stage emphasis changed to written tests of a formal nature. Thus, given the utilitarian driving force, curriculum, teaching methods organization and assessment seemed self-evidently to follow. As Geoffrey Howson (1982) reports, however, there were even then some dissenting voices.

Even the 1858 Newcastle Commission, whose report led to the 1870 introduction of universal primary education, expressed a concern not simply that many pupils in charity schools could not satisfactorily complete their sums, but that they were ignorant of any underlying principles, such as that to which we would now refer as the principle of place value. This suggests that there was some feeling that justification for arithmetic procedures was also important and could improve performance and application.

This feeling was enunciated by Thomas Tate, a mathematical engineer and educator, who became principal of Battersea Teacher Training College:

> All tricks and clap-traps of mental calculation should be conscientiously avoided. The boy [sic] called upon to give the answer should give the process of investigation.
>
> (Tate 1854: 140)

Tate was a utilitarian who followed the contemporary 'exercise' theory of learning. Nevertheless he emphasized what we would call certain aspects of 'number sense' and 'practical problem-solving' over rote calculation and argued a more progressive case, incorporating a respect for the intellectual development of pupils:

> Teachers of elementary schools would confer a great benefit on society, by teaching the fundamental principles of estimation, rather than waste the time of their pupils in giving 'sums' . . . those investigations which have the greatest bearing invariably form the most healthful and instructive exercise to the intellectual powers.
>
> (Tate 1854, quoted in Howson 1982: 120)

Tate's progressive principles extended to the intellectual development of teachers:

> a good teacher will vary his methods of instruction . . . his judgement must be exercised in selecting those methods which are most suited to the existing conditions of his school.
>
> (Tate 1854, quoted in Howson 1982: 120)

He was also ahead of his time in proposing a five stage theory of child development, not dissimilar to that of Piaget; he felt that teachers should in determining the form of instruction not demonstrate a 'blind unreasoning attachment' to any particular system of teaching, but take into account the stages of the pupils and the context of the school, and should foster self-development and self-instruction. He also followed a liberal line in believing in a wide curriculum, extolling especially the virtues of geometry.

The Senior Inspector (HMI) of the day (and poet) Matthew Arnold also took a progressive stance denouncing the system of state control of curriculum via national tests. He wrote in his 1869/70 Report that however brilliant the committee who drew up the curriculum, 'the teacher will in the end beat us . . . by [getting] children through the . . . examination . . . without their really knowing of these matters'. He noted that although the children 'sedulously practised all the year round', the failure rate in arithmetic was 'considerable' since children were not taught arithmetical principles 'or introduced into the science of arithmetic'. In general he believed the system 'gives a mechanical turn to the school teaching . . . and must be trying to the intellectual life of the school' (quoted in Howson 1982: 121).

Thus in the last century we can see the emergence of principles for curriculum and teaching methods, but with some powerful dissenting voices who would sow the seeds of future development:

- *Curriculum 1*: the curriculum should produce obedient young people who are trained for routine employment through having accurate, speedy and neatly recorded performance of arithmetic (including knowledge of times tables, fluent oral calculation and standard written algorithms).
  (Dissenting voices: but is not 'number sense', based on a grasp of underlying principles, useful to help avoid errors? Is not practical problem solving also important?)
- *Teaching methods 1:* arithmetic is best taught by demonstration and practice.
  (Dissenting voices: practical problem solving nurtures qualities such as autonomy and intelligence; different teaching methods may be appropriate for children at different stages and in different schools, and teachers should have flexibility in selecting.)
- *Grouping and differentiation 1:* children should be allocated to classes according to their attainment, not their age, to make whole-class methods effective.
  (Dissenting voices: academic needs should not override the social needs of children.)
- *Assessment 1*: external assessment by inspection and examination is necessary for accountability and to maintain standards.
  (Dissenting voices: high stakes arithmetic testing leads to superficial learning and unthinking activity.)

It may seem odd to seek principles underpinning the arithmetic curriculum as far back as 150 years ago, but there is no doubt that some nineteenth-century (Victorian) values still underpin to a remarkable (and perhaps increasing) extent what happens in schools at the beginning of the twenty-first century. One could make the case that so far as the principles underpinning the teaching of arithmetic, some politicians, parents and the media have not moved on. For example, the current Secretary of State for Education, David Blunkett, is quoted in the first White Paper issued by the new Labour government as saying that his aims were that pupils should be able to 'read, write and add up'. More recently he elaborated this: 'The new daily maths lesson will ensure that children know their tables, can do basic sums in their heads, and are taught effectively in whole class settings' (DfEE 1999c). Recent interviews with teachers as part of the Leverhulme Numeracy Research Programme based at King's College London also show that when asked for their main curricular aims for their class they rarely divert from the curriculum specified in 1862.

In the next part of this chapter developments in each of the aspects mentioned above are described separately.

The twentieth-century curriculum

There was little radical change in the arithmetic curriculum until the 1960s. Nevertheless the calculations gradually became rather less punishing and more realistic, as the notion of repetitive drill as mind-training and good for the soul lost ground and was replaced by a more humanistic approach to children, perhaps reflecting the growing influence of women in primary education. The more tortuous calculations also decreased as the more obscure imperial units fell into disuse, and there was a little more emphasis on the metric system and therefore on decimals, although abstract manipulation of fractions beyond what could be justified in practical application was retained. The aim of knowledge of times tables, fluent oral calculation and standard written algorithms still predominated.

Between the 1960s and 1980s, however, radical changes took place in England, as in many other countries, due to a number of converging factors which occurred over different timescales but tended to work in the same direction:

- with the advent of computers and calculators, and more automated industry leading to the need for a more autonomous and educated workforce, there was no longer any consensus about what skills were needed in employment;
- universal secondary education meant that primary education could now be seen as the first stage of a broad academic education for all children rather than having to contain all minimal employment skills;
- the expected replacement in industry and commerce (in 1975) of all imperial units by metric units was thought to provide some additional space for new material in the primary mathematics curriculum;
- secondary mathematics was also in a process of radical change, due to the world-wide modern mathematics movement adapting to changes in university mathematics, and, especially in England, pressure for the inclusion of new applications in statistics and computing;
- the changes in secondary mathematics, together with the growing influence of Piagetian psychology, encouraged a shift in emphasis away from computation drill and towards mathematical structure in primary curricula;
- the introduction of comprehensive secondary education in most areas meant that there was a relaxation of the curricular control on primary schools previously exercised by the eleven-plus selection test for secondary education;

- growing evidence from Piagetian and other research that pupils had many misconceptions which led to errors in applying arithmetic, which appeared to cast doubt on the efficacy of narrowly skills-based teaching.

Primary schools were free to choose their own curriculum, and some did elect to stay with traditional textbooks, at least until the 1980s. Nevertheless the result of these pressures was a steady movement towards the replacement of arithmetic by mathematics, and by a change of emphasis from efficiency in procedures to an understanding of underlying concepts and principles. Many people and projects were associated with the changes, each with slightly different emphases, in particular Elizabeth Williams and Hilary Shuard, Edith Biggs, Geoffrey Matthews and the Nuffield Primary Teaching Project, and Harold Fletcher.

The new curricula were broad, and included statistics, logic and sets, graphs and elementary algebra, and geometry (properties of shapes, angles and transformations). The broad structural principles underlying arithmetic included one-to-one correspondence, cardinality and ordinality, commutativity, associativity and distributivity, and inverse operations.

This movement contributed to an additional principle for the primary arithmetic curriculum:

> *Curriculum 2*: primary arithmetic should be seen not as narrowly vocational but as one aspect of a much broader primary mathematics curriculum which underpins and leads continuously onto a broad secondary mathematics curriculum; it should be based on a sound grasp of the structure of numbers and of number operations.
>
> *(Still contested: do we need the breadth, or should the curriculum in the primary school contain only number and be vocationally oriented? Is an understanding of structure really necessary for effective performance?)*

It was thought that a greater understanding of structural principles would save some time in calculation practice. While there was no national agreement that there should be less emphasis than before on accurate mental and written calculation, it is perhaps not surprising that this belief, together with the broadening of curricula and aims (and some change in teaching methods, described in the next section) should at least be perceived to have led to weaker performance in calculation. There was certainly a drop in the English performance in the common arithmetic items set in the first and second IEA international mathematics studies (FIMS and SIMS, for which the main testing took place in 1964 and 1980/81 respectively), although this was in line with changes in performance in most other countries (Robitaille and Garden 1989).

It was a general concern about national standards and the liberalization of the primary school curriculum that led to gradual revision of the policy of local determination of the curriculum that had lasted for more than 50 years. This government intervention and creeping control happened gradually and progressively over the period from 1974 to 1999, under governments which were Labour (1974–79), Tory (1979–97) and finally Labour again (1997–). The steps affecting the arithmetic curriculum, in chronological order, were:

- a national agency (the Assessment of Performance Unit or APU) to monitor standards (1974);
- a 'handbook' from Her Majesty's Inspectors (HMI) on primary mathematics suggesting appropriate aims and detailed objectives (DES/HMI 1979);
- the setting up and reporting of a 3-year inquiry into the teaching of mathematics in schools (the Cockcroft Report, DES 1982) which listed some recommendations relating to the curriculum (1979–82);
- another HMI advisory report specifying detailed mathematics objectives (DES 1985);
- the announcement (1987) and development of a national curriculum specifying statutory content for each key stage of education, revised twice in quick succession and again after a five year interval (1989, 1991, 1995, 2000);
- statutory national testing at ages 7 and 11 (and 14) against a framework of criteria for attainment of progressive levels, with results at age 11 for each school published nationally (1988);
- a National Numeracy Project aimed at increasing standards in low performing local education authorities (1996);
- a National Numeracy Strategy building on the National Numeracy Project, providing a suggested programme of specific skills to be taught in each week of each primary school year (DfEE 1999a), and concentrating mainly on a repertoire of strategies for mental calculation and, later on, the use of standard written algorithms (1999).

It was clear over this whole period that the government's agenda (including both major political parties) was concentrated on strengthening calculation skills, both mental and written. This concern, which was fed by views from industry, higher education, and to some extent from aspiring parents who were becoming a more articulate force, was supported by the relatively weak English performance in number in several international tests, including the second and third international mathematics studies known as SIMS (tested in 1980/1 and reported in 1988) and TIMSS (tested in 1994 and reported in 1996).

The educators' line, expressed in the Cockcroft Report (DES 1982), was that the changed situation with regard to calculator and computer technology should shift the emphasis yet further away from neatly presented standard written algorithms, and also away from the pure mathematical aspects of structure (such as sets), onto utilitarian ends and an 'at-homeness with number', and, to a lesser extent, pure mathematical investigation. The focus was to be on mental skills, understanding of the meaning of numbers and number operations in order to be able to select the correct operations to solve real-life problems, with a strong emphasis on estimation.

The developments in the 1980s and 1990s listed above represented a sequence of engagements between the government and the educational establishment, and led by the year 2000 towards a third principle for the curriculum which has official support, although with some areas that are contested by educators:

> *Curriculum 3:* the emphasis should be on ensuring a fluency with mental calculation and estimation, and later on in the primary school with standard written algorithms and calculators, in order to be able to use these methods effectively in other areas of primary mathematics such as space and shape and data handling, and with the aim of becoming competent in solving 'real-life' problems.
>
> *(Still contested: the weight to be given to number in the mathematics curriculum; the balance and the relationship between meaning/understanding of numbers and number operation, calculation procedures, pure mathematical puzzles/ investigations and problems set in real-world contexts; the choices between the use of calculators and written arithmetic for more complex calculations, in particular whether there is any need for standard written algorithms.)*

The three statements of principles governing the curriculum referred to here have followed in chronological order, and it is clear that they represent something of a dialectical process in that there is a thesis, and antithesis and then a synthesis. However the notion that this will represent a stable final state should clearly be resisted; as society develops, as the distribution of power moves between the representatives of different viewpoints, and as dissatisfaction grows yet again with the results of previous initiatives, it is likely that there will be continuing changes in the primary mathematics curriculum.

Teaching methods, grouping and differentiation

The Victorian inclination for drill and practice was first relaxed in the younger age groups as a result of the adoption of theories and practices from Europe and, to a lesser extent, the United States. Mainly through the influence of teacher training colleges, more practical activities based on counters, cubes, beads and rods (first the Stern apparatus, much later the structural equipment associated with Cuisenaire and then Dienes) were gradually introduced for younger children. This reflected a general principle that practical hands-on activities with attractive and colourful materials were appropriate for young children, incorporating elements of play. More specifically, however, they reflected the belief that concepts and meanings can be usefully introduced and later internalized via manipulation of structural apparatus which embodied models of number (e.g. cardinal, ordinal, place value). This principle was underpinned by the work of Piaget, which started to become available in English translation in the 1930s. The philosophy was encapsulated in the Nuffield Project in the 1960s with the project motto 'I do and I understand'.

Although the purer form of this doctrine was used in some schools, in many others the reluctance to forgo pencil and paper led, at least in infant schools (up to age 7), to a sequence of:

practical activity → pictures (worksheet/book) → symbols

which had greater similarities with Bruner's formulation of a learning sequence 'enactive–iconic–symbolic'.

With older children the changes from a diet of routine calculation and stereotyped word problems, which involved looking for word-cues to spot the operation involved, took much longer. However by the mid-1980s almost all schools were using the sequence above, often with the practical activity omitted, so that colourful textbooks with diagrams were used to demonstrate meanings prior to purely symbolic work. There was no national advice about which diagrams or symbolism should be used; these varied according to the views of the textbook authors.

Thus the second principle underpinning teaching methods was:

Teaching methods 2: children need to use spatial ideas, through concrete apparatus and/or diagrams, in order to develop meanings for number and number operations.

This principle, although widely supported, did not go completely unquestioned; some (e.g. Hart *et al.* 1989) argued that the practical work did not always relate directly to the symbolic mathematics, either logically or in children's perception.

During the twentieth century a growing concern for egalitarianism (and administrative tidiness) had also gradually led to a situation in which all school pupils born within a single year were taught together. (In small rural schools several age-groups might have to be in the same class). This meant that a wide span of attainment was present in each classroom, which made it difficult to teach the whole class together, especially when the focus shifted to understanding of concepts and away from practising algorithms. Simultaneously, Piagetian studies demonstrated and provided theoretical support for individual rates of development, and empirical results quoted in the Cockcroft Report indicated that 11-year-olds could differ in their mathematical development by as much as the equivalent of seven years. Many teachers dealt with this range of ability by allowing pupils to work on their own through the textbooks, since the attractive illustrations and careful explanations in the post-1960s generation of textbooks appeared to make this feasible. Pupils were also usually separated into attainment groups so that they could work together when appropriate; some teachers kept each group together and taught each group separately.

Grouping and differentiation 2: children born in the same year should be taught together; teachers need to differentiate by individualized working and/or separate teaching of attainment groups within the class.
(Still contested: the amount of differentiation, whether to set by attainment/ability across classes or year-groups.)

While there is some evidence that individualized methods were appropriate for the development of understanding, they were probably partly responsible for the comparatively low performances in number. Individual work from a book did not encourage mental fluency with number, and it allowed pupils to continue with strategies that were often primitive; teachers were able more easily to monitor whether written answers were correct rather than whether methods used were efficient. It was partly the shortcomings of such individualized working that led to the inclusion within the Cockcroft Report (DES 1982) of three ingredients of 'good practice', *investigation, problem solving* and *discussion*, alongside the more familiar *practical work, exposition* and *practice*.

In fact the tradition of investigation and problem solving reflected an earlier move in English primary schools generally towards children being more autonomous and working in small groups on theme-based cross-curricular investigations. This derived originally from Dewey's work, and was recommended by the two major government reports on primary education this century, the 1931 Hadow Report (Board of Education 1931) and the 1967 Plowden Report (CACE 1967). Investigation and problem solving in mathematics was further emphasized, especially by Edith Biggs, an HMI, in publications and in her professional development courses which were attended by large numbers of teachers between 1960 and 1980.

Nevertheless the post-Cockcroft emphasis on investigations was a target for the 'back-to basics' political lobbies of the 1980s, and while both investigations and real problem solving are covertly encouraged by many of the people involved at all levels in the National Numeracy Strategy, their presence in the official documents is minimal.

Teaching methods 3: open problem-solving and investigation, either individually or in groups, assist motivation, learning and application.
(Still contested: whether there is any place for investigations and cross-curricular problem-solving, as opposed to mathematical word problems.)

However the Cockcroft emphasis on discussion has been strengthened both theoretically and in policy terms. The earlier emphasis on individual physical/spatial/logically-based cognitive structures has been replaced by a more recent focus on sociocultural language-based aspects of learning. Meanwhile continual pressure to return to a high proportion of whole-class teaching, from the Chief Inspector and from influential educators who are pressing the need to copy the methods of the Pacific Rim, also provide some support for whole-class discussion.

Teaching methods 4: classroom discussion, including pupils sharing their own ideas and methods with the class and with each other, improves learning.
(Still contested: the balance between whole class teaching, group and individualized work.)

Twentieth-century assessment

The nineteenth-century position on assessment referred to earlier, relying on national written testing and inspection, was reasserted in the 1990s. Yet for most of the century the only assessment affecting primary arithmetic was a locally set eleven-plus test to select an increasing proportion of primary pupils for academic schools. While this was by no means the test of 'pure intelligence' it was designed to be, it did not in most cases have a strong backwash effect. Nevertheless its removal in most areas coinciding with a radical movement in primary education, blessed by the Plowden Report (CACE 1967), enabled schools to implement changes in their teaching and curriculum in arithmetic without fear or constraint.

Two influences affected the initial proposals for national assessment which accompanied the proposals for the National Curriculum in 1989. The first was the much wider and more process-based aims that had developed in primary education during the twentieth century and flowered especially in the 1960–80 period. In particular the Cockcroft Report (DES 1982) suggested that short written examinations would not be able to assess these wider aims, and that they could only be addressed by coursework assessment during the year, which included more protracted assignments, such as practical problem solving and investigation.

The other influence was a concern for ongoing and criterion-based assessment that reported what children knew rather than what order they came in the class or cohort. If done regularly, this could inform the planning for differentiated teaching, which was felt necessary following evidence of a wide range of attainment even following similar teaching input.

Assessment 2: Formative assessment by teachers and pupils using a variety of tasks, including longer problems and investigations, gives more valid information than tests and, by ensuring a better match between attainment and curriculum, helps to raise attainment.
(Still contested: the reliability of formative assessment, what is possible in a reasonable workload.)

While both these features were present in the proposals, the political will under both Conservative and Labour governments focused on providing a measure of the relative success of different primary schools rather than any diagnostic or comprehensive information about the attainment of individual pupils. This policy, backed by teachers' concern about the additional load of formative and coursework assessment, favoured the 'objective' short external tests that are now in place, and which give rise to the same concerns that they did in the last century.

Conclusion

Thus it can be seen that the teaching of arithmetic in England encompasses a variety of principles, some deeply embedded in educational history, each of which is itself underpinned by an ideological position. One reason for the difficulties of the role of a teacher is that the curriculum, the teaching methods and the assessment must all represent balances between these conflicting principles, including some which may not correspond to the ideology of the individual teacher. Over time these balances are continually shifting according to the degree of power held by different interests, and in particular depending on the changing degree of centralization.

The adjustments needed in what would be a complex task, even in stable conditions, can be potentially exciting but can also be potentially exhausting and undermining of confidence and self-esteem. Getting the degree of centralization and the pace of change right is something which we in England have not yet achieved.

4

Realistic mathematics education in the Netherlands

Marja van den Heuvel-Panhuizen

Introduction

This chapter can be seen as a guided tour through some main aspects of the Dutch approach to mathematics education and will focus on the number strand in primary school mathematics. The main questions that will be considered are:

- How do we teach arithmetic in primary schools in the Netherlands?
- What does our arithmetic curriculum contain?

This guided tour will not take you into classrooms nor will it provide you with a representative sample of Dutch classroom practice (this can be seen in the chapter by Julie Menne in this volume). Instead, it will introduce you to a theoretical framework of teaching mathematics and the teaching activities that are in tune with the ideas this involves. What it will do is show you attainment targets identified in the Netherlands regarding mathematics, and give you an idea of the position that we want to reach in the end. Do not expect to get complete answers and a thorough overview of the Dutch approach to mathematics education from this trip as our approach to mathematics education is too complex. Moreover, the difficulty is that there is not a unified Dutch approach. Instead, there are some shared basic ideas about the what-and-how of teaching mathematics.

These ideas have been developed over 30 years and the accumulation and repeated revision of these ideas has resulted in what is now called Realistic Mathematics Education (RME). Inherent in RME, with its founding idea of mathematics as a human activity, is the idea that it can never be considered as a fixed and finished theory of mathematics education. We see RME as 'work under construction' (van den Heuvel-Panhuizen 1998). The different accentuations are the impetus for this continuing development. (For a more detailed discussion about the RME approach by means of developmental research, see Chapter 11, this volume.)

This chapter will outline key characteristics in the teaching approaches now widely adopted in the Netherlands and will identify the thinking and research that has led to these ideas. It will show some of the work that is done to implement the RME approach in classroom practice.

The Dutch approach to mathematics education

History and founding philosophy

The development of Realistic Mathematics Education started almost 30 years ago with the foundations laid by Freudenthal and his colleagues at the former IOWO, the oldest predecessor of the Freudenthal Institute. The impulse for the reform movement was the inception, in 1968, of the Wiskobas project, initiated by Wijdeveld and Goffree. The present form of RME was mostly determined by Freudenthal's (1977) view that mathematics must be connected to reality, stay close to children and be relevant to society. Instead of seeing mathematics as subject matter that has to be transmitted, Freudenthal stressed the idea of mathematics as a human activity. Education should give students the 'guided' opportunity to 'reinvent' mathematics by doing it within a process of progressive mathematization (Freudenthal 1968).

Later on, Treffers (1978, 1987b) explicitly formulated the idea of two types of process, distinguished as 'horizontal' and 'vertical' mathematization. In horizontal mathematization the students come up with mathematical tools that can help to organize and solve a problem located in a real-life situation. Vertical mathematization is the process of reorganization within the mathematical system itself, for instance, finding shortcuts and discovering connections between concepts and strategies, and then applying these discoveries. In short, horizontal mathematization involves going from the world of life into the world of symbols, while vertical mathematization means moving within the world of symbols (Freudenthal 1991: 41–2).

Misunderstanding of 'realistic'

Despite this clear statement about horizontal and vertical mathematization, RME became known as 'real-world mathematics education'. The reason, however, why the Dutch reform of mathematics education was called 'realistic' was not only because of the connection with the real world, but was related to the emphasis that RME puts on offering the students problem situations that they can imagine. The Dutch translation of 'to imagine' is 'zich REALIS-Eren.' It is this emphasis on making something real in your mind, that gave RME its name. For the problems to be presented to the students this means that the context can be a real-world context but this is not always necessary. The fantasy world of fairy tales and even the formal world of mathematics can be very suitable contexts for a problem, as long as they are real in the student's mind.

Principles underpinning teaching methods in the Netherlands

RME reflects a certain view of mathematics as a subject, of how children learn mathematics and of how mathematics should be taught. These views can be characterized by the following six principles,[1] some of which originate more from the perspective of learning and some of which are more connected to the teaching perspective.

1 Activity principle

The idea of mathematization clearly refers to the concept of mathematics as an activity which, according to Freudenthal (1971, 1973), can best be learned by doing (see also Treffers 1978, 1987b). The students, instead of being the receivers of ready-made mathematics, are treated as active participants in the educational process, in which they develop by themselves all sorts of mathematical tools and insights. According to Freudenthal (1973), using scientifically structured curricula, in which students are confronted with ready-made mathematics, is an 'anti-didactic inversion'. It is based on the false assumption that the results of mathematical thinking, placed in a subject-matter framework, can be transferred directly to the students. The consequence of the activity principle is that the students are confronted with problem situations in which they can, for instance, produce fractions and can gradually develop an algorithmic way of multiplication and division, based on an informal way of working. Related to this principle, students' own productions play an important role in RME.

2 Reality principle

In RME the overall goal is that the students must be able to bring into action mathematical understandings and tools when they have to solve problems. This implies that they must learn 'mathematics so as to be useful' (see Freudenthal 1968). The reality principle is, however, not only recognizable at the end of the learning process in the area of application; reality is also conceived as a source for learning mathematics. Just as mathematics arose from the mathematization of reality, so must learning mathematics also originate in mathematizing reality.

In the early days of RME it was already emphasized that if children learn mathematics in an isolated fashion, divorced from experienced reality, it will be quickly forgotten and the children will not be able to apply it (Freudenthal 1971, 1973, 1968). Rather than beginning with certain abstractions or definitions to be applied later, one must start with rich contexts demanding mathematical organization or, in other words, contexts that can be mathematized (Freudenthal 1968, 1979). While working on context problems the students can develop mathematical tools and understanding.

3 Level principle

Learning mathematics means that students pass various levels of understanding: from the ability to invent informal context-related solutions to the creation of various levels of short cuts and schematization, to the acquisition of insights into the underlying principles and the discernment of even broader relationships. The condition for arriving at the next level is the ability to reflect on the activities conducted. This reflection can be elicited by interaction.

Models serve as an important device for bridging this gap between informal, context-related mathematics and more formal mathematics. First, the students develop strategies closely connected to the context. Later on, certain aspects of the context situation can become more general which means that the context can assume, more or less, the character of a model, and as such can give support for solving other, but related, problems. Eventually, the models give the students access to more formal mathematical knowledge. In order to fulfil the bridging function between the informal and the formal level, models have to shift from a 'model of' a particular situation to a 'model for' all kinds of other, but equivalent, situations (see Streefland 1991; Treffers 1991a; Gravemeijer 1994b; van den Heuvel-Panhuizen 1995). The bus context (van den Brink 1989) is an example of a 'daily life' context which can evolve to a more general and formal level. In the beginning the situation is more or less pictured to describe the changes at the bus stop (see Figure 4.1). Later on the bus context has become a 'model for' understanding all kinds of number sentences. Then the students can go far beyond the real bus context. They can even use the model for backwards reasoning (see Figure 4.2).

An important requirement for having models functioning in this way is that they are rooted in concrete situations and that they are also flexible enough to be useful in higher levels of mathematical activities. This means that the models will provide the students with a foothold during the process of vertical mathematization, without obstructing the path back to the source.

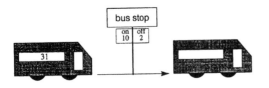
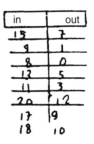

Figure 4.1   At the bus stop
Source: Streefland (1996: 15, 16)

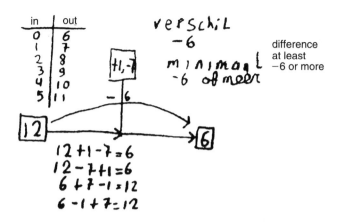

Figure 4.2   Two number sentences
Source: Streefland (1996: 17)

The strength of the level principle is that it both guides the growth in mathematical understanding and it gives the curriculum a longitudinal coherency. This long-term perspective is very characteristic of RME. There is a strong focus on the connection between what is learned earlier and what will be learned later. A powerful example of such a 'longitudinal' model is the number line (see Figure 4.3). It begins in first grade as (a) a beaded necklace on which the students can practice all kinds of counting activities. In higher grades this chain of beads subsequently becomes (b) an empty number line

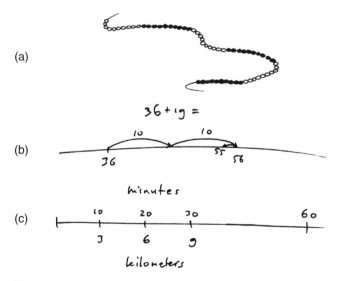

Figure 4.3   Different appearance of the number line

for supporting additions and subtractions (see the chapter by Julie Menne about her Jumping Ahead programme for underachievers in the early grades and Ruthven, Chapter 12) (c) a double number line for supporting problems on ratios, and (d) a fraction/percentage bar for supporting working with fractions and percentages.

4 Intertwinement principle

Characteristic of RME is the fact that mathematics as a school subject is not split up into distinctive learning strands. From a deeper mathematical view the chapters within mathematics cannot be separated. Moreover, solving rich context problems often means that you have to apply a broad range of mathematical tools and understandings. For instance, the mirror activity in Figure 4.4 clearly shows how geometry and early arithmetic can go together. The strength of the intertwinement principle is that it gives coherency across the curriculum.

5 Interaction principle

Within RME, the learning of mathematics is considered as a social activity. By listening to what is found by others and discussing these findings, the students can get ideas for improving their own strategies. Moreover, the interaction can evoke reflection which enables the students to reach a higher level of understanding. The significance of the interaction principle implies that whole-class teaching plays a very important role in the RME approach to mathematics education. This, however, does not mean that the whole class is proceeding together and that every student is following the same track and reaching the same level of development at the same moment. On the contrary, within RME, children are considered as individuals, each following an individual learning path. This view of learning often results in pleas for splitting classes up into small groups of students each following their own learning trajectories. In RME, however, there is a strong preference for keeping the class together as a

Figure 4.4   Mirroring and counting
Source: TAL Team (1998)

unit of organization. Instead of adapting lessons to the different ability levels of the students by means of ability grouping, differences between students are catered for by providing them with problems that can be solved with different levels of understanding.

6 Guidance principle

One of Freudenthal's (1991) key principles for mathematics education is that it should give students the 'guided' opportunity to 're-invent' mathematics. In RME both the teachers and the curriculum have a crucial role in steering the learning process, but not in a fixed way by demonstrating what the students have to learn. This would be in conflict with the activity principle and would lead to pseudo-understanding. Instead, the students need room to construct mathematical insights and tools by themselves. In order to reach this position the teachers have to provide the students with a learning environment in which this constructing process can emerge. A requirement for this is that teachers must be able to foresee where and how they can anticipate the students' understandings and skills that are just coming into view in the distance (see also Streefland 1985). Educational programs should contain scenarios which have the potential to work as a lever to reach shifts in the students' understanding. Crucial for these scenarios is that they always keep in view the long-term teaching/learning trajectory based on the goals one wants to attain. Without this perspective it is not possible to guide the students' learning.

What are the determinants of our mathematics curriculum?

Unlike many other countries, at primary school level the Netherlands does not have centralized decision making regarding curriculum syllabuses, textbooks and examinations (see Mullis *et al.* 1997). Teachers have flexibility with respect to their teaching and can make many educational decisions either by themselves, or as a school team, including choice of textbooks and even what curriculum to teach. To give some examples, teachers are allowed to make changes in their timetable without asking the director of the school (who often teaches a class too), and the teacher's advice at the end of primary school, and not a test score, is the most important criterion for allocating a student to a particular level of secondary education. Despite this freedom in educational decision making, the mathematical topics addressed in primary schools do not differ a lot between schools. In general, all the schools follow the same curriculum. This takes me to the question: what determines this curriculum?

Until recently, there were three important determinants for mathematics education in primary school:

- the mathematics textbooks series;
- the 'Proeve' – a document that describes the mathematical content to be taught in primary school; and

- the key goals to be reached by the end of primary school as described by the government.

The determining role of textbooks

Many reform movements around the world appear to be aimed at getting rid of textbooks. In the Netherlands, however, the contrary is the case. Here, the improvement of mathematics education depends largely on textbooks, which have a determining role in mathematics education and are the most important tools that guide the teachers' teaching. This is true of both the content and the teaching methods, although regarding the latter the guidance is not sufficient to reach all teachers. Many studies have, for example, provided indications that the implementation of RME in classroom practice is not yet fully achieved (Gravemeijer *et al.* 1993; van den Heuvel-Panhuizen and Vermeer 1999).

Currently, about 80 per cent of Dutch primary schools use a mathematics textbook series which was inspired, to a greater or lesser degree, by RME. Compared to even 10 or 15 years ago, this percentage has changed considerably; at that time, only half of the schools worked with such a textbook series (De Jong 1986). The development of textbook series is done by commercial publishers (chapter by Kees Buys in this volume). The textbook authors are independent developers of mathematics education, but they can also make use of the ideas for teaching activities resulting from developmental research at the Freudenthal Institute (and its predecessors) and at the Dutch Institute for Curriculum Development (the SLO).

The 'Proeve': a domain description of primary school mathematics

Looking back at our reform movement in mathematics education, it is clear that the reform proceeded in a very interactive and informal way. There was no interference from the government. Instead, developers and researchers, in collaboration with teacher educators, school advisors and teachers, worked out teaching activities and learning strands. Later on, these were included in textbooks. An important aid to the development of textbooks has been the guidance which, since the mid-80s, comes from a series of publications called the 'Proeve van een Nationaal Programma voor het reken-wiskundeonderwijs op de basisschool' (Design of a national programme for mathematics education at primary school) (Treffers *et al.* 1989). It is of note that the title refers to a 'national programme' while, in fact, there was no interference from the government.

Treffers is the main author of the 'Proeve' and work on this series is still going on. The documents contain descriptions of the various domains within mathematics as a school subject and, although it is written in a very accessible style with a lot of examples, it is not written as a series for teachers. Instead, it is meant to be a support for textbook authors, teacher trainers and school advisors, many of whom are significant contributors to the series.

The key goals for mathematics education

Until recently there was no real interference from the Dutch government regarding the content of the educational programmes. A few years ago, however, the policy of the government changed. In 1993, the Dutch Ministry of Education published a list of attainment targets, called 'key goals'. For each subject these goals describe what has to be learned by the end of primary school. For mathematics the list consists of 23 goals, split up into six domains (see Table 4.1).

Compared to goal descriptions and programmes from other countries it is notable that some widespread mathematical topics are not mentioned in this list, such as, for instance, problem solving, probability, combinatorics and logic. Another striking feature of the list is that it is so limited. This means that the teachers have a lot of freedom in interpreting the goals. At the same time, however, such a list does not give much support to teachers. As a result the list actually is a 'dead' document, mostly put away in a drawer when it arrives at school.

Nevertheless, this first list of key goals was of importance for Dutch mathematics education. The publication of the list by the government confirmed and, in a way, validated the recent changes in our curriculum. The main changes have been that:

- more attention is paid to mental arithmetic and estimation;
- formal operations with fractions are no longer in the core curriculum;
- geometry is officially included in the curriculum;
- insightful use of calculators is incorporated.

However, not all these changes have yet been reflected in the textbooks or implemented in our present classroom practice. This is especially true for geometry and the use of calculators.

In the years after 1993 discussions emerged about these 23 key goals (see De Wit 1997). Almost everybody agreed that these could never be sufficient to give support for improving classroom practice, nor to assess the outcome of education. The latter is conceived by the government as a powerful tool for safeguarding the quality of education. For both purposes, the key goals were judged to fail; simply stating goals is not enough to improve practice, and the key goals are not formulated precisely enough to provide yardsticks for testing.

Blueprints of longitudinal learning/teaching trajectories

For several years it was unclear which direction would be chosen to improve the key goals: whether for each grade a more detailed list of goals expressed in operational terms would be created, or whether a description that supports teaching rather than pure testing would be developed. In 1997, the government chose tentatively the latter and asked the Freudenthal Institute to work

Table 4.1   Dutch key goals of primary school mathematics

General abilities	1	The students can count forward and backward with changing units.
	2	The students can do addition tables and multiplication tables up to ten.
	3	The students can do easy mental-arithmetic problems in a quick way with insight in the operations.
	4	The students can estimate by determining the answer globally, also with fractions and decimals.
	5	The students have insight in the structure of whole numbers and the place-value system of decimals.
	6	The students can use the calculator with insight.
	7	The students can convert into a mathematical problem, simple problems which are not presented in a mathematical way.
Written algorithms	8	The students can apply the standard algorithms, or variations of these, for the basic operations, addition, subtraction, multiplication and division, in easy context situations.
Ratio and percentage	9	The students can compare ratios and percentages.
	10	The students can do simple problems on ratio.
	11	The students have understanding of the concept percentage and can carry out practical calculations with percentages presented in simple context situations.
	12	The students understand the relation between ratios, fractions, and decimals.
Fractions	13	The students know that fractions and decimals can stand for several meanings.
	14	The students can locate fractions and decimals on a number line and can convert fractions into decimals; also with the help of a calculator.
	15	The students can compare, add, subtract, divide, and multiply simple fractions in simple context situations by means of models.
Measurement	16	The students can read the time and calculate time intervals; also with the help of a calendar.
	17	The students can do calculations with money in daily-life context situations.
	18	The students have insight in the relation between the most important quantities and the corresponding units of measurement.
	19	The students know the current units of measurement for length, area, volume, time, speed, weight, and temperature, and can apply these in simple context situations.
	20	The students can read simple tables and diagram and produce them based on own investigations of simple context situations.
Geometry	21	The students have some basic concepts with which they can organize and describe a space in a geometrical way.
	22	The students can reason geometrically for which they use buildings of blocks, ground plans, maps, pictures, and data about place, direction, distance, and scale.
	23	The students can explain shadow images, can compound shapes, and can devise and identify cut-outs of regular objects.

on curriculum development for mathematics. This decision resulted in the start of the Tussendoelen Annex Leerlijnen (TAL) (Intermediate Goals Annex Learning/Teaching Trajectories) Project (1998) which the Freudenthal Institute is carrying out together with the SLO and CED with the purpose of enhancing classroom practice starting with the early grades. (SLO is the Dutch Institute for Curriculum Development. CED is the school advisory centre for the city of Rotterdam. Probably in the near future the National Institute for Educational Measurement or CITO will also officially participate in the TAL Project.)

Starting with a trajectory blueprint for whole number: a new approach to goal description as a framework to support teaching

The first focus of the project has been on the development of a description of a longitudinal learning/teaching trajectory on whole-number arithmetic. In November 1998 the first descriptions for the lower grades (4- to 8-year-olds) were published. The definitive version followed one year later (Treffers *et al.* 1999). The project continues with a whole-number trajectory for the higher grades. Later on, other strands will be worked out.

In the whole-number trajectory, arithmetic is interpreted in a broad way to include number knowledge, number sense, mental arithmetic, estimation and algorithms. Actually, the description is meant to give an overview of how all these elements of number are related to each other, both in a longitudinal and in a cross-sectional way. Crucial to the trajectory blueprints are the stepping stones which the students will use (in one way or another) on their way to reaching the goals at the end of primary school. These stepping stones can be seen as intermediate goals. As end goals, however, they differ in many respects from the usual end-of-grade goal descriptions, which are usually very rigid in order to be appropriate as a direct basis for testing. The intended blueprints for the learning/teaching trajectories are, in several respects, the opposite to goal descriptions traditionally supposed to guide the curriculum. Instead of unambiguous goal descriptions in behavioural terms, the learning trajectories will provide teachers with a narrative sketch of how the learning process can proceed provided that a route is followed.

The trajectory blueprints are in no way meant as recipe books, rather they are intended to provide teachers with a mental educational map that can help them, if necessary, to make adjustments to the textbook. Another difference from the traditional goal description is that there is no strictly formulated structure. In addition, the learning processes are not regarded as a continuous process of small steps, nor are the in-between goals considered as a checklist in which the ticks tell you how far your students have gone. Such an approach neglects the discontinuities in the learning process and does not take into account the degree to which understanding and skill performance are determined by the context and differ between individuals. Instead of a checklist of isolated abilities, the trajectory blueprints try to make clear how relevant skills and understanding are built up in connection with each other.

The binding force of levels and the didactical use of them

It is this level characteristic of the learning processes that brings coherence to the learning/teaching trajectory. A crucial implication is that children can understand something on different levels and several can be working on the same problems without being at the same level of understanding. This distinction of levels in understanding, which can have different appearances for different subdomains within the whole number strand, is very fruitful for working on the progress of children's understanding. It offers footholds for stimulating this progress.

As an example one might consider the levels in counting that we have distinguished for the early stage of the development of number concept in the early years (see TAL Team 1998):

- context-connected counting;
- object-connected counting;
- (towards) a more formal way of counting.

To explain this level distinction and to give an idea of how it can be used for making problems accessible to children and for eliciting shifts in levels of understanding, one could think of the ability to count up to ten. What do we have to do if a child does not make any sense of the 'how many' question (see Figure 4.5)? Does this mean that the child is simply not able to do the counting?

That this is not necessarily the case may become clear if we move to a context-connected question. This means that a plain 'how many' question is not asked, but that a context-connected question is used, such as:

- How old is she (while referring to the candles on a birthday cake)? (Figure 4.6)
- How far can you move (while referring to the dots on a die)?

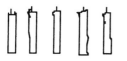

Figure 4.5 How many . . .?

Figure 4.6 How old . . .?
Source: TAL team (1998: 26)

- How high is the tower (while referring to the blocks of which the tower is built)?

In the context-connected questions, the context gives meaning to the concept of number. This context-connected counting precedes the level of the object-connected counting in which the children can handle the direct 'how many' question in relation to a collection of concrete objects without any reference to a meaningful context. Later on, the presence of the concrete objects is also not needed anymore to answer 'how many' questions. Through symbolizing, the children have reached a level of understanding in which they are capable of what might be called 'formal counting', which means that they can reflect upon number relations and that they can make use of this knowledge. Regarding the field of early calculating in Grade 1 (with numbers up to 20), the following levels have been identified (see Treffers *et al.* 1999):

- calculating by counting: calculating 7 + 6 by laying down seven 1-guilder coins and six 1-guilder coins and counting one by one;
- calculating by structuring: calculating 7 + 6 by laying down a 5-guilder coin and 1-guilder coins;
- formal calculating: calculating 7 + 6 without using coins and by making use of number knowledge about 6 + 6.

In the higher grades when students are doing calculations on a formal level the above levels can be recognized in the three different calculation strategies for addition and subtraction up to 100:

- the 'jumping' strategy, which is related to calculating by counting: it implies keeping the first number as a whole number, e.g. $87 - 39 = \ldots 87 - 30 = 57 \ldots 57 - 7 = 50 \ldots 50 - 2 = 48$;
- the strategy of splitting numbers in tens and ones, which is related to calculating by structuring: it implies making use of the decimal structure, e.g. $87 - 39 = \ldots 80 - 30 = 50 \ldots 7 - 7 = 0 \ldots 50 - 2 = 48$;
- flexible counting, which is related to formal calculating: it implies making use of knowledge of number relations and properties of operations, e.g. $87 - 39 = \ldots 87 - 40 = 47 \ldots 47 + 1 = 48$

These ideas about counting on a number line as a base for counting up to 100 are further developed in the chapter by Julie Menne in this volume.

Didactical levels

Insight into such didactical levels provides teachers with a powerful mainstay for getting access to children's understanding and for working on shifts in understanding. After starting, for instance, with context-connected questions ('How old is she?') the teacher can gradually push back the context and come to the object-connected questions ('How many candles are on the birthday cake?'). The level categories for calculations up to 20 and 100 differ considerably from, for instance, levels based on problem types and levels based on the size of the numbers to be processed. They also deviate from the more general concrete–abstract distinctions in levels of understanding and from level distinctions ranging from material-based operating with numbers to mental procedures; verbalizing is seen as an intermediate state.

As far as some of the main ideas behind the trajectory blueprints are regarded, we are just at the beginning of work on them. We do not yet know how they will function in school practice and whether they can really help teachers. Investigations to date (De Goeij *et al.* 1998; Groot 1999; Slavenburg and Krooneman 1999), however, have given us the feeling that the latter might indeed be the case and that we have triggered off something that can bring not only the children to a higher level but also our mathematics education. The interesting thing for us was to discover that making a trajectory blueprint was not only a matter of writing down in a popular and accessible way for teachers what was already known, but that the work on the trajectory also resulted in new ideas about teaching mathematics and involved revisiting our current thinking about it.

To conclude

In this chapter I have attempted to outline the main characteristics of an approach to arithmetic teaching that has been, and continues to be developed in the Netherlands. The metaphor of a guided tour through the Dutch landscape has a special meaning for Dutch mathematics educators as it was Freudenthal (1991) who called the last chapter in his last book, 'The landscape of mathematics education'. This chapter probably inspired Treffers when he took a well-known poem of the famous Dutch poet Marsman to summarize Dutch mathematics education in primary school. Let me conclude with this poem.

Thinking of Holland

Thinking of Holland
I see wide rivers
winding lazily through
endless low countrysides
like rows of empty number lines
striping the horizon
I see multibase
arithmetic blocks
low and lost
in the immense open space
and throughout the land
mathematics of a realistic brand.

(after H. Marsman's 'Denkend aan Holland'; adapted by A. Treffers 1996)

Note

1 This list of principles is an adaptation of the five tenets of the framework for the RME instruction theory that have been distinguished by Treffers (1987): phenomenological exploration by means of concepts; bridging by vertical instruments; pupils' own constructions and productions; interactive instruction; and intertwining of learning strands. Out of the six principles described in the present section, the first three have remarkable consequences for RME assessment (see van den Heuvel-Panhuizen 1996).

◯− Part III

Classroom practices in arithmetic teaching

The chapters of this section explore classroom practices in England and the Netherlands from a variety of perspectives. The first two chapters present issues that have been the focus for research and discussion in the UK, while the following three chapters, written by Dutch educators, identify particular contributions to curriculum developments in the Netherlands. Central to each of the chapters is the role of research in influencing teaching approaches and in the development of resources to support learning.

Ian Thompson is a senior lecturer in Mathematics Education at the University of Newcastle upon Tyne and has been a member of the Advisory Group for the National Numeracy Strategy as well as advisor to the government Qualifications and Curriculum Authority (QCA). In Chapter 5, he writes about three particular areas of interest that have featured high on the agenda for discussions in England leading up to the launch of the National Numeracy Strategy: *mathematics texts*, *models for teaching number* and *methods of calculation*. He identifies some of the classroom resources, such as the 'empty number line' and 'arrow cards', which he suggests constitute a different model for developing number sense and mental calculation strategies. Despite approaches involving such materials appearing theoretically more appropriate than the arithmetic blocks that were widely used in the past, he identifies some difficulties associated with their use and calls for more research to evaluate their effectiveness. Overall, he questions the way curriculum changes have been introduced in England and calls for more consideration of the classroom implications, and the validation through research of their effectiveness.

In the next two chapters, Julia Anghileri and Julie Menne look in some detail at specific research, with the implications their findings may have for changing practices in the primary classroom. As a member of the Advisory Group for the National Numeracy Strategy and consultant to the government Qualifications and Curriculum Authority, Julia Anghileri has been involved in discussions about curriculum changes and the way these may be implemented in the classroom. Her research has focused on the way children learn arithmetic and she considers the relationship between children's intuitive methods for solving problems and the written procedures they learn in school. In Chapter 6, she reports on a study that involved collaboration with Dutch colleagues from Leiden University in making a direct comparison between calculating methods for solving division problems used by English and Dutch Year 5 pupils. In discussing the results of this study, she considers the importance of pupils' understanding and the difficulties that can arise in the progression from mental to written calculation methods. She ends with a proposition that two different purposes exist for written calculation that need to be made explicit: on the one hand, *arithmetic for solving problems* requiring the solution to particular numerical problems with a focus on modelling and interpreting the result; on the other hand, more analytical approaches used in *arithmetic for exploring procedures*, which will generate understanding of the mathematical rules and relationships involved in calculating processes. Introducing this distinction, she suggests, will make clearer to children the priorities in their ways of working with numbers.

The following two chapters in this section, by Julie Menne and by Kees Buys, give illustrations of the way the Realistic Mathematics Education approach is being used in classroom practice. Julie Menne is a teacher who is researching at the Freudenthal Institute into different approaches for teaching arithmetic. In her chapter she describes some of the particular activities she has developed and successfully used in the classroom, raising the achievement of pupils identified as weak in comparison to average scores on Dutch national tests. By concentrating on developing specific 'skills' with numbers, such as *counting, locating* and *jumping*, and on 'operations' with numbers, such as *completing to 10, splitting numbers up to 10* and *jumps of 10*, she has planned a 'training program' of fundamental skills. These skills constitute 'reproductive practice' with repeated rehearsal that enables them to become automated and to be used alongside 'productive practice', where the children make up problems for themselves, sometimes with the help of an imaginary parrot named Waku-Waku.

Kees Buys has responsibility for developing a new generation of textbooks based on the Realistic Mathematics Education approach. He outlines one of the learning strands (for addition and subtraction up to 100) from a Dutch textbook series, *Wis en Reken* (an abbreviation of 'mathematics and arithmetic'). He gives typical examples of the way mental arithmetic, or 'using your head' in a wider sense, has come to occupy a central position in the Dutch curriculum.

Meindert Beishuizen is a senior lecturer in the Department of Education at Leiden University in the Netherlands and, as a psychologist, he has undertaken extensive research into the way children learn arithmetic. Most recently his research has included the evaluation of teaching programmes based on new approaches to teaching calculation methods involving an 'empty number line'. His familiarity with the approaches to calculation that are common in USA, English and Dutch schools, enables him to focus on the way mental calculation strategies are learned, and leads to a comparison of 'sequential',

N10, methods based on counting, and 'split tens', 1010, methods that reflect a place value approach. He refers to research work in the Netherlands with weaker pupils showing some examples of the way counting strategies can be modelled using the empty number line. In considering the appropriateness of introducing such approaches to English pupils, he suggests that even where place value strategies are well established, there are merits of introducing the empty number line to support the development of alternative methods.

For the reader, this section presents a stark contrast between the Dutch contributors, who show confidence that their methods have been validated through research, and the English contributors, who reflect more on the difficulties that are inherent in different ways of calculating. The discussion introduces some fundamental questions about the arithmetic curriculum, for example whether 'counting' or 'place value' methods provide the most appropriate base for calculating, and whether these different approaches can be compatible in classroom practice. Overall, the contributions on the English curriculum appear to be more negative about the changes that are taking place and do not identify those elements of innovative practice that have been more successful, for example the introduction of more open-ended questioning and investigative approaches, that give ownership to the pupils and develop their self-confidence. It perhaps reflects unease in the UK research fraternity about the way changes are being implemented with extreme haste and without the validation of research into their effectiveness.

It is certain that debates about the arithmetic curriculum will continue if educators are to meet the needs of pupils who must gain efficiency in calculating while retaining and developing their understanding of the relationships that exist among numbers. Through the discussions presented in this section it is envisaged that the reflective reader will be encouraged to identify relative strengths and weaknesses in particular calculating strategies, and share such thoughts with their colleagues and their pupils. The ultimate choice of which calculation strategies to use must, after all, be the informed choice of individual pupils who are motivated to make judgements on mathematical as well as utilitarian grounds.

⊖ 5

Issues for classroom practices in England

Ian Thompson

Introduction

Writing in the *International Handbook on Mathematics Education*, Becker and Selter (1996: 550) argue forcibly that there is a need for research to lead to improvement in classroom teaching practices, and express concern over the fact that it often appears that 'the development of desperately needed practical suggestions for elementary teaching practices is not regarded as a task worthy of scientific value'. In their chapter entitled 'Elementary School Practices', they classify mathematical education research into two types: 'analytical' research is compared with 'constructional' research, by which they mean research 'about what is' as opposed to research 'about what might be'. In the latter category they describe projects from four different countries. As part of the specific language used to describe these projects, 'in which instructional theories were developed and evaluated', the following phrases are used: 'progressive schematization', 'vertical and horizontal mathematization' (Holland); 'intertwined learning strands', 'a coherent conception of teaching units that is theoretically as well as empirically based' (Germany); and 'three non-verbal languages used to give children access to mathematical ideas' (USA) (Becker and Selter 1996: 511–64).

It was initially disappointing to find no English project had been selected for analysis. However, a few minutes' reflection raised several important questions for me, the answers to which would appear to provide ample justification for this exclusion. These questions were: 'Do we have any projects in England in which "instructional theories are developed and evaluated"?' and 'Do we, indeed, have the language to enable us to discuss ideas equivalent to those alluded to above?' Although we have established research in mathematics education, we have probably suffered in England from not having a recognized discipline of pedagogy, and from having no faculties of pedagogical sciences similar to those that exist in many European countries. Many of the topics and issues covered in courses on pedagogy are likely to be found in English courses for teacher education but they are likely to be embedded within the disciplines of philosophy, sociology or psychology. They are also hidden in the fine detail of the statutory requirements for courses of initial teacher training as found in Circular 4/98 (DfEE 1998b).

Preparation for the launch of the National Numeracy Strategy in September 1999 (DfEE 1999a) led to major changes in the teaching of arithmetic in England. Three particular areas of interest, which featured high on the agenda for discussions leading up to the strategy's implementation, have been selected for discussion in this chapter. These areas are mathematics texts, models for teaching number and methods of calculating.

Mathematics texts

Unlike most of Europe, textbooks in England do not need official approval, and consequently there is a plethora of commercial mathematics schemes available where publishing houses vie with each other for a larger share of the market. Millett and Johnson (1996) argue that the commercial mathematics scheme is the main resource for British teachers, and HMI (Ofsted 1993: 16) inform us that 'in over a third of classes there was an over-reliance upon a particular published scheme'. Desforges and Cockburn (1987: 127) report that many teachers see commercial schemes as 'conferring status on the definition of the content of a school's mathematics curriculum as they have been *devised by experts*' (my italics).

Despite the quality of some textbook series, the latter comment is quite worrying, because, if the books have been written by 'experts', then it is 'obvious' that they cannot really be questioned by a 'mere' primary teacher. The reality of the situation is, of course, that anyone in England can publish a scheme provided they can find a publisher to support their venture.

How, then, do English schemes compare with those from other countries? Harries and Sutherland (1999) carried out a detailed comparison of primary mathematics textbooks from five countries: France, England, USA, Hungary and Singapore. The schemes were compared and contrasted on a range of criteria. When analysing them in terms of their underlying principles the authors found that the schemes ranged from those that emphasized management aspects (England), through others that were mathematics education focused (France and the USA) to those that were mathematics focused (Singapore and Hungary). They commented that the organizational style of the scheme from England was as a whole more complex, and were critical of the fact that it was much more fragmented than the others. Bierhoff (1996) has argued that the rate of change of topic in English schemes is excessive, and that one consequence of this is that insufficient time is allowed for consolidation of basic concepts. This perhaps reflects the wider range of topics that pupils have been expected to study in English primary schools with the inclusion of 'data handling' and more geometry than many other countries.

Harries and Sutherland also found that the dominant characteristic of the teachers' guide for the English scheme was that of a resource from which the teacher was expected to construct the course; the American manual was seen as a lesson planning resource; and the other three were felt to be 'elaboration[s] of the text'. The authors' overall findings suggest that the English scheme provides much less immediate support and gives less emphasis to the mathematical content than the other schemes.

Origins of English schemes

As a teacher educator and a researcher, I have been critical of the authors of many English primary mathematics schemes for being too conservative and for perpetuating, rather than questioning and evaluating the teaching styles and rigorous mathematical approach of the original Nuffield Mathematics 5–13 project launched in 1964 (Thompson 1997a). This project was greatly influenced by developments in mathematics at the time, and by the views of the Bourbaki group of mathematicians in particular, being evident by the interest in set theory and focusing on mathematical precision and rigour. It was also influenced by the work of Piaget, who in the 1970s collaborated with the Nuffield team to produce assessment materials based on his clinical tests. Subsequent schemes and projects have perpetuated what later became known as the 'pre-number activities' approach to the teaching of early years mathematics that the Nuffield writers had developed. Few, if any, of these (with the notable exception of the Calculator-Aware Number, or CAN, curriculum project) attempted to trial and evaluate learning theories. Despite its influential impact on curriculum approaches and the wide interest it generated internationally, it is unfortunate that evaluation of the CAN scheme was never published as a piece of academic research in a peer-reviewed journal. The legacy of CAN's innovative practices is evident in some schools today and Kenneth Ruthven reports on some of the positive consequences in Chapter 12 of this volume.

The National Numeracy Strategy

The Department for Education and Employment (DfEE) would argue that the latest solution to the problem of commercial mathematics schemes lies in the National Numeracy Strategy's *Framework for Teaching Mathematics from Reception to Year 6* (DfEE 1999a). This document provides detailed guidance to supplement and develop the content of the *Mathematics in the National Curriculum* (DfE 1995), and provides the foundation for the new National Curriculum that is its successor (DfEE 1996). The Framework contains a set of structured yearly teaching programmes illustrating how mathematics can be planned and taught throughout the primary age range and has been welcomed as guidance by many primary practitioners. All teachers, practising or in training, received a copy, and school staff development for teachers has included training to help them implement this National Numeracy Strategy (NNS).

Two of the four key principles underpinning the NNS are:

- direct teaching and interactive oral work with the whole class and groups; and
- controlled differentiation.

These are deliberately aimed at helping teachers to plan for more whole-class teaching and to become less dependent on commercial schemes – particularly those that have in the past led to children being left to work individually through them at their own pace (see Brown in this volume).

My criticism of the Nuffield Project has been that it was, perhaps, too mathematical and too abstract (Thompson 1997a). Much emphasis was placed on ensuring that the content reflected current developments in mathematics, but this appears to have been at the expense of ensuring that the teaching suggestions were pedagogically practical. What is worrying is that publishers are again moving into uncharted territory. We have little or no recent experience in England of explicitly teaching mental calculation strategies, developing written algorithms from them, using interactive whole-class teaching methods, and so on. Consequently, current scheme writers have no earlier texts to fall back on, and are solely dependent on their own interpretation of the content and approach of the Framework (DfEE 1999a). Nor do they have a base of research findings to guide them in designing curriculum content and appropriate progression in skills and understanding that can be developed at each stage. This situation has the potential to be problematic as the NSS's 'message' is cascaded through the education system, becoming more and more distorted with each new interpretation. A few examples to illustrate this anticipated distortion will be provided in the following sections.

The above discussion raises the question: 'Is the time now ripe to address the issue of "official" approval of commercial mathematics schemes, or do the disadvantages that might accrue from this outweigh any advantages?'

Models for teaching number

The main items of practical equipment (or 'manipulatives') used in England for the purposes of teaching children about numbers larger than 10 are Dienes base-10 blocks consisting of unit cubes, rods of 10 and flat cuboids of 100. The use of this apparatus is considered to be the best way of teaching children about hundreds, tens and units and is particularly recommended in many texts for teaching the 'exchange' and 'decomposition' aspects of the standard written algorithms for addition and subtraction. Lack of success in teaching children these standard methods has led to a drive in some quarters of the English mathematics education world to shift the emphasis to alternative, more 'mental-calculation friendly' manipulatives.

The number line

The Framework (DfEE 1999a) strongly recommends that teachers should make more use of number lines in their teaching. Number lines have been used in the

Dutch Realistic Mathematics Education (RME) approach for some time, and their use subject to research, as is evident from the extended discussion in the chapters by Menne, Beishuizen, and Buys in this volume. In England, on the other hand, the number line is not so well established and teachers are given guidance in how to implement its use in the classroom. They are exhorted to have a large, long number line, preferably below the blackboard where children can touch it (as in Hungary) as well as smaller versions on their children's desks. Given this emphasis, it is worth considering what guidance on the use of number lines a conscientious teacher would find in the literature.

Several publications recommend that children extend their knowledge of 'counting-on using objects' to 'counting-on using the number line'. Let us compare the structure of the counting-on procedures used in these two different situations by calculating 7 + 5. Using objects, I say '7 . . . 8, 9, 10, 11, 12' assigning to each of the five objects in turn the number names that follow 'seven' in the learned sequence, and I stop when I have assigned a number name to the last object in the count. In this situation the answer is the last number name spoken. With the number line, once I know how to begin (and that is not as obvious as it seems) I proceed as follows (as recommended in many books): put my finger on 'seven' on the line; move my finger to the next numeral to the right and say 'one'; move my finger to the next numeral and say 'two'; continue this procedure until I say the number 'five'; and then stop and read off the numeral that my finger is on. These two operations are quite different in the words that are uttered and the actions involved, and one implication is that children who can successfully count-on using objects should not be automatically expected to count-on using a number line. As a consequence, great care needs to be taken when teaching children to use a number line for calculation purposes.

One particular commercial scheme, *Abacus* (Merttens *et al.* 1996), appears to be trying to make the two types of 'counting-on' equivalent by suggesting the following algorithm for calculating 7 + 5: place one finger of one hand on the seven on the number line; raise five fingers of the other hand; count-on using the raised fingers and say 'eight, nine . . .' stopping when you have matched the final finger with a number name, while at the same time moving your other finger onto the next number as you say it. This seems to be a complicated mental and physical algorithm, and given that the answer is found when the final finger is tagged, the immediate question that springs to mind is: 'What purpose is the number line serving?'

As part of a discussion about the appropriateness of using test items involving number line diagrams to assess the understanding of whole number operations, Ernest (1985) recommends several stages in young children's use of this aid. His recommendations are based on the widely accepted and well-documented levels of addition strategies used by young children when solving simple word problems: 'count-all', 'count-on from first' and 'count-on from larger'. However, when translated into number line representations these strategies appear to be somewhat confusing and unlikely to lead to much useful learning.

Some texts recommend the use of fully numbered lines for adding or subtracting two-digit numbers (Webber and Haigh 1999). However, even though it is suggested that children jump along the number line in tens, the presence of the individual points on the line means that children can resort to lower level strategies involving counting in ones. In fact, a foolproof algorithm for those who can count accurately will enable any two-digit addition or subtraction to be done, provided the line is long enough. For example, to find 34 + 27 proceed as follows: put your finger on 34 and count 27 places to the right. The answer is the number that your finger is on. To find 34 – 27 put your finger on 34 and count 27 places to the left. All that needs to be remembered is the direction in which to move. It is obvious that few number relationships are being learned and even fewer useful mental strategies are being developed while this process is being executed with a calibrated number line.

For the addition and subtraction of two-digit numbers the Dutch, by contrast, recommend progressive and structured teaching involving the empty number line (ENL) to discourage 'low level strategies' like counting in ones. In England such an approach has not yet been adopted, and the examples discussed above suggest that we have to work out clear 'learning trajectories' for work with number lines.

An alternative model

A different model for developing number understanding, recommended in some books and articles, is the Gattegno chart, which is a grid of numbers arranged to highlight their place value, to be used together with related place-value or arrow cards (Wigley 1997; DfEE 1999a; Anghileri in press). This model offers an alternative approach to place value (or at least what the English call 'place value') and aim to develop children's understanding of the structure of multidigit numbers in such a way that they do not think of 35, in the first instance, as a three in the tens column and a five in the units column, but rather as *thirty* plus *five*. This way of interpreting a number, in terms of the quantities it represents, is useful for the mental addition and subtraction of two-digit numbers, because most strategies for these calculations also involve some level of partitioning into multiples of tens and ones. This 'quantities' interpretation is also closely related to the language we use to read such numbers – language that the Gattegno approach is designed to develop. In English, 35 is, of course, read as 'thirty-five', and so it is more natural to interpret the number as being made up of a *thirty* and a *five* than *three tens* and *five units*. In Japanese this number would be read as 'three tens five' – an interpretation more useful for written than for mental algorithms.

The Gattegno approach would, therefore, appear to be logically more appropriate for supporting mental calculation than Dienes blocks, which closely model standard written algorithms, although some would suggest this is only possible for those who already understand them (Hart 1989). Freudenthal in the Netherlands was critical of the use of multibase blocks at a time when Dienes was advocating their use, and as a consequence they never became an intrinsic part of the Dutch teaching approach as they did in England. The place-value or arrow cards constitute a different model for developing number sense and for supporting mental calculation (Anghileri in press). However, despite the approach appearing theoretically more appropriate, to my knowledge, its effectiveness has not been formally evaluated.

Methods of calculation

One of the key principles underpinning the National Numeracy Strategy is 'an emphasis on mental calculation', a principle that has been operationalized by the inclusion of oral practice in mental calculation in each daily mathematics lesson. For the vast majority of practising primary teachers this has necessitated a major change in their classroom practice and presents opportunities to develop pupils' thinking strategies in a way that have not been possible in pencil and paper calculations.

The Cockcroft Report (DES 1982) argued for the reinstatement of mental arithmetic in the mathematics curriculum claiming that working 'done in the head' was an important and intrinsic part of mathematics. The National Curriculum, which had various incarnations in the late 1980s and early 1990s (see Brown, this volume), fixed the ability to add and subtract mentally any pair of two-digit numbers at level 4 (originally interpreted as the level of performance of an 'average' 11-year-old). However, the excessive demands made on teachers at that time in terms of the structure, language and subject knowledge relating to the National Curriculum meant that very little support was provided to help teachers get their children to attain this level of performance in mental calculation. The Framework (DfEE 1999a) specifies that this is now an expected objective for all children by the end of Year 4 (age 9).

Criticisms of the English 'obsession' with the teaching of formal written algorithms to young children have been voiced over many years by various writers (Plunkett 1979; Ofsted 1993; Beishuizen and Anghileri 1998; Thompson 1999b). One major impetus for a swing back to mental arithmetic, however, was the performance of English pupils on the number items in international tests and surveys. *Worlds Apart?* by Reynolds and Farrell (1996), a review of international surveys that involved England, raised the issue of mental arithmetic. It quoted the Bierhoff report (1996), a publication that was ostensibly a comparison of primary textbooks from different European countries, but which looked in some detail at the differing approaches to mental calculation in these countries. The report states that: 'Mental calculation is regarded on the continent as a priority, to the exclusion of formal pencil and paper algorithms until the age of nine' (Bierhoff 1996: 22).

These and other influences contributed towards the decision to ensure that a substantial emphasis was given to mental work in the National Numeracy Project, launched in 1996, and now described (post-hoc!) as a pilot for the National Numeracy Strategy. The final report of the Numeracy Task Force

(DfEE 1998a: 51) said: 'The Task Force's view [is] that mental calculation methods lie at the heart of numeracy'.

A recommendation that written algorithms should be developed from children's own mental methods has appeared in several official government documents. For example, the *Mathematics Non-Statutory Guidance* (NCC 1989: E2) informs us that 'such mental methods are the basis upon which all standard and non-standard written methods are built.'

If an emphasis on mental calculation is expected to lead to the development of written algorithms based on these strategies then it is important to ask why we need to introduce subtraction by decomposition (expanded notation) in Year 3 (DfEE 1999a, section 5: 45). This appears to represent a confusion in the aims and, to my knowledge, there are no references in the research or professional literature, on children's idiosyncratic mental algorithms, to any children having invented or discovered the decomposition algorithm for themselves. Hart (1989) has illustrated the difficulties that children experience in making connections between the activities they perform with apparatus (Dienes blocks in this case) and the written algorithms that these activities are designed to model. It appears that decomposition – a written algorithm definitely not based on mental methods – at age 8 is inappropriate. For a discussion of alternative approaches based on progressive development of different mental strategies see the chapters by Anghileri, Beishuizen and Buys in this volume.

The language of mental methods

The terminology used in the Framework (DfEE 1999a) to describe such methods is 'mental calculation', deliberately chosen instead of the more traditional 'mental arithmetic'. Politicians and the media, of course, prefer 'mental arithmetic' because it conjures up the idea of tried and tested methods and a return to good old-fashioned mental arithmetic tests with their requirement for number facts and 'times tables' to be recalled at great speed. The phrase 'mental calculation' is used to stress the fact that the calculation strand – the 'figuring out' or 'using strategies' aspect of mental work – is at least as important as the 'recall' strand, and needs to be carefully taught in a structured way. This strand is often ignored in the plethora of publications appearing on the market which purport to be written for the 'daily mathematics lesson', but which, in many cases, are 1990s rewrites of older books. These texts often provide little more than pages of practice questions testing multiplication tables and other number facts.

It is also interesting that, even though the Framework and associated training materials use the words 'recall' and 'mental strategies' to describe mental calculation, the National Curriculum Mental Tests produced by the Qualifications and Curriculum Authority (QCA) are designed specifically to assess recall and 'mental agility'. Apparently, 'mental agility' is concerned with 'ways of finding answers to questions'. The image conjured up by the word 'agility', with its gymnastic connotation of leaping lightly from one piece of equipment to another, does not sit comfortably with the important idea of children and teacher discussing and sharing mental strategies or with the notion that strategy development is inevitably a slow process. Where is there space in this model for children to acquire experience of the range of 'jottings' and 'images' emphasized in QCA's (1999a) own guidance on teaching mental calculation strategies? By focusing solely on the assessment of recall and agility in these tests QCA is illustrating a more limited conception of the nature of mental calculation than that described in the Framework.

Given that a decision has been made in England to assess mental calculation in a separate test, what can be done to improve a situation that inevitably leads to 'teaching to the test'? Are we just testing what is easy to test rather than what is important? Can we learn from our neighbours? Which other countries assess mental calculation? How do they do it? Thompson and Smith (1999) have developed a model comprising five levels of increasingly more sophisticated strategies that children were found to use to mentally calculate two-digit additions and subtractions. However, it needs to be asked whether it is feasible, or even desirable to assess children on the level of sophistication of their strategies? In the Netherlands the idea of flexibility is emphasized in the use of mental strategies. Is this what we should be trying to assess? Or should we not be bothering at all? There would appear to be a need for further research in this area.

Conclusion

Returning to Becker and Selter (1996), quoted at the beginning of this chapter, it is impossible not to agree that there is a need for more classroom-based research into the teaching of mathematics to help teachers improve their practice. There is no doubt that a wealth of useful information will accrue from King's College's Leverhulme Numeracy Research Programme (1997–2002) discussed in Chapter 10. However, it is ironic – but par for the course – that we, in England, set up a project, funded to the tune of one and a half million pounds, to look in detail at pupils' attainment in numeracy, and at effective ways of improving standards in this area shortly before we launch a National Numeracy Strategy with a completed *Framework for Teaching Mathematics from Reception to Year 6* (DfEE 1999a). This, of course, means that the National Numeracy Strategy will not be able to make use of or build upon the findings of this wide-ranging project. Compare this with the approach taken in the Netherlands where the Wiskobas project, begun in the early 1960s, led to the gradual development of the instructional theory of Realistic Mathematics Education (RME) (see van den Heuvel-Panhuizen, this volume). As van den Heuvel-Panhuizen makes explicit in her chapter, this theory and the related practice are still being developed in a variety of different forms, where the results of research, such as that pertaining to the empty number line, are fed into the education system through close work with teachers and published texts.

In the latter part of the 1990s an anti-research climate was developing amongst a small but powerful group of individuals in England. This can be clearly seen in a survey of published educational research, *Educational Research – a Critique* (Ofsted 1998). In the foreword to this survey (the Tooley Report), Chris Woodhead, Her Majesty's Chief Inspector of Schools, argues that educational research is not making a sufficient contribution to the raising of standards in the classroom. He states, more strongly than the contents of the report would appear to warrant, that, 'Much that is published is, on this analysis, at best no more than an irrelevance and distraction' (Ofsted 1998:1).

However, even when research is available, those in positions of power often seem to remain unaware of its existence, or make deliberate attempts to disregard it. For example, in the 1991 Key Stage 1 Standard Assessment Tests (SATs) 7-year-old children had to perform single-digit additions and subtractions 'by using recall of number facts only, not by counting or computation'; they were effectively being banned from using those 'derived-fact strategies' which four years later became an important aspect of the Dearing adaptations to the National Curriculum (DfE 1995). Research on derived-fact strategies had been in the public domain for many years (Carpenter and Moser 1983; Steinberg 1985), but was completely ignored.

Similarly, in the 1997 pilot mental arithmetic tests, children were penalized for including any marks to show working, other than the answer on their papers. 'Working' included 'any memory-jogging words, figures or pictures'. The resulting negative feedback from academics and teachers led, encouragingly, to a complete U-turn, and by the time the 1998 mental tests appeared children were allowed to make any 'jottings' that they wished (Bramald 1998). The English perception of a clear distinction between 'written' and 'mental' work was being questioned – even though few, if any, other countries made this fine distinction. Beishuizen (1999: 161) has argued that, 'mental' versus 'written' does not seem to be a good contrast (but a commonplace one), because the real distinctions are between the different types of strategies and procedures [used].'

One particular example where the evidence has been totally ignored and misinformation has been deliberately fed to the media for political reasons is in the area of calculator use. The government's own research and inspection evidence is fairly positive about the use of calculators as a teaching aid rather than a calculating tool and yet an official press release in July 1998 informed teachers of a ban on the use of calculators up to the age of 8 (Thompson 1999a). It is not clear that this ban has any official status but I feel there is a certain irony in a situation where a government, professing itself to be committed to the effective use of information and communication technologies (ICT), then proceeds to ban the most accessible, portable, user-friendly and cheapest form of ICT currently available. It is heartening that more recent guidance for teachers includes judicious and appropriate use of the calculator at all stages of primary schooling (QCA 1999a).

So, we have a government that espouses a policy of research and evidence-based practice in education, and we have a body of evidence backed by reliable research findings in many of the areas where decisions have to be made, and yet those decisions taken by government bodies invariably appear to ignore this research. The challenge for this millennium is going to be to develop strategies for ensuring that decision makers at all levels – teachers, advisers, university lecturers, and, last but not least, politicians – are made aware of educational research findings, and that those in power take account of this information when making important educational decisions.

6

Intuitive approaches, mental strategies and standard algorithms

Julia Anghileri

The need for change

Many teachers will have personal experiences in learning arithmetic that precede the integration of calculators and calculating aids into society. Their experiences will be based on the well established tradition of written calculations that has been described by Margaret Brown in this volume. These calculations involved standard procedures that were practised by repetitive use, with numbers that steadily increased in size. Most teachers will have been successful at this type of classroom arithmetic and many will value the satisfaction that such experiences can give. Unfortunately, this has not been reflected in the general population; the Cockcroft Report (DES 1982, para. 13) noted that:

> There are indeed many adults in Britain who have the greatest difficulty with even such simple matters as adding up money, checking their change in shops or working out the change of the cost of five gallons of petrol . . . [and] are hopeless at arithmetic.

This quotation identifies a mismatch between the abstract exercises that constituted school arithmetic and its application to real-life problems. It can also be used to indicate the changing role that arithmetic will take in a developing society. Although this quotation dates only from 1982, shopping today is dominated by machines that not only total the bills but also calculate the change, and petrol pumps dispense fuel according to the amount to be spent, eliminating the need for change altogether. Educational needs have changed from reflecting the needs of a society where all calculators were human, to a society where all important calculations are undertaken by machines, designed or programmed specifically for the task. The emphasis in teaching arithmetic has changed from preparation of *disciplined human calculators* to developing children's abilities as *flexible problem solvers*.

This change in emphasis requires new approaches in teaching that will develop children's confidence in their own methods rather than replicating taught procedures, and that will enable them to understand the methods used by others. Recommendations of the 1998 Numeracy Task Force state that 'the curriculum should have a greater emphasis on oral work and mental calculation' with more formal recording of calculation methods emerging progressively from 'personal jottings' and 'discussing and comparing different part-written, part-mental methods' (DfEE 1998a: 52).

It is acknowledged that 'standard written methods offer reliable and efficient procedures' but that the wider aspect of numeracy extends beyond the skills of computation to embrace some fundamental principles of problem solving and ways of thinking in mathematics. In the definition given for *numeracy*, the Task Force includes 'a proficiency that involves a confidence and competence with numbers and measures' and 'an inclination and ability to solve number problems in a variety of contexts' (DfEE 1998: 11). It is the relationship between mental and written strategies, and the way progression may help or hinder children's 'inclination' for solving problems, that will be the focus for the discussion in this chapter.

Mental strategies to written algorithms

In many existing textbooks and schemes of work there appears to be a development *from* mental calculations *to* more formalized written procedures with an implication that the final goal is competence with the standard algorithm. This is clearly illustrated in the teaching of multiplication and division where there has been a traditional belief that a hierarchy exists from mental methods to the standard algorithms, as shown in Figure 6.1.

Progression is certainly necessary in the direction indicated because the algorithms are dependent on mental calculation, and often jottings as well (e.g. to make estimates for the long division algorithm), but the development needs to be in both directions. Learning written methods should strengthen mental calculations and facilitate jottings (which are probably the most widely used calculating strategies in adult life) by helping to structure a calculation.

The need for different approaches can be seen in the following calculations:

25 + 39
25 + 17
25 + 26

Each of these calculations involves addition of two-digit numbers, but it is probable that each one will provoke a different strategy for mental calculation. Although they could all be solved using a vertical addition algorithm, there appears to be little *progression* from the mental approaches that reflect relationships among the numbers, to the formal procedure of the algorithm.

This is equally marked in all the operations and an example of division shows clearly some of the difficulty children may experience in making the

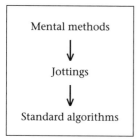

Figure 6.1   Traditional progression in calculating

transition from mental to written algorithm. In the calculation 96 ÷ 4 a mental strategy might involve the 'chunking' of 96 into 40 and 40 and 16 as numbers that are divisible by 4. Alternatively, halving 96 to get 48 and halving again would give the answer. The traditional algorithm 4)96 begins by asking the question 'how many fours in 9?' with the answer 'two' placed precisely above the 'nine'. This written procedure uses 'nine' rather than the 90 in 96, and the response 'two' is recorded as the 'tens' part of the final answer. These steps are not easy to reconcile with the holistic approach to numbers used in the mental strategies (Anghileri 1995b; in press). There are advantages to an algorithmic approach and for many adults the algorithms have become mental methods where they are easy enough to apply, for example 639 ÷ 3, but the same algorithm will present many complexities in other situations, such as 200 ÷ 3. In such cases an alternative approach may well be more effective.

Moving away from intuitive methods

Before the standard algorithms are taught in school, children's first approaches to solving numerical problems reflect the understanding they have of each individual situation. Multiplication and division provide rich problems for studying individuals' strategies because children will already have considerable experience with numbers and problem solving. Research on children's strategies for solving multiplication and division problems reveals that intuitive approaches children use in the early years appear to be replaced in the later years by standard taught procedures (algorithms). Mulligan and Mitchelmore (1997: 309), in a study of Australian children in Grades 2 and 3, found that

> children [in the early years] acquire an expanding repertoire of intuitive models and that the model they employ to solve any particular problem reflects the mathematical structure they impose on it.

Even when the algorithms are introduced there is evidence that children persist in employing their own methods with better success. Murray *et al.* (1991: 50) in South Africa found that young children invent powerful non-standard algorithms alongside school-taught algorithms: that they prefer to use their own algorithms when allowed to . . . and that their success rate when using their own algorithms is significantly higher than the success rate of children who use the standard algorithms or when they themselves use standard algorithms.

This flexibility and confidence with their own methods does not persist as children try to conform to the algorithmic procedures that have a high profile in mathematics teaching. In a study of Japanese students (Grades 2, 4, 6 and 8) to identify strategies used to mentally compute it is reported that: 'the range of strategies (initial and alternative) used to do mental computation was narrow, with the most popular approach reflecting a mental version of a learned "pencil/paper" algorithm' (Reys *et al.* 1995: 304).

This suggests that even in Grade 2 children are conforming to an algorithmic procedure. The inclination and ability to match a mental method to the numbers in the problem is overtaken by a more mechanistic approach reflecting what has been taught in school rather than the more intuitive methods evident in younger children's strategies. Reporting on a study of US students in Grades 6, 7 and 8, Silver *et al.* (1993) considered pupils' responses to the problem involving '540 (532, 554) people to be transported on 40 seater buses' (the three numbers in brackets represent different items). They found that: 'All the students' performances indicated use of an algorithm . . . 70% used the long division algorithm . . . 20% used other algorithmic procedures such as repeated subtraction.' The researchers concluded that:

> Student performance was adversely affected by their dissociation of sense making from the solution of school mathematics problems and their difficulty in providing written accounts of their mathematical thinking and reasoning.
>
> (Silver *et al.* 1993: 123)

Conflict with the development of problem-solving skills

The focus on written algorithms in school appears to be in conflict with the development of children's personal skills in problem solving, and teachers will be familiar with children who are more concerned to know the 'right way' to tackle a calculation than thinking through a method for themselves. The algorithm has advantages in that it provides a concise structure for written recording and, if used correctly, will usually be an efficient way to calculate. The fact that it may become a mechanical procedure can be an advantage where it relieves the need to think about the calculation, enabling a better focus on the problem to be solved. Critics of the algorithm (Plunkett 1979; DES 1982; Thompson 1997b; Anghileri 1997; Anghileri and Beishuizen 1998) have, however, been suggesting for many years that this advantage is outweighed by the difficulties that are encountered in the abbreviated formal recording that is required. The introduction of the standard algorithm has been shown to lead to errors where it is incompatible with intuitive approaches (Anghileri 1998, in press). If the emphasis in teaching is to develop flexible mathematical thinkers who are skilled in communicating their ideas, it is time to stop teaching the algorithm and encourage efficiency in the children's own written methods.

When larger numbers are involved and mental calculations are difficult, pencil and paper recording becomes necessary for keeping track as the problem is broken down into manageable stages. Ruthven (1998: 31) identifies two distinct purposes for written recording: 'to augment working memory by *recording* key items of information' and 'to cue sequences of actions through *schematising* such information within a standard spatial configuration'. Intuitive approaches are supported by jottings that may initially be idiosyncratic in providing a personal record that is difficult for others to follow. The algorithms, while providing a procedure that is efficient, standardized and succinct, are difficult for children to understand. Where the algorithm is difficult to reconcile with an individual's understanding it will be difficult to reproduce, and without understanding the steps involved, children may reconstruct a procedure that looks approximately right. Ruthven and Chaplin (1997) refer to 'the improvisation of malgorithms' to describe pupils' inappropriate adaptations of the procedures for the algorithm. Little support appears to be given in school to helping children structure better their own ideas; more emphasis appears to be given to replacing their thinking with a standard procedure.

A study of children's strategies for division problems

The cognitive complexities involved in moving from intuitive yet inefficient strategies, to the curtailed recording involved in the traditional standard algorithms, have been a focus for a recent study undertaken by contributors to this book (Anghileri *et al.* 1999; Anghileri in press), analysing children's methods for solving division problems. This comparative study of English and Dutch pupils in Year 5 (Grade 4) looked at the intuitive strategies used and the way approaches to calculations changed after additional teaching. Pupils in the same year groups in England (n = 276) and in the Netherlands (n = 259) were tested in January and June, before and after teaching that involved division calculations.

What are intuitive approaches?

A test involving ten problems with one and two-digit divisors was constructed with each type of problem presented in a context and in a parallel 'bare' symbolic sum (see Table 6.1). The numbers were chosen to encourage intuitive approaches even where the size of the numbers went beyond the children's experiences of division. By asking children to write down the way they worked out the answer, including their thinking, their strategies were compared before and after five months had elapsed, and across the two countries. The children's work in the first test included 'low level' strategies such as direct modelling of the problems with tally marks, and repeated adding or subtracting, which was inefficient where large numbers were involved. For some children the different contexts stimulated methods that appeared to model the question, particularly the shopkeeper question, which was illustrated by some children using a 'sharing' strategy (see Figure 6.2).

This method was generally unsuccessful except for a few children who 'shared' larger portions (fives and then tens and twenties), keeping a running total until they reached the required number. The bare problems, which were presented symbolically without a context, were not solved in this way and appeared to stimulate more procedural calculating approaches. In the second test the numbers used were the same but context and bare problems were interchanged to reduce the impact of memory. The greatest improvements in terms of the number of correct solutions were in those problems that changed from bare to context. Little change in success rates was seen in those that changed from context to bare. This study showed that providing a context will help children identify an appropriate solution strategy that could be used instead of the algorithm.

In this study, it was clear that certain approaches, although appearing to be intuitive, had been encouraged by teachers, in order to lay the foundation for the structured algorithmic approaches. Although it appears to relate to an intuitive way of thinking about division, repeated subtraction of the divisor (e.g. calculating $98 \div 7$ as $98 - 7 = 91$, $91 - 7 = 84$, etc.) was only used by the Dutch children (3 per cent in test 1) as it forms the basis for the standard Dutch algorithm. Repeated subtraction was not used at all by the English children, a number of whom preferred repeated addition (9 per cent in test 1 and 7 per cent in test 2) even where the numbers were very large. Some Dutch children used repeated addition in test 1 (3 per cent) but none used such 'low level' strategies in test 2. More English children persisted with a 'low level' strategy in the second test (7 per cent) while all the Dutch children introduced some efficiency into their attempts in the second test and none used repeated addition or subtraction (see Table 6.2).

Table 6.1   Ten problems used to compare strategies of English and Dutch children

Context problem		Bare problem
1 98 flowers are bundled in bunches of 7. How many bunches can be made?	6	$96 \div 6$
2 64 pencils have to be packed in boxes of 16. How many boxes will be needed?	7	$84 \div 14$
3 432 children have to be transported by 15 seater buses. How many buses will be needed?	8	$538 \div 15$
4 604 blocks are laid down in rows of 10. How many rows will there be?	9	$804 \div 10$
5 1256 apples are divided among 6 shopkeepers. How many apples will each shopkeeper get? How many apples will be left?	10	$1542 \div 5$

1256 apples

1256 apples are divided among 6 shopkeepers.
How many apples will every shopkeeper get?
How many apples will be left?

Working:

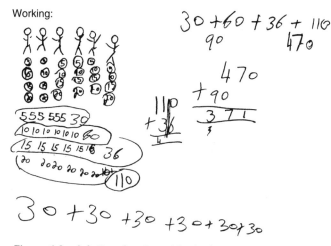

Answer:................

Figure 6.2 Solution showing a 'sharing' strategy

Classifying the strategies

In order to identify progression in the different approaches, each individual strategy was classified for all 10 problems in each of the tests (n = 5350 items). 'Low level' strategies, **1(S)**, included tallying and direct addition or subtraction of the divisor. Other strategies used place value to partition the dividend, the divisor, or both, operating with the digits independently, **2(P)**. Sometimes this involved wrong assumptions about the way the numbers could be partitioned (e.g. 64 ÷ 16 was attempted as 6 ÷ 1 and 4 ÷ 6). More efficiency was evident in strategies that used doubling, or halving, or repeated subtraction of other multiples of the divisor in 'low level chunking' **3(L)** (e.g. using chunks of 30 when dividing by 15) or 'high level chunking' **4(H)** (e.g. using chunks of 150). In the Netherlands, children are taught a standard lay-out (algorithm) for recording these procedures of repeated subtraction. The traditional algorithm **5(AL)** was used to structure a procedure based on place value and sometimes involved additional jottings. Where an answer was given but no working shown, this was classified as a mental strategy **6(ME)**. Sometimes a wrong operation was used **7(WR)** or the method was unclear **8(UN)**. Table 6.2 shows the strategies used in each of the tests.

Overall, the results showed development towards efficiency in the strategies used in both countries with more correct solutions among the Dutch children in the first test (47 per cent) compared with the English (38 per cent). Despite a 'higher' initial position, a bigger increase in correct solutions in the second test was evident for the Dutch children (68 per cent correct) while the English results were some way behind (44 per cent correct). These results reflect not only the explicit teaching of division by a two-digit divisor in Grade 4 (Year 5) in the Netherlands, which is not common in England, but also the progressive development from informal strategies to a standard procedure for 'high level chunking' which constitutes a standard algorithm in the Netherlands (Anghileri in press). It is notable that half the items (49 per cent) in test 2 were attempted by the English children using the traditional algorithm and only about half of these attempts were successful (25 per cent of all attempts).

Differences in the taught algorithms?

In English schools, teaching in Year 5 usually includes the introduction of a standard procedure for division by a single-digit divisor. The traditional algorithm, referred to as short division, is based on the place value of the digits and involves a structured written record using prescribed steps. Two-digit divisors are introduced later as the algorithm is adapted to long division, involving more complex stages.

In the Netherlands, division is a focus for Grade 4 (Year 5) teaching in the second half of the year and a different algorithm, based on repeated subtraction, is used. Sometimes the calculation is started by making a list of multiples of the divisor which may be used to identify appropriate steps (see Figure 6.3). Progressive stages are introduced to improve efficiency by subtracting larger 'chunks' that are multiples of the divisor.

The same holistic approach is used in the Netherlands for one-digit and two-digit divisors. Children have the flexibility to use 'chunks' of their own choice to subtract. This technique leads to varying degrees of efficiency as children progress, unlike the traditional algorithm, which has a precise shortened format and requires a precise calculation at each step.

Using a standard procedure for single-digit divisors

Because two-digit division is not introduced in the English schools, in the study discussed above a comparison was made of the four problems involving a single digit divisor, 96 ÷ 6, 98 ÷ 7, 1542 ÷ 5, 1256 ÷ 6. In both countries, the relevant standard procedure was the most common approach used by the children – the traditional short division algorithm in England, and an algorithm based on high level chunking in the Netherlands. The Dutch children were more successful, particularly with larger numbers (see Table 6.3).

From these results it is clear that, even with only a single digit divisor, the English children are less successful at using the algorithm for larger numbers

Table 6.2 Summary of strategies used in test 1 and test 2

	Dutch test 1		English test 1		Dutch test 2		English test 2	
	attempts (%)	correct (%)	attempts (%)	correct (%)	attempts (%)	correct (%)	attempts (%)	correct (%)
1(S)	10	4	17	7	1	1	11	6
2(P)	7	1	5	0	6	2	3	0
3(L)	16	7	6	2	6	5	8	4
4(H)	41	28	8	5	69	51	7	3
5(AL)	4	1	38	18	3	1	49	23
6(ME)	9	6	9	5	11	7	11	5
7(WR)	5	0	3	0	1	0	2	0
8(UN)	2	0	4	1	1	0	3	0
missing	8	0	9	0	2	0	8	0
overall		47		38		68		44

Note: Figures rounded to the nearest whole number.

1542 ÷ 5

Kladblaadje:

Working:

$$\begin{array}{r} 0\,3\,08\,r2 \\ 5\overline{\smash{)}1\,5\,4\,2} \end{array}$$

5) 15 (2) 308   rest 2
500   100x
1042
1000   200x
42
40   8x
2

Answer: 308 r2

Antwoord: 308 r 2

English algorithm   Dutch algorithm

Figure 6.3   English and Dutch algorithms

and many errors occurred. Although the Dutch children found the large numbers more difficult, their holistic approach led to greater accuracy. Errors with
the traditional algorithm in England included inappropriate use of separate
digits, incorrect identification or use of a remainder, and missing the zero in
the answer (see Figure 6.4). Where this algorithm was attempted inappropri-
ately, for example to solve 64 ÷ 16, it appears that the English children could
not 'change back' to a more informal approach (such as doubling) that would
have enabled them to find a solution.

From intuition to algorithm

There is not only a question of which standard procedure to teach for each of
the operations in arithmetic, but how to develop progressively children's
understanding, and how to retain their flexibility to tackle different problems
using appropriate approaches. Although the mechanization of a standard procedure can have advantages, it is important that the calculation does not
become detached from the meaning of the problem and automatically applied
in all cases. Intuitive approaches to division, for example, are developed from
ideas of sharing and grouping using experiences of calculating, including
doubling, halving, adding, subtracting and place value, and it is important

Table 6.3   Use of algorithms for problems in test 2 involving a one-digit divisor

	$96 \div 6$	$98 \div 7$	$1542 \div 5$	$1256 \div 6$
English (n = 276)				
traditional algorithm	66% (51)	66% (52)	70% (34)	67% (21)
Dutch (n = 259)				
Dutch algorithm: repeated subtraction of large chunks	78% (69)	76% (69)	71% (52)	72% (50)

Note: The figure in brackets is the proportion of these attempts that were correct.

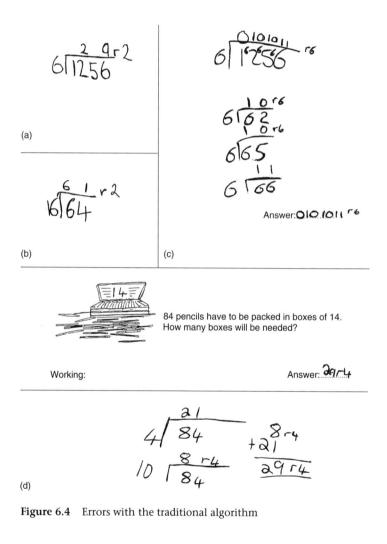

Figure 6.4   Errors with the traditional algorithm

that children are guided to greater efficiency and effective ways to record their calculations without reducing their understanding.

Teachers will be able to assess pupils' different understanding where long-winded and inefficient methods are recorded. These methods reflect a stage of understanding that is the starting point for gains in efficiency. At this stage it is important that pupils are helped to organize their recording without losing the personal nature of these strategies.

In the study referred to above, many children's illustrations showed that they were thinking of the problem as a sharing or grouping situation. It has been shown that such ideas hold an enduring position in pupils' intuitive thinking (Fischbein *et al.* 1985; Anghileri 1995b) and may not easily be reconciled with taught procedures. The images associated with such approaches suggest that children's intuitive thinking will need considerable adaptation before the algorithm can 'fit' their understanding of the problem. If they are to use a standard approach to all division problems, they will need to know that calculations will not follow intuitive understanding of a particular problem. This is perhaps the strongest argument for developing individual approaches to their greatest efficiency, rather than replacing an inefficient personal procedure with a standard approach (Anghileri 1997, in press).

Even where strategies are accepted to be detached from the context of a problem, the relationship of any calculation to a child's existing understanding of number operations needs to be taken into account. Many wrong calculations in the division study stemmed from an approach based on place value, generalizing the distributive rule to break down a calculation into steps. The approach used for partitioning numbers for multiplication using the distributive rule, for example $8 \times 14 = (8 \times 4)+(8 \times 10)$, was, for example, used for division to calculate $64 \div 16$ as $6 \div 1$ and $4 \div 6$ (with the 4 and 6 often reversed to make the calculation 'possible') (see Figure 6.4b). Where children have learned the vertical algorithms for addition, subtraction and multiplication, which require digits to be carefully lined up in structured recording, and which encourage more mechanical operating with the digits separately, there appears to be a tendency to work similarly with division instead of trying to understand what the operation means.

Calculating with digits rather than whole numbers in a division problem is not easy to reconcile with the place value *meaning* of the digits. Sometimes, even where place value meanings are correctly applied, this working can make a problem more complex than necessary as the attempt in Figure 6.5 illustrates. This problem becomes much easier if 1256 is partitioned into 1200 (12 hundreds) and 56.

Steps in developing an algorithm

Teaching approaches in English and Dutch classrooms are characterized by significant differences in the ways children are encouraged to think about arithmetic (see other chapters in this volume). There is a strong tradition in the United Kingdom to make place value the central structure that will enable

1256 *apples*

1256 apples are divided among 6 shopkeepers.
How many apples will every shopkeeper get?
How many apples will be left?

Working: $100 \times 6 = 600$ Answer: *1.36*.....

$1000 \div 6 = 106 r 2$

$200 \div 6 = ~~180~~ ~~18 120~~ ~~188~~ 21 r 2$

$50 \div 6 = 8 r 2$

$6 \div 6 = 1$

$106 + 21 + 8 + 1 = 136$
          127   9

$2 + 2 + 2 = 6$

Figure 6.5   Division strategy using place value partitioning

efficient approaches to calculating. Materials used in the classroom reflect this emphasis and Dienes apparatus, number cards and number fans promote the partitioning of numbers into hundreds, tens and units from an early stage. It is not surprising that written recording is identified with this view of numbers, as digits placed in specified positions, to facilitate the working in any given calculation. Recent directives (DfEE 1998a) propose that written calculation procedures are not introduced until the latter part of Year 3 (8-year-olds) but the emphasis on place value remains. Published advice for teachers notes that 'progression in understanding about place value is required as a sound basis for efficient and correct mental and written calculation' (SCAA 1997c).

In the Netherlands the mathematics curriculum has been developed using Realistic Mathematics approaches, which focus on the systematic development of more naïve strategies like counting. The development of support materials includes the bead string and the empty number line to support mental calculating (see Menne and Buys, this volume). In a process referred to as 'progressive mathematization' the Dutch children are led through progressive stages from mental to written calculations; for example, division starts with repeated subtraction and written recording develops efficiency through 'chunking' using appropriate multiples of the divisor. This is often explicitly linked with the counting patterns that children learn (see Menne, this volume), for example a listing of doubled multiples ($1\times$, $2\times$, $4\times$, $8\times$) may be written at the start of a division calculation for reference. At all stages, the holistic approach to numbers is retained and this method will never achieve the condensed format characteristic of a place-value approach.

Concern has been expressed about the limitations of counting as a basis for calculating as overdependence on such naïve approaches 'will limit the development of "strategic methods" (SCAA 1997c). Preference is given to the more traditional written methods that achieve the greatest efficiency but can be the most difficult for children to understand. Advice included in the QCA guidance for teachers (QCA 1999b) does not distinguish between 'counting in ones', which is limiting in the way suggested, and counting in multiples other than ones, which can provide a powerful approach to calculations. It is not made clear what are meant by 'strategic methods', but other countries besides the UK do not support the development of counting strategies as the Dutch do. The 'chunking' that is central to the algorithm taught in the Netherlands is a development of counting and has been referred to as 'basically a "guess and check"' strategy by Silver *et al.* (1993).

Apparent 'dismissal' of some approaches is again evident in advice for teachers in England with detailed examples in the National Numeracy Framework (DfEE 1999a) identified as 'informal' and 'part written' calculations, while the objective remains to achieve standardization. The Framework appears to indicate a hierarchical development towards the 'formal written methods' that have been traditional with a progression in the size of numbers involved but not in the approach. Alternative recording methods are illustrated but have been 'devalued' by their label as 'informal'. There is, however, an optimistic note in the legislation of the new National Curriculum for England and Wales, statutory from August 2000 in Key Stages 1, 2 and 3. The replacement of a requirement for 'standard written methods', by a requirement for 'efficient written methods', will go a long way to enable teachers to encourage children to develop the methods that they understand to greater efficiency, without loss of ownership.

Whatever the approach, it will not be effective to teach a compact standard procedure if the pupils' level of understanding makes the explanation underlying this method inaccessible. In attempting to replicate a method that they cannot themselves re-create, it will be inevitable that lapses in memory will mean that errors are introduced that the children themselves do not have the ability to detect and rectify.

Making clear the agenda for learning

Some people will argue that when calculations cannot be done in the head, they should be done on a calculator. It has been known for some time that adults do not use the standard algorithms they were taught in school (DES

1982) but use idiosyncratic methods and personal jottings. Across the developed world, all the important calculations in society today are done by a skilled operator using a machine (calculator or computer). The world of school is, however, different and it is not the sole purpose in a calculation to find the answer, although this is not always made explicit to children. There is knowledge and understanding to be gained through *doing* calculations that can initiate children into the world of mathematics, revealing the patterns and relationships that will empower them to go on to more complex calculations, and that will be the basis for working with more abstract higher mathematics.

The time has come in the mathematics curriculum to clearly identify the agenda for arithmetic teaching and, where necessary, to have separate purposes for activities with numbers. *Arithmetic for solving problems*, where the main purpose is to find a solution, may require a different (convergent) methodology from the more analytical (divergent) approaches that are reflected in *arithmetic for exploring procedures*, where the purpose is to generate understanding of mathematical relationships underlying the processes involved in finding a solution.

In *arithmetic for problem solving* only one approach will be necessary in order to find a solution and it may not always be appropriate to debate the most succinct written method for calculating. The focus will be on interpreting the information for a given problem, modelling the situation arithmetically, and applying the result of a numerical calculation to find a meaningful solution. For the problem 'How many buses are needed to transport 532 people on 15 seater buses?', initial identification of the operation as division could lead to the answer 35.466667 which would need to be interpreted in terms of the number of buses needed. This problem provides a good example of the way calculations may lead to mathematical thinking, even where a calculator is used.

In contrast, *arithmetic for exploring procedures* will involve exploration of the many different ways to tackle a single calculation and the effectiveness of different approaches. The purpose will be to identify links among numbers, and among the operations, that will help to develop children's understanding of number relationships. An example may involve possible ways to calculate 300 – 158, and include the relationship between addition and subtraction, and the use of 'near doubles'. Particular types of calculation may be formalized in a written record to make explicit the rules and relationships that underpin the different approaches that may lead to generalizations.

Clearly these different purposes for arithmetic could be combined but children need to be aware of what they are to learn from any activity, and separating these two purposes may provide a clearer agenda. Each purpose will strengthen the skills and understanding gained from the other and the two should be seen as complimentary rather than separate, just as reading and writing are related elements in learning language. The purpose of written algorithms will be identified with their conciseness as written records, and the way they encapsulate rules and relationships among numbers in a formal procedure. Their elegance and rigour rather than their utilitarian nature could give them a valued position in mathematics learning.

Many mathematics educators have argued that algorithms are no longer needed while others argue just as forcibly for their continued inclusion in arithmetic teaching. In an argument that has long been a classic in debating the place of algorithms, Plunkett (1979) argued that the reasons for teaching the standard written algorithm are out of date and their utilization leads to 'frustration, unhappiness and a deteriorating attitude to mathematics'. Perhaps it is the objectives in teaching the algorithms rather than the algorithms themselves that now need to be questioned.

⊖ 7

Jumping ahead: an innovative teaching programme

Julie Menne

Introduction

Although the Realistic Mathematics Education (RME) curriculum has been received with enthusiasm in Dutch classrooms, many teachers still feel that the textbooks do not give them enough guidance on how to give effective, oral lessons that focus on the development of mental calculation strategies. This is a missed opportunity because interactive whole-class teaching can help the strong, as well as the weak mathematicians in a class, to solve their problems in a clever and flexible way. Such lessons may also increase the children's enjoyment of mathematics and may provide opportunities for differentiation (Treffers 1997).

Having these goals in mind, the Freudenthal Institute has started a research project, in cooperation with teachers of eight Year 3 classes, to look at improved ways of teaching arithmetic with numbers up to 100. (It is typical for the Dutch curriculum to work in stages with limited numbers, first up to 10, and then 20, and later up to 100.)

The experimental group for the research programme consisted of almost 200 children in eight Year 3 classes who were low achievers in mathematics. Of the sample, 60 per cent were Dutch second language speakers from countries such as Morocco and Turkey. Furthermore, half of the children were from disadvantaged social backgrounds. At the start of the programme the average test results for all children involved was far below the national average and some 40 per cent of them were among the bottom quarter when compared with national scores.

During the development of the programme it became clear that problems with mathematics were not only due to insufficient grasp of the language, but the children really had problems with the subject matter itself. Weak pupils often lack all sorts of fundamental skills, for example a lot of them do not know the counting sequence up to 100 and they cannot continue strings such as '40, 50, 60, . . .', '30, 35, 40, 45, . . .' and '92, 82, 72, . . .'. As long as the underlying structures in such number sequence remained obscure, it would be impossible to develop methods for abbreviated and efficient mental calculations. So, the training programme will first give children the opportunity to gather these fundamental skills. Number problems that can only easily be solved when something is known about structures in the counting sequence are kept for the second half of the programme.

I will describe the level at which low attaining pupils should be able to calculate at the end of Year 3 ('desired level'). How to get there is explained by so-called 'reproductive practice' (concentrated on fundamental skills: those concerning 'number concept' and 'number operations') and 'productive practice' (concentrated on own productions). In the section on classroom organization, guidelines are given for effective practice. The chapter ends with a summary of the results of the programme.

Desired levels

At the end of Year 3 children should be able to deal flexibly with different two-digit number problems, and to find abbreviated methods using the empty number line (see Thompson and Buys, this volume). This means, on the one hand, choosing a solution strategy dependent on the numbers given, and on the other hand calculating the correct answer in as few steps as possible. Treffers (1998) identified three increasing levels for a mental solution strategy:

- calculating by *counting* – supported by counting materials whenever needed;
- *structured* calculating – without counting but with the help of suitable models;
- *formal* calculating – using numbers as mental objects for curtailed and flexible calculating without the help of any structured materials or models.

At the beginning of the school year it is assumed that all children can solve calculations with numbers up to 20, at least by counting one by one. Such a counting strategy, however, is a poor method for calculations involving numbers up to 100. A 'jumping' method, on the other hand, provides possibilities for *abbreviated* ways of calculating, and links in a most natural way to what children can do already. Just as in calculating by *counting*, the first number is taken as a whole, and moving forwards or backwards in the number sequence can be modelled with jumping on a number line. An empty number line invites a jumping strategy that relates well to the children's own experiences. When the jumping strategy consists of shortened jumps, a child calculates at the level of so-called *structured* calculating. This level of structured calculating is the minimum goal for all kinds of number operations. Ideally, after one year of practice, all the children should be able to solve any sum up to 100 at least at this (second) level.

Let us have a closer look at what this means for a context problem such as: 'On the bus are 43 people. At the bus stop 18 people get off. Nobody gets on. How many people are still on the bus?' (Janssen *et al.* 1992). One can solve

'43 – 18' by jumping 20 back in one go, and then, because you have gone too far, you have to take a jump of two in the opposite direction. It is also possible to carry out this calculation in a less abbreviated way by jumping back 10 followed by eight hops of one. Figure 7.1 shows how these more and less shortened methods can be visualized on the empty number line.

Of course, within this structural level one can think of intermediate forms of shortened calculations. It happens, for example, that a jump of 10 can be combined with partitioning using complements in 10. This can be done by first taking a hop of three back to 40, then a jump of 10 to 30, and finally a hop of five, all in the same direction. It is interesting that only 53 per cent of Dutch Year 3 children could solve this problem correctly in a national arithmetic test.

Reproductive practice

Reproductive practice is identified with procedures that first focus on finding the right answer, and later focus on the way the answer has been found. For being able to calculate at level two (*structured* calculating) children should be familiar with some fundamental skills. These skills may be divided into those relating to numbers, and those relating to operations with numbers. Skills concerning number concepts are:

- counting from any number;
- locating numbers in relation to each other;
- identifying jumps towards a number.

Skills concerning number operations are:

- complements in 10;
- splitting numbers up to 10;
- jumps of 10.

In the next section examples of training for each of these fundamental skills are given. Of course, actual lessons will consist of several activities for each type of practice.

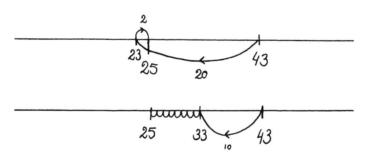

Figure 7.1   More and less shortened jumping solutions on the empty number line

Skills concerning number concepts

Counting

As can be seen in Figure 7.1, for the less shortened jumping solutions children are in fact counting from any number in either direction. Learning the counting sequence is therefore an important building block for a practice repertoire. At the beginning of Year 3 learning how to count is not much more than learning a rhyme. As they can already count and use numbers at least to 20, they now start learning the bigger counting sequence. First the children need to know the tens as landmarks: 10, 20, 30 . . . 100, 110 . . .

If they do not know what comes after '27, 28, 29' they will get stuck time and time again. Furthermore, a lot of practice is needed in counting on from *any* number. At this stage the mechanical character of counting is emphasized and for this purpose, whole-class activities such as the following can provide effective practice:

> Start with the teacher walking around the classroom while counting aloud. At a certain moment she touches a child who then takes over by counting on while themselves walking around the classroom. When the teacher gives a sign to stop, the nearest child is given a turn, and so on. This kind of practice is very efficient as hardly any time is lost in instruction and all the children are participating in silence, as they could be picked out at any moment!

In the beginning, this type of 'chronological counting' in order is often preferable practice over sums like '4 plus 5' or '15 minus 12'. These number operations are based on insight, while counting has essentially a mechanical character. Learning how to count concerns nothing more than that the numbers one to nine interwoven with the nice, round numbers (with the exception of 11, 12 and 13 whose sounds do not quite fit the system – this is also true for 14 in the Dutch language). For solving a sum such as '4 plus 5', however, you have to combine a couple of skills. For example, you can think of doubles like 4 and 4, or 5 and 5. If you choose double 4, you have to know that 5 is one more than 4; that 4 and 4 is 8; that 8 is one less than the final answer; that 8 and 1 is 9. Extending the counting sequence to 100, or even further, is an easier way to help children gain some insight into the structure of the number sequence, which will be useful for the number operations later.

Locating

As well as learning the counting sequence, it is important that children develop some ideas of the location of numbers in relation to each other. Locating numbers is a fundamental skill, because it builds foundations for calculating later on. When you can determine beforehand how one number is related to another, you can decide which (close) numbers to use, depending on which will give the most convenient calculation. In the more shortened solution in

Figure 7.1 'minus 18' is converted into a jump of 20 back and two forward. For this choice of solution strategy, you have to know that 18 lies closer to 20 than 10. Eventually, it is also desirable that children decide to solve '43 – 38' in a way that is different from that shown for '43 – 18'. In the case of '43 – 38' they would hopefully bridge the difference by going from 43 directly to 38, or the other way round from 38 to 43. In doing so, they have not only been able to 'see' that there is a relation between subtraction and addition. Experience is also needed in estimating distances between number positions to figure out whether bridging is indeed the shortest solution to a given calculation.

During the activity walking around the classroom while counting, the children will have already discovered something about the relation between numbers; starting with 88 brings you to 100 in no time; starting from 18, it will take more time. By participating in such activities, they are developing a model, namely an imaginary number line. This number line can then be used to practice locating numbers. In order to give all the children the same point of view, an agreement is made that the line goes from left to right at the front of the classroom. Set the left as 0 and the right as 100. Now it is possible to play *locating* activities where children guess which number they, or someone else, are standing on.

Kamal is standing somewhere on the imaginary number line. A Post-it sticker with the number 83 is stuck on his sweater in such a way that he cannot see it. He cannot see which number it is. Children take turns to help him identify his number as quickly as possible by getting him to move to the right or left. When everyone agrees he is standing about right, he guesses, '80?'. 'Very hot,' concludes Hamdi. '90?' 'A little bit too high', says Tugba. Meanwhile the teacher draws an empty number line on the blackboard and keeps track of the numbers that are suggested.

In the beginning, it is not that important to guess the number quickly, but it is much more important for the development of children's insight that they learn to make use of each others' suggestions. For locating numbers more precisely they need points of reference, for instance that 50 is halfway between 0 and 100. A chain of 100 beads with the ten structure shown in two colours of beads can be displayed in the front of the classroom as a supporting aid. The relation between the mark for 50 on the empty number line and the amount of 50 on the chain of beads can be made by using a peg after 50 beads (Whitney 1973). The highest level of locating is reached when all the children can play a game like 'Guess my number' on the empty number line in as few turns as possible.

Jumping

Children also have to understand how numbers are built up. In the process of jumping, numbers structures are analysed and the relations between jumps and numbers can be discovered. These activities follow naturally from the process of counting and are an important preparation for number operations.

Considering the structure of the counting sequence, it is logical to start with jumps of 10 and hops of one. From now on, the number 18 can be read as a jump of 10 and eight hops. Children jump towards numbers along an imaginary number line on the floor, an empty number line drawn on the board, or on a chain of beads. Jumping along an imaginary number line on the floor has the big advantage that the size of numbers can be experienced physically by the children.

'To which number do I jump?' A pupil takes three jumps forwards and then one hop back. A couple of children think that he has landed at thirty-nine. On the chain of beads or on the empty number line the jumps can be reconstructed to see if this is the case (see Figure 7.2).

After some time, jumps are supplemented with big hops of any size from two to nine. This leads to further abbreviations. When asked, 'To which number do I jump?' it will be necessary to give the information about how big the hop is, otherwise it will not be possible to say precisely which number is meant. By the way, an interesting variation is, which numbers are possible with a jump, another jump and a big hop?

Jumping towards numbers and jumping away from numbers can develop into recording the related sums. At first, calculations can be derived from jumping on an empty number line. The written calculation will serve as a record of the jumping activity. Later the empty number line can serve as a suitable model for solving sums. In Figure 7.3 Sabir is jumping in different ways to the number 45. When he is finished, he writes his sums next to it.

Number operations

Completing to 10

During the activity of jumping towards numbers it becomes clear that children need some knowledge of the number bonds up to 10 (the pairs of numbers that together make 10). For instance, it is only possible to change your mental image of 18 (beads) when you realize that two beads should be left out when you take a second collection of 10. Also, for the problem 43 – 18 it is necessary to see that you have to make a hop of two forwards after having taken a jump

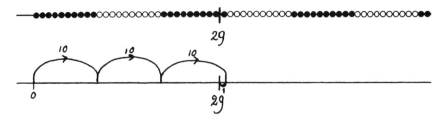

Figure 7.2 Jumping towards 29 on a chain of beads and an empty number line

Name: Sabir

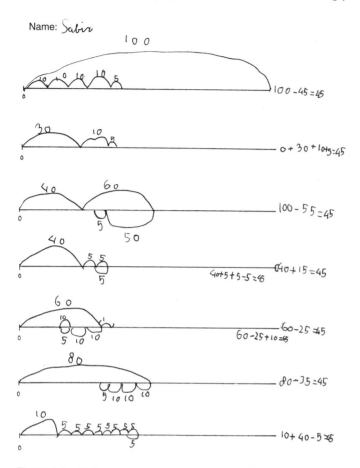

Figure 7.3 Different ways of jumping towards 45 and deduced sums

of 20 backwards. Memorizing the number bonds of 10 offers a lot of advantages for calculations up to 100 (besides, completing to 10 is always available for the children: you have 10 fingers, five on each hand).

In the Netherlands a bead frame with 10 beads on the upper bar and 10 on the lower bar is used to help visualize the bonds to 10. Just like children's fingers, these bars consist of 10 beads with a five-structure. Levels of working include touching and moving the beads, just looking at the beads, and only thinking of the beads when the transfer is made to a mental level. Here, the so-called 'hearts in love' are introduced. A couple of hearts in love always make 10 together (Menne and Veenman 1997).

When the children know the 'hearts' or complements to 10, knowledge of these bonds is practised in a variety of ways and extended to 100. Suggestions for further practice are:

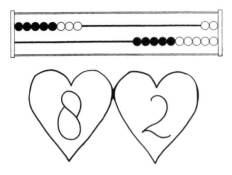

Figure 7.4 Hearts of love are derived from the arithmetic frame

- How many is: 10 – 6, 3 + 7 and then 30 – 6, 43 + 7?
- Friends of 100 are: '80 and 20', '50 and 50';
- Own productions of 'families' of sums: 8 + 2, 38 + 2, 98 + 2. Who knows another which fits in?

Splitting numbers up to 10

As well as putting two numbers together, there is the skill of 'splitting' numbers. Weak mathematicians have many difficulties in memorizing different ways to 'split' numbers. In the experimental training programme we started with splitting numbers into two equal parts: 'You get as many marbles as your brother'. This appeals to children because equal division is fair and can be considered as the inverse of doubling. The notion of doubles appears to be a fundamental one and is found in primitive counting systems, for instance, with the word 'three-three' meaning six (Zaslovsky 1984). When pupils have learned that six is the same as double three, they can use this knowledge for a more complex splitting such as '7 is 3 and . . .'

Just like completing to 10, doubles are introduced with an emotional context: twins who both have the same amount of marbles or stickers. Twins can also be derived from the arithmetic frame. When the children know what three and three is, they can be asked the reverse question: 'How many marbles each if they have six altogether?' The twin is turned over to check (see Figure 7.5).

During the school year activities with the doubles are extended with examples such as the following:

- sums such as 4 + 4, 8 – 4;
- big doubles: 40 + 40, 200 – 100;
- other related sums: 44 + 4, 140 – 40;
- The game of the doctor and the half deaf patient. The doctor does not believe his patient can only hear half. So he says a number, for example 22 and the patient standing in the corner repeats: '11'.

Figure 7.5   Twins: 'Together 6, so each . . .?'

Jumps of 10

The last, but not least, fundamental skill is the ability to jump 10 at a time from any number. It is a great increase in efficiency when the sum 43 – 18 can be solved by taking away the 10 out of the 18 all at once by making a jump of 10.

Children can discover the 10 jump on a chain of beads. As an additional learning aid a so-called '10 catcher' can be constructed (see Figure 7.6). A '10 catcher' can catch exactly 10 beads. (Fewer beads is also possible, but then this will not match the name.) When you want to go 10 further on from 21, you can do this all at once. Catch the next 10 beads and pull them up a bit. Children who do this repeatedly will try to express in words what they notice: 'You constantly catch one bead of the next colour.' This discovery of the structured pattern is crucial, because after a couple of times most children can make jumps of 10 without a '10 catcher'.

For the time being, the focus on naming the number of beads is avoided on purpose. Instead, children are asked to think in advance how many beads you will get when making a jump of 10. In this way, transfer is stimulated to mental imagery of the action of the '10 catcher'. The goal is reached when the children can make a jump of 10 from any number on the empty number line.

Of course, money can also play a modelling role in learning a jump of 10 because of its 10 structure. 'You have 25 pence in your savings. If you save another 10 pence, how much money do you have?' It is logical to think of two 10-pence coins and five more pence. A new 10 pence can be added to the other two. The new total is now made up with three 10-pence coins and five pence. Not every context, however, reminds the children of money. For all the other cases they should learn to make jumps of 10 on the empty number line.

Exercises such as 'add 10' or 'subtract 10' should become a regular part of the practice activities as soon as possible. Gradually this skill is extended with calculations such as 43 + 11, 43 – 9, 43 + 20 and 43 – 18, in bare sums as well as in a problem context. These sums can be all calculated with an empty number line.

When jumping on an empty number line, all types of addition and subtraction problems can be included. Children can also learn multiplication and division by making repeated jumps. However the final goal is to do calculations at

Figure 7.6   Jump of 10 from 21 with a '10 catcher'

a more formal level. The empty number line is only a supporting model. For jumping as a strategy at the highest level an arrow notation is very useful (see Figure 7.7). This arrow notation follows naturally from jumping on the empty number line; it is still dynamic, visual and mathematically correct.

Productive practice

Apart from *reproductive* practice, *productive* practice plays an important role in the research programme. Here productive practice is characterized as sums that the children make up for themselves, called 'own productions'. When children get the opportunity to think of sums, many structures in the counting sequence are being discovered as well as relationships that exist between numbers. Throughout the programme the children are encouraged to make up as many sums as they can for their talking parrot, Waku-Waku (Menne 1997). From time to time, this speaking bird learns to say a new number and to make him look clever, the children think of a lot of sums with his number as the answer. At first these numbers correspond to sums that can be made on the arithmetic frame, but later numbers such as 1, 2, 50 and 100 are learned by the parrot. Working with Waku-Waku stimulates the children in a great variety of oral practice with mental and later written calculations. They learn a lot from each other when discussing their own productions. Figure 7.8 illustrates how their friend, Waku-Waku, is not only very popular, but provides many opportunities for differentiation. These examples also illustrate how the answer '1' appears to provide good opportunities for emphasizing the relation between addition and subtraction.

Classroom organization

The choice of interactive, whole classroom teaching has the great advantage that the teacher can receive direct feedback that gives insight into the skills of each individual child. In the case of a wrong answer, she can immediately switch back to the arithmetic frame, or to the chain of beads to provide the

$$43 - 18 \qquad 43 \xrightarrow{\ -20\ } 23 \xrightarrow{\ +2\ } 25$$

Figure 7.7   Arrow notation at a formal level

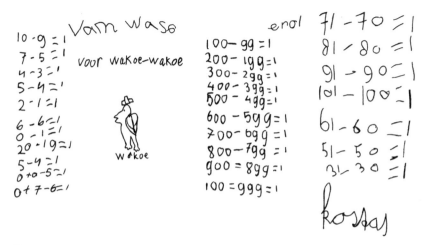

Figure 7.8 Waku-Waku says: '1'

children with modelling images that will help them to understand. Another positive point is that children are being made more aware of what they already know and which skills could be mastered in the near future.

Practice is only useful if it is done on a regular basis. These types of skill training sessions should take place at least three times a week for a quarter of an hour. Fundamental skills like counting on from any number are only memorized, and made automatic, by rehearsal over and over again. Moreover, a variety of practice activities will give children confidence and the opportunity to warm up. They learn what is coming later and they can demonstrate what they can already do. Ideally, every training lesson should start with a short succession of familiar or less well known exercises. In the plenary, elaborations can be offered. After some time, items like 'hearts in love' or 'twins' disappear into the background and acquired number facts take over.

The technique of giving turns needs special attention. When the teacher calls a name before asking a question, there is a strong chance that the majority of the children will not be thinking about the answer. To keep everybody's attention, it is better to present a problem, give a few seconds thinking time, and then call a name. The pupils' attention is also engaged most effectively by using the voice in a variety of ways (e.g. whispering, different pitches, different tempos) and moving flexibly from one question to another.

Conclusion

After a year of teaching and training, preliminary results show that the children in the experimental programme have made good progress. The number of children who initially belonged to the 25 per cent of lowest scores on the national arithmetic tests has been halved. The better pupils have also advanced their levels of attainment and on average, all the children of the experimental group improved to just a little below the national average. Furthermore, the children performed better on a problem like 43 – 18 than the reference group, with 66 per cent answering it correctly. Looking at the children who are Dutch second language speakers separately, one can be positive again, as 59 per cent gave the correct answer.

When a training programme like this one becomes part of the mathematics curriculum in a primary school, it is expected that children's performances in calculating will be greatly improved, lost pleasure will be recovered and, in particular, that second language speakers will eliminate much of their backlog. Actual classroom practice will, of course, be dependent on the personal style of the teacher, but the types of activities described above will stimulate not only effective, but also motivating and even exciting oral practice lessons.

Note

A more extended report of this research appears in the author's forthcoming PhD dissertation: 'Jumping Ahead'.

8

Progressive mathematization: sketch of a learning strand

Kees Buys

Introduction

Mental arithmetic as a topic in primary mathematics education has a long tradition in the Netherlands, but it is also a tradition with its ups and downs. There have been times when it has been given equal emphasis in the curriculum alongside column-wise arithmetic, but also times when it was given hardly any attention at all. During the 1980s and 1990s there was a revival of mental arithmetic due to the growing influence of the Realistic Mathematics Education (RME) movement in the Netherlands, which is discussed by van den Heuvel-Panhuizen in this volume. Today, mental arithmetic is seen more and more as the 'heart of the curriculum', while column-wise arithmetic is moving to a less central position. Given the fact that algorithmic procedures are now becoming increasingly obsolete in everyday life, as a consequence of the large-scale use of pocket calculators, this seems to be a logical development that has not yet come to an end.

The new Dutch textbook series *Wis en Reken* (abbreviation of *Mathematics and Arithmetic*; Buys *et al.* 1999) is a typical example of the development mentioned above; mental arithmetic or 'using your head' in a wider sense occupies a central position in this textbook series. This is true not only for the number domain up to 100, but also for the number domain up to 1000. In the following pages a concise description will be given of the learning strand for addition and subtraction up to 100 that is pursued in this textbook series. I will illustrate this with examples of worksheets and pupils' work taken from Group 4 (corresponding with the English Year 3). Our central aim is to clarify the overall outline of the learning strand, and to show how the different types of mental strategies are introduced successively in a process that can be characterized as a process of 'progressive mathematization'.

Outline of the learning strand for addition and subtraction up to 100

The target of the learning strand is a fluent and flexible use of mental addition and subtraction strategies up to 100, which in practice means that children learn a variety of methods for solving a number problem like 46 + 38 in a competent way. See the following examples:

46 + 30 = 76	40 + 30 = 70	40 + 30 = 70	46 + 40 = 86
76 + 4 = 80	70 + 6 = 76	6 + 8 = 14	86 – 2 = 84
80 + 4 = 84	76 + 8 = 84	70 + 14 = 84	
(sequential method)	(mixed method)	(split method)	(compensation method)

The main part of the learning strand is a systematic investigation into such calculation strategies, and practice in learning to use them in an increasingly efficient way. The total learning process takes about one and a half years during Year 3 and Year 4 (Groups 4 and 5, 7 to 9-year-olds). Below I have sketched in a nutshell how children go through a four-phase process of progressive mathematization within the framework of this learning strand.

Phase 1: exploring the number domain itself

Various contextual situations (like skipping, collecting savings stamps and throwing the javelin) are used to make the pupils confident with the numbers up to 100. By exploring the numbers within these situations they become acquainted with different aspects of the numbers, such as the structure of the number sequence, the 'environment' of a number (approximate numbers, round numbers, etc.), place on the number line, various meanings of numbers in real life, and so on. Activities for developing these ideas are to be found later in this chapter and in Chapter 7, by Menne, in this volume. There is also an informal exploration of adding and subtracting problems in this phase, mostly focusing on counting strategies as a rather primitive way of solving these problems (August–October in Group 4).

Phase 2: initiating arithmetic up to 100: jumping in tens and jumping across tens

When addition and subtraction problems are being explored, counting strategies soon turn out to be quite wordy. To cope with this problem, two fundamental abbreviations of counting are introduced:

- jumping in tens (for example: calculating 46 + 20 by making two big jumps of 10: 46, 56 (10 added), 66 (another 10 added)); and
- jumping across tens (for example: calculating 46 + 8 by making two bigger jumps: 46 + 4 = 50; 50 + 4 = 54) (November–December in Group 4).

Phase 3: introduction of the sequential method (N10) on the
empty number line

A general method of solving any problem up to 100 is introduced first: the
sequential method, based on the two abbreviations mentioned above. With
this method the first number is taken as a whole, whereas the second number
is added (or subtracted) in various chunks. The empty number line is introduced as a support to carrying out this strategy (January–March in Group 4).
But pupils soon start to use this strategy by just writing down their steps in
number language, for instance, in the case of 46 + 28 (see Figure 8.1).

Phase 4: extension to two other types of strategies: the split tens
(1010) method, and varied strategies

When the pupils are sufficiently confident with the sequential method, they
are made more and more aware of two other types of strategies: the *split tens*
method, 1010, which serves as a second general method to solve any problem
up to 100 (for instance: solving 46 + 28 by splitting up both numbers: 40 + 20
= 60; 6 + 8 = 14; 60 + 14 = 74); and various methods that are based on elementary properties of numbers and operations, like *compensating* (solving 46
+ 28 by saying: 46 + 30 = 76; 76 – 2 = 74), *transforming* (46 + 28 = 44 + 30 = 74),
and *adding up* (solving 46 – 38 by saying: from 38 to 40 is 2; from 40 to 46 is
6; in total 2 + 6 = 8). (April–June in Group 4.)

Two ways of using the empty number line

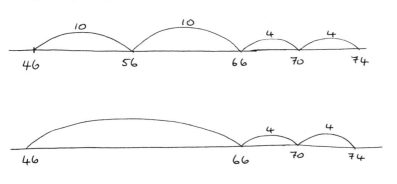

One way of writing down your steps in
number language

46 + 20 = 66
66 + 4 = 70
70 + 4 = 74

Figure 8.1   Recording a solution for 46 + 28

Teaching within the phases

Phase 1: exploring the number domain itself

An important precondition for an easy exploration of adding and subtracting up to 100 is a good understanding of the numbers up to 100 themselves. These numbers need to gain substance and meaning for the pupils. Everyday life situations can serve as a starting point for this exploration, in which several aspects of the numbers are investigated. For instance:

- the counting row up to 100 in combination with counting forwards and backwards, correct number notation, and the special meaning of multiples of tens as landmarks;
- clever counting of large quantities by making use of groups of 5, 10 and 20 as a way to make the counting well organized;
- measuring aspects of numbers, positioning on the number line among multiples of 10, the question of neighbouring numbers, the order of magnitude of numbers.

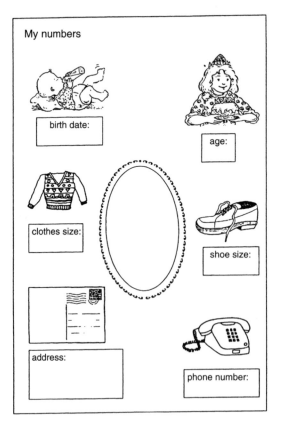

Figure 8.2a Work card: 'depicting your own numbers'

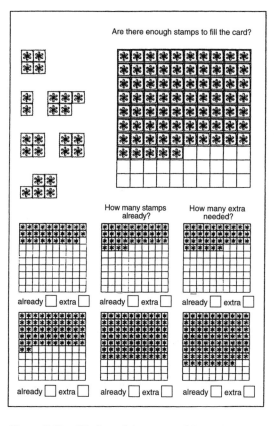

Figure 8.2b   Work card: 'stamp cards': are there enough stamps to fill the card?

All these aspects are presented to children in a number of realistic contexts where number representations are embedded in everyday situations: skipping, counting and tallying, charts for stamps, throwing the javelin, etc.

It is expected that such a 'realistic' instructional design (with regular whole-class discussions and exchanges of ideas, strategies, etc.) will contribute powerfully to the development of a strong number sense in children, and that, given such a conceptual base, the exploration of arithmetical strategies will proceed relatively easily.

Phase 2: initiating arithmetic up to 100: jumping in tens and jumping across tens

The most natural way of solving arithmetical problems up to 100 is counting. That is what children do first when they are presented with a problem such as (in terms of the stamp card context from the previous section): 'You have 46 stamps on your card, then you get 3 more; how many is that altogether?'. Counting on is an obvious strategy: 46, 47 (1 counted on), 48 (2), 49 (3). However, this approach soon turns out to be a time-consuming and wordy strategy for larger problems. For instance: 'The king has a box of 46 gold coins; then he gets 18 more. How many will he have altogether?'

Two essential abbreviations can be used to surpass the counting strategy: jumping in tens and jumping across tens:

- *jumping in tens*: calculating 46 + 10 by making a jump of 10: 46, 56; similarly 46 – 10: 46, 36;
- *jumping across tens*: calculating 46 + 8 by splitting up 8 into two smaller jumps: 46 + 4 towards 50, followed by 50 + 4 towards 54; a similar strategy for 46 – 8.

Particularly notable in these abbreviations is that they are natural continuations of informal counting strategies: the first number is conceived as a whole, and the second number is added (or subtracted) in one, two or more 'chunks'. Both abbreviations are underpinned in *Wis en Reken* by the so-called 'gold board' and the '100 beads string', in relation to other activities around number exploration. These are illustrated in Figure 8.3. This approach uses the quantitative aspect of numbers to make both of these abbreviations more meaningful to children.

The empty number line, introduced as a schematization of the bead string, is then used as a model for the schematic visualization of both of these abbreviated strategies (Figure 8.4).

Jumping in tens is particularly intensively explored and this strategy is also practised in short, whole-class, oral activities using a money box where tens (10-guilder notes) go in and out.

Phase 3: introduction of the sequential method on the empty number line

Once the children are sufficiently familiar with these two abbreviations of the counting strategy, doing calculations with larger numbers is explored by presenting problems like 46 + 38, 46 – 18, etc. The children themselves offer

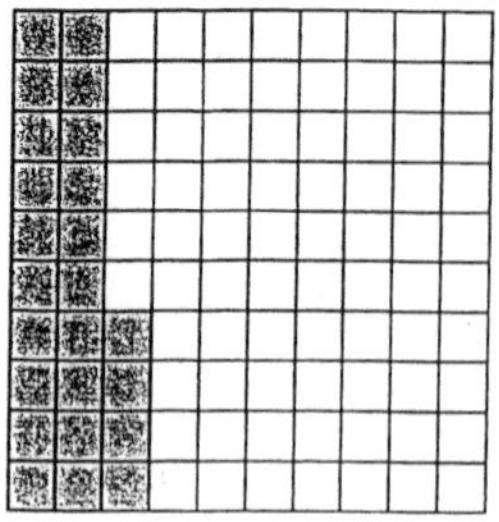

Figure 8.3a   Gold balance

Figure 8.3b   10-bar added

Figure 8.3c   New gold board

Figure 8.3d   24 beads on a string

Figure 8.3e   8 added; 32 beads on a string

suggestions (guided by the teacher) of how they can solve such problems on the empty number line. Several methods of problem solving will emerge, such as those shown in Figure 8.5.

The advantages and disadvantages of these different calculation procedures are weighed against each other in whole-class discussion, and the children are made aware of the fundamental characteristic in all of them: the first number is taken as a whole, and the second number is partitioned and added in parts.

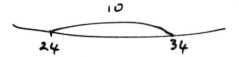

Figure 8.4a   24, 10 added is 34

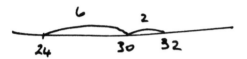

Figure 8.4b   24, 8 added is 32

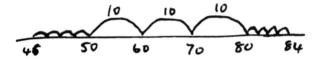

Figure 8.5a   Four jumps of 1; then three of 10, then another four of 1

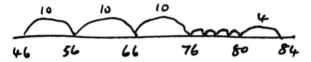

Figure 8.5b   Three jumps of 10; four jumps of 1, and another one of 4

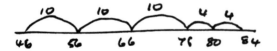

Figure 8.5c   Three jumps of 10; then two jumps of 4

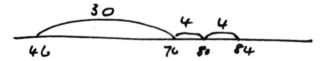

Figure 8.5d   One big jump of 30; then two jumps of 4

For subtraction the procedure is the same, but now the second number is taken away in parts. Various contexts are used to make children more familiar with this sequential calculation method (referred to as N10 by Beishuizen, this volume) in different problem situations, for instance the problems illustrated in Figure 8.6.

Verbalizing solutions that the children have constructed themselves plays

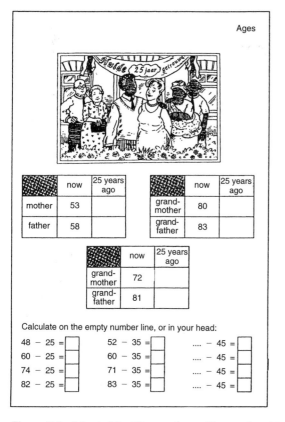

Figure 8.6 Married for 25 years; how old were they 25 years ago?

an important role in the learning process. Consequently, several abbreviations begin to emerge in the solution strategies. A number of children soon proceed to a more mental level of calculating problems in their head (without support of the number line) and during further practice on worksheets they are given ample opportunity for extending this mental facility.

Phase 4: Notation in formal number language; extension to two other types of strategies: the split tens method, and varied strategies

In this period more and more children begin trying to do every calculation in their heads. In order to prevent them from losing track, a transition to the notation of mental steps in number language is introduced: the children are encouraged to write down on scrap paper every step they can carry out mentally. These activities result in descriptions of the sequential approach, N10, at a more formal level. For example, in the calculation of 84 – 38 we see notations such as:

$84 - 4 = 80$ $84 - 30 = 54$
$80 - 30 = 50$ $54 - 8 = 46$
$50 - 4 = 46$

Some children prefer to rely for a bit longer on the support of the empty number line, but more and more change to the notation of purely mental steps in formal number language. Other children move on to writing down just a few steps rather than every one, or no steps at all, only the intermediate answers. And, of course, more and more children change to purely mental or 'in the head' calculation.

There is soon a move towards a second, basic mental calculation strategy, already explored at a lower level: the one we call the (base-ten) split method (referred to as 1010 by Beishuizen, this volume). Shopping situations are used to make children aware of the difference in the calculation procedure, because now both numbers are split into tens and units (for example, If you buy two items costing 46 and 38 guilders, how much do you pay? If you buy an item costing 84 guilders with 38 guilders discount, how much do you pay?). This time, notation in formal number language is explicitly employed to describe the various split methods of calculation. For example, in the case of $46 + 38$ and $84 - 38$ the following methods are seen:

$46 + 38 =$	$46 + 38 =$	$84 - 38 =$	$84 - 38 =$
$40 + 30 = 70$	$40 + 30 = 70$	$80 - 30 = 50$	$80 - 30 = 50$
$70 + 6 = 76$	$6 + 8 = 14$	$50 + 4 = 54$	$4 - 8 = -4$ (4 short)
$76 + 8 = 84$	$70 + 14 = 84$	$54 - 8 = 46$	$50 - 4 = 46$
mixed (split) method:	split method:	mixed (split) method:	split method:
units added sequentially	carrying units	units subtracted sequentially	how many units 'short'

For addition, in particular, the split method soon becomes a popular strategy; for subtraction, however, this method is less convenient, and therefore interest in it is not often stimulated.

Lastly, a third category of calculation methods is explored: the so-called varied strategies, not useful for every calculation but very useful for certain problem types. For instance, solving a problem like $46 + 39$ by jumping first $+40$ and then -1 (compensation); or solving a problem like $84 - 79$ by taking the difference between both numbers (completion). Such varied strategies are explored from appropriate context situations (see Figure 8.7), but are not imposed; the children are made aware that, depending on the situation and number particulars as well as their own preferences, they can choose to use them or not.

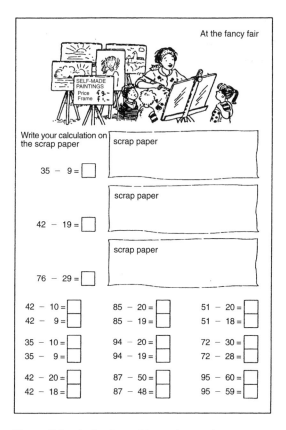

Figure 8.7   At the fancy fair: exploring the compensation strategy

Conclusion: gradual further increase in level and flexibilization of strategies

The learning process described above takes place in Group 4 (Year 3), but that is not the end of the story. The process of further abbreviation and increase in level of calculation strategies will develop further in subsequent school years. At the same time, the number domain is extended up to 1000 (later on beyond 1000), and the children will explore similar, efficient calculation strategies for these much larger numbers. At this stage they will profit greatly from their new knowledge base of arithmetic up to 100. This knowledge has to be elaborated and consolidated, so that children can grow in their confidence in mental strategies and will become increasingly flexible in choosing a suitable calculation method for each problem type. For that reason more detailed attention is given in Group 5 (Year 4) to the varied strategy of complementary addition (instead of subtraction). Moreover, practice in mental strategies up to 100 is continued in short, sharp oral lessons, in which fluent mental calculation, verbalizing solution steps, and reflection on differences between methods, are important didactic ingredients. In this way the children learn to move around with increasing speed and skill in the number domains up to 100 and up to 1000.

Acknowledgements

Thanks to Angela Bennett for her assistance with the English version.

9

Different approaches to mastering mental calculation strategies

Meindert Beishuizen

Introduction

In this chapter, the following proposition will be elaborated for discussion: 'Proper mastery of a (place value based) split tens method for calculating is preferable to low level mastery of a (number-line based) sequential strategy'. This statement might be surprising coming from a Dutchman, but contrary to earlier publications (Beishuizen 1997; Beishuizen and Anghileri 1998) the discussion of mental strategies will be viewed from the British point of view, which is also traditional in the USA and many other countries. The line of argument taken will be underpinned with empirical data, but this time more from British and American research, where the place value based 'separate tens' (1010) strategies are used much more in classrooms than 'sequence tens' (N10) strategies (Beishuizen *et al.* 1997b; Fuson *et al.* 1997). (See Figure 9.1 and 9.3 for examples of these strategies for addition and subtraction in the number domain up to 100 and the chapter by Buys in this volume.)

In particular the studies of Carpenter and others, carried out in a number of schools participating in the project 'Cognitively Guided Instruction' (CGI), are relevant in this respect, because they focus on the development of children's invented mental strategies in a US curriculum, with base-ten apparatus and corresponding solution methods (Carpenter and Fennema 1992; Carpenter 1997; Carpenter *et al.* 1998; Carpenter *et al.* 1999). An experts' meeting at Leiden University on research in teaching arithmetic (Beishuizen *et al.* 1997b) was the venue for an exchange of ideas and experiences. At this meeting, Carpenter expressed views that identified many similarities between the Dutch Realistic Mathematics Education (RME), which was discussed by van den Heuvel-Panhuizen in this volume, and the American approaches, both CGI and that described by Yackel earlier in this volume. Each emphasizes the development of children's early number concepts and number operations in 'progressive mathematization' of intuitive mental strategies, and asks children to solve many real-world problems guided by interactive teaching instead of direct instruction in standard algorithms.

Although there are clear differences in the preparatory learning trajectories (see Yackel and van den Heuvel-Panhuizen, this volume), could it be that children reach comparable levels in understanding and flexibility of strategy use? What is seen in the publications, with examples of CGI-children's work and examples given by Yackel, is a good mastery and a flexible use of a rich variety of mental strategies, mainly based on the base-ten split method, 1010. It might therefore be interesting to take a closer look at this research from the British perspective. It is not suggested that this is a better approach than that of the Dutch RME, but because the place value based calculation methods are more central in both the US and the UK than in the Dutch early number curriculum, it might be that many useful suggestions can be found in this research as to how to raise the current level of mental calculation in British and American classrooms.

The risk of a low modelling level for new strategies on the empty number line

In Dutch (RME) primary mathematics teaching, the sequential strategy, referred to as N10, where the first number is *not split* but kept intact, is introduced first on the number line, as a continuation and abbreviation of counting (see Menne this volume). This is followed later in Year 3 by the split tens method, referred to as 1010, where tens and units are separated, as a second basic mental calculation strategy. (See Buys, this volume, as well as Beishuizen and Anghileri 1998, for arguments as to why the order of introduction is N10 first and then 1010.) Later on, in Years 4 and 5, these strategies will evolve into mixed and varied methods, employing personal preferences and short-cuts, while standard written algorithms are also introduced (see Anghileri in this volume for a discussion of the standard approaches). During this development the emphasis shifts from specific strategies, towards general aspects like recording mental calculation steps in formal number language, discussing the efficiency of solutions, and similar considerations. In an experiment with the empty number line the explicit introduction of short names that children could use for the different strategies proved to be quite successful (Klein *et al.* 1998). Such general aspects have also been put forward as official British arguments for introducing more mental calculation into the early number curriculum, first in the SCAA discussion paper (SCAA 1997c) and later in the National Numeracy Strategy (DfEE 1998a) and Framework (DfEE 1999).

Psychological research has shown that fluency and flexibility in mental calculation procedures (Hope and Sherrill 1987), or the drive for cognitive economy by keeping memory load to a minimum (Baroody and Ginsburg 1986), can become strong incentives for further development of mental strategies. These characteristics, however, need a good deal of initial practice and automatization before they begin to yield profits (see Menne, this volume). In the Netherlands, the lesson was learned during the first implementation of RME in the 1980s, that neglecting basic number aspects may hamper a really fluent and flexible use of mental strategies (Beishuizen 1997). Askew *et al.* (1997a), and Ruthven (1998), emphasize the same point in their research with British children. In the Netherlands, this was one of the reasons for publishing a revised primary mathematics curriculum (Treffers and De Moor 1990) discussed by van den Heuvel-Panhuizen in this volume, with more attention being paid to basic number skills, and modelling and sequencing of basic mental strategies, as a carefully designed learning trajectory (see also Buys in this volume).

This introduces a second argument in support of the proposition: the risk that the introduction of the empty number line and sequential strategies like N10 into British classrooms may *stagnate* at a low level of mastery. In earlier publications (Beishuizen 1997; Beishuizen and Anghileri 1998) this possibility had not been considered, but now with the publication of the National Numeracy Strategy *Framework for Teaching Mathematics from Reception to Year 6* (DfEE 1999a) it appears that this pessimistic prospect may be a possibility. Of course, it is encouraging to see the positive adoption of the empty number line as a transparent model for children in so many British publications, in workshops for teachers, and now in the Framework. Its introduction in the latter, however, is rather piecemeal. It also appears that different types of mental calculation strategies (1010, N10, etc.) are being introduced simultaneously. According to the Dutch view and experience, these conditions are not the best for promoting new mental strategies (see Thompson, this volume).

Using the empty number line

Figure 9.1 shows some examples of how to use the empty number line at a low 'modelling' level as might be expected in the British situation where it is a new experience. They are taken from a short experiment (six lessons) in a British school, where pupils in Year 3/Year 4 learned to solve difference problems (Rousham 1997; Beishuizen and Anghileri 1998). Because such difference problems were quite unfamiliar to the pupils, performance on the pre-test was rather low (31 per cent correct), and mostly 1010 or 10s (a sequential variant of 1010) strategies were used. Pupils adopted N10 and A10 strategies (Figure 9.1), when they were introduced on the empty number line, quite easily and improved strongly on the (same) post-test (75 per cent correct). However, in spite of this promising outcome, it must be emphasized that most solutions were still carried out at a *low* 'modelling' level of number line support and still proceeded in small steps at a *low* procedural level (see Figure 9.1).

Much more practice would be needed to bring the new N10 and A10 strategies to a higher and real mental level for these pupils. It is necessary also to draw attention to the fact that the children's own repertoire was already established at a higher level of formal number language with multiples of ten as

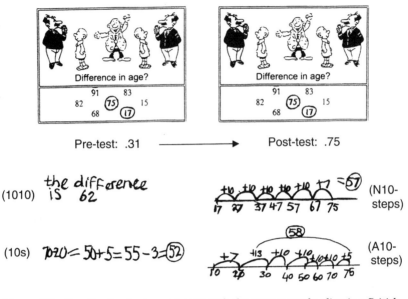

Figure 9.1 Results of a short experiment with the empty number line in a British school

much larger steps (Figure 9.1). Therefore, instead of pointing to the better scores attained on the empty number line, it should be asked if there was any lasting value, and whether it would not have been more profitable to improve the pupils' existing 1010 and 10s strategies for solving difference problems?

Development of mental strategies in British children: the 1987 APU study

More evidence and additional lines of discussion can be found in larger-scale empirical data concerning current mental strategies used by British children. Two such studies will be discussed briefly. While staying at Homerton College in 1997 the APU survey studies of Foxman *et al.* (1991) presented an intriguing study into the mental skills of 11-year-olds (n = 256) interviewed in 1987. Beishuizen and Foxman decided to cooperate in a reanalysis of the data, which might be interesting in the light of the current British discussions on mental calculation and newer categories for mental calculation methods. First results became available in 1999, and are being published elsewhere (Foxman and Beishuizen 1999). The results of two questions will be used to illustrate the present argument.

In Tables 9.1 and 9.2 the solution methods for two questions are summarized in categories, which have been made a little broader to include several methods covering all problems. The category 'complete number methods' includes sequential N10 strategies for subtraction or addition (small and large 10-jumps), but also the use of the unsplit number 25 (or chunks of 25) as a starting point in multiplication calculations. The category 'split number methods' encompasses all 1010-like calculations operating separately on tens and units (including calculations on split numbers in multiplications). When these split-off tens and units were in fact handled, and verbalized, as single digits this strategy was classified as 'separate digit methods'. Some children apparently used the standard 'algorithm' as a mental model (calculating from right to left), and some answers fell into the category 'unclassified' or 'no response'.

One of the surprising results of the reanalysis is that at the end of primary school about one-third of British pupils appeared to use complete number methods like N10 for the subtraction of 64 – 27, although they were unlikely to have been taught them in 1987. On the other hand the split tens method 1010 also proved to be widely used, often in the sequential 10s variant for 64 – 27 (60 – 20 + 4 – 7). However, the success rate of this split method turned out to be much lower than for the complete number methods (an interesting confirmation of Dutch research, see Beishuizen and Anghileri 1998). From a British perspective it is a remarkable outcome that the algorithmic procedure proved quite successful for a problem like 64 – 27, but unsuccessful for the multiplication problem 16 × 25 where misconceptions of place value and errors of the single-digit type occurred more frequently. Overall, the reanalysis of the APU data seems to confirm some weaknesses of the 1010 mental strategy and of the standard algorithm, in particular a loss of (whole) number sense during the calculation procedure. This latter result could be taken as an argument for giving priority to improving these place-value based calculation methods, but questioning the traditional way of teaching, because they are already so widely used in British classrooms.

Table 9.1   Reanalysis of question 1 in the APU study

Question 1: 64 – 27=	*Frequency of use (%)* *n = 256*	*correct (%)*
Complete number methods 64 – 20 – 7 64 – 30 + 3 27 + 10 + 10 + 10 + 7	33	80
Split number methods 60 – 20; 7 – 4 or 40 – 3 60 – 20 + 4 – 7	27	36
Algorithm	29	71
Unclassified/No response	10	19
Overall		59

Note: Figures rounded to the nearest whole number

Table 9.2   Reanalysis of question 2 in the APU study

Question 2: 16 × 25=	Frequency of use n = 256	correct (%)
Complete number methods $4 \times 25 \to 100, \times 4$ $6 \times 25 + 10 \times 25$	33	75
Split number methods $(10 \times 20 + 6 \times 20) + 16 \times 5$	8	10
Separate digit methods $5 \times 6 + 1 \times 2$ $5 \times 6 + 1 \times 20$	14	0
Algorithm	22	14
Unclassified/No response	23	0
Overall		29

Note: Figures are rounded to the nearest whole number

Development of mental strategies in British children: a study in Newcastle in 1999

Further evidence in the same direction can be found in a similar study into mental calculation strategies, carried out by Thompson and Smith (1999) in 18 schools in the Newcastle area. From each class (Year 4 and Year 5; age 8 to 10) teachers selected six pupils (two of below-average, two of average and two of above-average mathematics attainment, n = 144), who were to be interviewed about the way they tackled two-digit calculations such as 23 + 24 and 68 – 32 as well as more difficult questions like 37 + 45 and 54 – 27. The graphs in Figure 9.2 give the outcomes in terms of mental strategies used for addition and subtraction problems. The classification of mental strategies is comparable to those used in the APU study, but there are some minor differences. At the bottom (1) 'counting in ones and/or tens' is distinguished as a separate category, while (2) 'manipulating digits' also includes the standard algorithm used mentally. Within the broad category of the place-value based split tens methods, a distinction is made between (3) the 'partitioning' or 'split' 1010 method, and (4) the sequential variant or 'split-jump' 10s method, including some complementary additions for solving subtraction problems. The last category (5) includes the sequential N10 'jump' method as well as the compensation 'jump-over' method N10C.

What is seen in 1999 in Figure 9.2 is more or less a confirmation of the outcomes of the APU study in 1987, particularly when the subtraction strategies are compared with those in Table 9.1 (64 – 27). Once again the (5) 'jump' strategy N10 (and N10C) is used quite a lot, although these pupils have probably not been taught this sequential strategy. The 'counting' strategy (1) is used more frequently than in the APU study, which is not a sign of mathematics

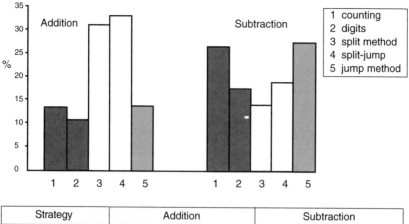

Strategy	Addition	Subtraction
1	13.2%	25.7%
2	10.4%	16.7%
3	30.6%	13.2%
4	32.6%	18.1%
5	13.2%	26.4%

Figure 9.2   Mental strategies used in the Newcastle study

improvement (but may be due to sample differences, see below). Although Thompson and Smith (1999) do not report error scores, their data point to the frequent use of low-level strategies like counting and manipulating digits (both known to be error-prone) for difficult subtraction problems. So the results of this study also reveal that improving existing strategies should be made a first priority.

The Newcastle study contains further relevant information, emphasizing this priority even more forcefully. The diagrams in Figure 9.2 demonstrate how the profile of mental strategies for addition problems is quite different from subtraction, with a more frequent use of the base-ten split methods (3) and (4). This is in line with an earlier study by Thompson (1994), which concluded that these latter calculation methods are the most common mental strategies used by British children, but that was for addition problems only. For subtraction problems Figure 9.2 reveals quite a change of strategy use towards low-level (1, 2) methods on the one hand and high-level (5) on the other. The explanation for this differential effect can be found in mathematics ability level. The study provides a separate analysis of the three ability subgroups (see above), showing a big difference between the more able pupils, where (5), sequential N10, is the most frequent strategy, and the less able pupils, where (1), counting, and (2), single-digits, were used in more than half of their solutions. This latter disappointingly low level of mental two-digit calculations in Year 4 and Year 5 is, perhaps, another strong argument for working to improve children's current mental strategies. Finally, Thompson and Smith (1999) give a separate overview of types of strategy use in Year 4 and Year 5, and their conclusion is a 'lack of progress in the development of more sophisticated mental methods' – surely another argument and further evidence in favour of the viewpoint stated in the initial proposition for discussion?

A Dutch experiment with a computer program enhancing spontaneous strategy development (before the empty number line)

Before the empty number line was introduced into the Dutch early number curriculum (Treffers and De Moor 1990) to invite and support sequential strategies like N10 in a better way, the split tens method was also used much more in Dutch classrooms. One of the reasons was that the materials which were popular during the 1980s (arithmetic blocks and hundred squares) were not too effective in modelling N10 strategies, in particular not for weaker children. In that period (1985–90) a research project was undertaken, in which two experimental computer programs were developed and compared for teaching addition and subtraction up to 100: an 'adaptive tutoring' program taking pupils through stages of gradual strategy change 1010 → 10s → N10, and a 'direct instruction' program giving immediate practice in N10 (Beishuizen *et al.* 1990). In Figure 9.3 a brief outline is given of the consecutive learning stages in the adaptive tutoring program.

The tutoring program was based on the observation in Dutch classrooms that pupils using a 1010 strategy sometimes adapt that strategy into the sequential 10s, when they come across difficult subtraction problems including carrying (Figure 9.3). This *adaptation* is a clever way out of the (1010) impasse of how to subtract the larger units from the smaller units in a subtraction carry problem. Later on, after more practice with 10s, these pupils sometimes *discover* N10 as an efficient abbreviation of the first calculation steps in 10s (Figure 9.3). The neo-Piagetian theory of Case and Bereiter (1984)

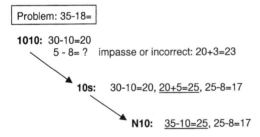

Figure 9.3 Supposed trajectory of spontaneous strategy development: 1010 → 10s → N10

was used as a theoretical framework, stating that the spontaneous development of rule-based behaviour towards a higher level may be blocked because children overlook, or do not encode, the essential information of new problem features. Therefore, bringing this information to the pupils' attention is an important supporting condition for cognitive development. This idea was implemented in the computer program by means of tutoring dialogues designed to draw pupils' attention to new problem features and suggesting alternative solution methods (like 10s without imposing them (Figure 9.4).

The impression formed was that in school practice it is largely the better and not the weaker pupils who show traces of this spontaneous strategy development $1010 \rightarrow 10s \rightarrow N10$. The purpose of the tutoring program was to enable more pupils to achieve such adequate strategy adaptations. However, the computer program, particularly the tutoring dialogues, proved rather ineffective because, compared to current standards, its design was somewhat primitive (without the use of visual models, etc.). On the other hand it appeared that the direct instruction in N10 was more effective than expected, so the results of the study were inconclusive and not convincing (Felix 1992).

Interestingly, the previously mentioned data from British pupils in the APU study (Foxman and Beishuizen 1999) and in the Newcastle study (Thompson and Smith 1999) seem to provide more evidence for this supposed strategy development trajectory ($1010 \rightarrow 10s \rightarrow N10$) than could be collected from the Dutch computer program study. In particular the rather frequent use of the N10 sequential strategy – which might be considered as mostly 'untaught' in British classrooms – could be taken as evidence of the spontaneous 'invention' of this more efficient strategy. But the 10s strategy adaptation is also used rather frequently by both British and American pupils. When describing the learning process occurring in two CGI-classrooms, Carpenter (1997: 46) mentions this adaptation explicitly for subtraction problems like $83 - 27$: 'Most

Pupil:	Computer:	
35-18=23	The answer is not correct. Another solution method will be demonstrated.	
Your method:	Another method:	Attention:
30-10=20	**30-10=20**	
5 - 8=3	**20+5=25**	**Add 5 to 20**
20+3=23	**25-8=17**	**Subtract 8**
42-17=....	Try this method on a new problem:	

Figure 9.4   Example of a tutoring dialogue in a Dutch experimental computer program

students either shifted from a combining-units-separately strategy to a sequential strategy or modelled the problem with base-ten materials'. From the examples given it is clear that a shift is meant from 1010 to 10s strategies.

Some conclusions from innovative US research focusing on the development of mental strategies in a place-value oriented curriculum

In summary, the examples quoted from American and British research suggest that the development of mental strategies along the 'invention' line 1010 → 10s → N10 might be a viable option, with the advantage of an immediate start from the children's current (place value based) strategies. Another advantage might be that immediate attention could be given to general aspects of mental calculation, including:

- making children more aware of what they are doing (number sense);
- recording the procedural steps of number operation;
- verbalizing and discussing alternative mental calculations;
- becoming more aware of inefficient and efficient mental strategies through interactive teaching;
- adaptation and development of strategies towards higher levels of proficiency.

These arguments might also apply to the current role of standard algorithms in the American and British curricula. In an earlier publication Thompson's (1997b) proposal to emphasize the split tens method mental strategies in the British curriculum was discussed because these are more similar and closer to standard algorithms than the N10 sequential strategy. At the time criticism was made of this and other British ideas about mental calculation as 'not going far enough' (Beishuizen and Anghileri 1998), but this criticism was from a Dutch (RME) viewpoint, while a different perspective is taken in this chapter.

The place of algorithms

There is a striking conclusion to a recently published study by Carpenter *et al.* (1998) after a three-year longitudinal study into strategy development, emphasizing children's invention and understanding of multidigit addition and subtraction (in US Grades 1 to 3). Apart from the emphasis on mental strategies, standard algorithms were also introduced in Grades 2 and 3. Compared to a control group following a traditional curriculum, pupils in the experimental group not only did better on mental strategies but *also* on standard algorithms, which can be taken as a confirmation of Thompson's proposal. However, another conclusion, from Carpenter *et al.* (1998: 13) should also be mentioned, namely that pupils in the experimental group did not abandon their invented mental strategies once they had learned the standard algorithms. The final comment in this article goes much further, suggesting that teachers taught the standard algorithms because of curriculum pressure, and that a strong case could be made for *not teaching the algorithms at all*, given the widespread availability of calculators for more complex calculations (Carpenter *et al.* 1998: 19).

This last example of innovative US research not only answers the proposition discussed in this chapter, but also poses new questions about the primary mathematics curriculum; in other words, the discussion has only just begun and the end is not yet in sight. Empirical studies with new experimental programmes may contribute to the discussion by making alternative instructional designs, and their possible effects, more concrete. For example, in a new research project at Leiden University in the Netherlands with special-needs pupils, there is a focus on the introduction of sequential N10 strategies at a later stage than in a traditional curriculum. Preliminary trials show hardly any effects because these pupils hold on to their previously acquired split method 1010 strategies. Cobb *et al.* (1997) have also struggled with the question of how to adapt the introduction of the number-line model for (US) children who have already been exposed to place value based number concepts and strategies (see Yackel, this volume). Such options might be relevant to the implementation of the new *Framework* (DfEE 1999a) in the UK, and hopefully empirical studies with experimental programme variations in British schools will contribute to this (international) discussion and research (see Thompson and Anghileri, this volume).

Mental imagery

A final and critical comment has to be made about the popular role of 'modelling strategies' (Carpenter 1997) or 'drawing mental images' (Atkinson 1992), which is strongly associated with the role of base-ten arithmetic blocks in the development of split tens strategies. In the RME view, however, the use of concrete materials might result in too much support and too little mental activation, so, in fact, might slow down instead of stimulate children's strategy development to a higher level. Working with the empty number line could also result in holding on too long to a modelling level, and the risk of such inappropriate use is the second argument in support of the question for discussion in this chapter. According to the RME view, reference to real-world, contextual situations should be used first to give numbers a concrete meaning for children. Soon after that, models could be introduced and used on a more abstract level for emphasizing number structure and number relations (Gravemeijer 1997b).

The role of models is one of the differences in 'progressive mathematization' between the CGI and the RME approach (Beishuizen *et al.* 1997a), and instead of 'modelling strategies' the previously mentioned emphasis on 'structuring' of number operations is given more attention (see also Menne, this volume). This 'structuring' level is soon followed by asking children to use 'formal number language' in their workings and recordings of mental calculations. This highest (formal) level of mental strategy use is practised a great deal in the

RME early number curriculum (see Buys, this volume), because it is believed that this is the level where fluency and flexibility of number operations will make real progress, much more than at the 'modelling strategies' level. So, in this respect, some aspects of the suggested strategy development trajectory $1010 \rightarrow 10s \rightarrow N10$ might be elaborated in a different way. What is important is the development of abstract thinking on different levels that will progress and become more curtailed, otherwise, the expected advantages of an earlier start on fostering the general aspects of mental strategies might get lost in the prolonged use of 'modelling strategies', even on the empty number line.

Acknowledgement

Thanks to Angela Bennett for her assistance with the English version.

◯ Part IV

Developmental research

The relationship between classroom practice in arithmetic teaching and educational research is not always as close as either researchers or practitioners would hope, but the approaches reported in the next two chapters show how interrelationships can be established that will inform and enhance both research and practice. While the previous section reported and discussed some individual aspects of research and their implications for the classroom, this section attempts to make clear how developmental research can establish a symbiosis for the mutual benefit of the whole community of curriculum developers, researchers, textbook writers, teachers and, not least, pupils.

In comparison to traditional research, the norms of justification for developmental research represent a shift from assembling facts that prove one curriculum better than another, to providing well substantiated theories about *how* these curricula work (NCTM Research Advisory Committee 1996). Rather than passively accepting principles based on research, teachers are encouraged to take the theories of researchers as conjectures, which they can test and modify in their own classroom. In this way, the teachers can produce their own contribution to the development of those theories instead of being consumers of knowledge produced by others.

Mike Askew is a senior lecturer at University of London's King's College, which has a long tradition of research in mathematics education, and he has many years of experience working on major research projects concerning primary classroom practices in arithmetic teaching. In Chapter 10, he discusses the way research has moved on to address some fundamental questions about learning, from the perspectives of individual teachers and the pupils they are involved with on a daily basis. He first identifies how curriculum development projects of the 1970s and 1980s in Britain, such as the Nuffield and PrIME projects, have suffered from lack of systematic research evidence, with resulting questions about their value in identifying effective teaching approaches. He then presents extracts from recent research to show how findings can be influential in developing approaches to teaching that enhance the experiences of pupils and teachers alike. From a theoretical position of learning mathematics as being change in participation, he suggests that developmental research needs to attend to the actual events in which pupils have the opportunity to engage. To examine some of the potential and actual opportunities offered by this change, he addresses two very fundamental questions: What does it mean 'to learn'? What does it mean 'to teach'?

In analysing developmental research, he identifies the distinction between numeracy *events*, which may be directly observed by a researcher or taken from accounts of others, and numeracy *orientations*, which are theoretical accounts for how, and why, mathematics events proceed in the way they do. From the data collected in a King's College research project, he suggests that such analysis of teachers' orientations can be related to their effectiveness in terms of learning outcomes. Current research at King's is moving the focus of attention away from the teacher, towards pupils' orientations in mathematics lessons. He notes that pupils' perspectives will be an integral part of a five year longitudinal study (Leverhulme Numeracy Research Programme) which is tracking some 1600 5-year-olds and 1600 8-year-olds across five years of schooling. The aims of this work will be to further understand the impact of specific practices as they are interpreted by particular pupils, and to consider the implications for teachers in their attempts to reconcile working with whole classes with responses to individuals. In suggesting directions for the future, rather than concentrate on the form of lessons, he argues that developmental research in England needs to attend more to the 'didactics' of teaching, that is the moment to moment interactions with pupils, and the teaching tools that are available to teachers.

Koeno Gravemeijer is a principal researcher at the Freudenthal Institute, Utrecht University, in the Netherlands and associate professor at Vanderbilt University in the USA. In Chapter 11, he argues that developmental research projects that primarily have an objective of instructional design or educational development can also contribute to theory development. He outlines the way Realistic Mathematics Education in the Netherlands combines the development of a theoretical framework for research, with development of new instructional materials. He notes that the traditional instructional design models that concentrate on learning objectives, focus on learning outcomes, while the process that leads to these learning outcomes is actually treated as a black box 'Certain *inputs* from the outside are fed in [to the classroom] . . . some *output* follows . . .' but it is not clear 'what is happening inside' and whether 'a particular set of new imputs will produce better outputs' (Black and Wiliam 1998: 1, original italics). In developmental research, he suggests, the teaching–learning process and especially the mental processes of the students are central. Key elements in this respect are the learning process of the researchers/developers, and the involvement of a larger community of practitioners and researchers.

Using the idea of a *learning trajectory*, teachers have to integrate their goals and directions for learning, with the trajectory of students' mathematical thinking and learning. An important outcome is that although the teacher may rely on theory and tasks developed by others, there is still room, and a need, for teachers to construe their own hypothetical learning trajectories. One of the outcomes is that, for application in the classroom, tasks developed through research will have to be adapted to the specific situation of individual teachers with their own goals, with their students, at a particular moment in time. Within the RME research community, by experimenting with mathematics education in practice and by reflecting on this experimental practice, one tries to answer the question of what mathematics education should look like that would fulfil the above educational philosophy. This reflection leads to the development of an educational theory, and this theory feeds back into new experiments.

◯ 10

What does it mean to learn? What is effective teaching?

Mike Askew

Introduction

A glance through the chapters of this book may give the impression that there is a stronger tradition in the Netherlands of research that might be directly described as developmental, than is the case in England. Based on a clearly articulated theoretical framework, the work of the Freudenthal Institute has developed, and continues to develop, the dual strands of furthering understanding of children's learning of mathematics, while at the same time recognizing that teachers need access to research based curriculum and assessment materials.

In England such symbiosis between research and teaching tends to be more in evidence at the secondary level. Research from the Centre for Science and Mathematics Education at Chelsea College, now King's College, produced a series of seminal research findings (Hart 1981, 1984; Hart *et al.* 1985, 1989; Brown 1989) which fed directly into the development of teaching and into assessment materials. Similarly the Shell Centre for Mathematics Education at Nottingham University developed research that was linked to classroom practices and processes (Bell 1986, 1993; Swan 1990).

Research in primary school mathematics

The picture, however, is rather different at the primary level. Historically, there has been a wider gap between those involved in researching the teaching and learning of primary mathematics, and those engaged in producing teaching materials. One notable exception to this was the Nuffield primary mathematics project which built on a Piagetian theoretical framework to produce teaching materials. Initially, materials directed only at the teacher were produced; the ideas therein were to be put into classroom practice (Nuffield Mathematics Project/British Council 1978a, b, c). The latterly produced Nuffield classroom scheme, while ostensibly based upon the project, consisted of classroom materials that were not directly linked to research, nor authored by the original research team.

The Primary Initiative in Mathematics Education (PrIME) Project (Shuard *et al.* 1991), the last major curriculum development in English primary mathematics teaching before the introduction of the National Curriculum in 1988, was notable for the extent of teacher involvement in the project. A structured cascade model for the development and dissemination of ideas was based on the belief that being involved in the process was more important than the development of particular products. The products of this project took the form of in-service training materials encouraging teachers to engage in reflective activities similar to those engaged in by teachers involved in the project. In retrospect, it seems surprising that there is a lack of systematic research evidence from the project charting the effectiveness of PrIME. This is particularly lamentable in the case of the CAN (Calculator Aware Number Curriculum) strand of the project given the wealth of favourable anecdotal evidence, the limited available evidence on how effective this curriculum was (Shuard *et al.* 1991), and the continued debate about the use of calculators in primary classrooms (Askew and Wiliam 1995; SCAA 1997a; Ruthven this volume).

In contrast to such projects producing materials for teachers, most materials published for use with pupils have authors who have come through the teaching and advisory route rather than being directly involved in developmental research. Publishers often make a virtue of this, promoting materials written by practising teachers, with the implication that they bring understanding of the realities of classroom practices in a way that academics in ivory towers may not (a perception fuelled by our press and government agencies in their attacks on educational research).

While not wishing to suggest that textbook writers are ignorant of research findings, there is the danger that the materials produced only recycle current practice and are judged more in terms of what is practicable within classrooms (a necessary consideration) rather than rooted in our growing understanding of how children learn mathematics.

So am I suggesting that there is no developmental research in primary mathematics in England? Well no, but I am suggesting that the story is not as clear cut as in the Netherlands. My intention here is to look at the current context of teaching mathematics in primary schools. The introduction of the National Curriculum for the first time provided a mandatory intended curriculum for all English primary schools. The National Numeracy Strategy (DfEE 1998a, 1999a) is providing teachers with a detailed framework of teaching objectives and learning outcomes for every year of primary schooling and training in how to structure and deliver mathematics lessons. While not mandatory, the Numeracy Strategy will doubtless have a major impact on teaching in primary schools.

We are, therefore, at a time of unprecedented change in the landscape of primary classrooms. My intention in this chapter is to examine some of the potential and actual opportunities for developmental research offered by this change. To do this, I shall address two very fundamental questions:

- What does it mean 'to learn'?
- What does it mean 'to teach'?

What does it mean 'to learn'?

There is currently a redefining of both the mathematics curriculum and, consequently, what constitutes mathematics per se. In a political climate where there
is a perceived need to 'return to basics' in primary education, based upon England's apparently poor performance in international comparisons, a National Literacy Project was set up alongside a National Numeracy Project. The choice of
'numeracy' was no doubt chosen to mirror 'literacy' and presumably thought to
be more acceptable than 'arithmetic', although the latter might have more hon-
estly reflected the government's intentions. (In the press release launching the
move, from a project, to a national strategy, much emphasis was placed on 'learning [multiplication] tables' as being at the heart of the strategy (Straker 1996).)

The meaning of numeracy

What is this beast *numeracy*, however? The intention does not appear to be
closely tied to Crowther's original concept of 'scientific literacy' (Crowther
1959). I shall not attempt to produce a definitive definition of the term as I
believe that terms come to be tacitly understood only through their use.
Rather I want to examine the way that the term is used in the documentation
supporting the National Numeracy Strategy.

I want to suggest that two strong senses of what it means to be 'numerate'
are embodied in the Framework for Teaching Numeracy (subsequently re-
named the *Framework for Teaching Mathematics from Reception to Year 6*,
although inside the reference is still to becoming 'numerate' as opposed to,
say, becoming mathematically literate) (DfEE 1999a).

Learning as acquisition

The first sense is that of 'numerate' as an adjective to describe pupils' 'states',
that is, their internal cognitions or dispositions. This is illustrated by the
following extract:

the numerate pupil should:

- know by heart number facts . . .
- calculate accurately and efficiently . . .
- explain their methods and reasoning using correct mathematical
  terms.

(DfEE 1999a: 4)

In the body of the Framework, there are detailed listings of teaching objectives and learning outcomes. For example, in Year 4 (8- and 9-year-olds):

pupils should be taught to:

- find a difference by counting up through the next multiple of 10, 100 or 1000;
- count on or back in repeated steps of 1, 10, 100, 1000;
- partition into hundreds, tens and ones;
- identify near doubles;
- add or subtract the nearest multiple of 10, 100 or 1000 and adjust.

(DfEE 1999a: 40)

I suggest that one way to read such lists is in line with the 'acquisition' metaphor for learning. As Lave points out, this is deeply embedded in our normative language for talking about learning (Lave 1990: 648). Learning as acquisition also buys into Gee's 'cultural myth' of commodities (Gee 1996). Such readings are consistent with the commodification and market place perspective brought to education under the Conservative government and largely maintained within the current climate.

One possible consequence of the 'acquisition' view of learning is a separation from teaching of the locus of responsibility for learning. Failure becomes the responsibility of the individual, either teacher or pupil. If the teacher, then this is because they lack the skills to 'pass on' the knowledge (or worse, wilfully withhold it). (In a radio interview about a small decline in national test results in mathematics at age 11, one of the government's ministers repeatedly referred to the fact that this was due to teachers not 'giving' pupils the skills they needed and that the government was committed to making sure that teachers would 'give' pupils the skills in future.)

Alternatively, if the 'fault' does not lie with teachers, then it must be that pupils are not capable of 'grasping' the ideas. Research into teachers' beliefs about pupils' learning (Askew *et al.* 1997b) suggests a continued presence of the need for pupils' 'readiness' to learn ideas, or that the mind is like a 'leaky vessel' (Shuard 1986a: 936) with pupils lacking the ability to retain (i.e. hold onto) what has been taught.

Learning as acquisition theories can be regarded broadly as 'mentalist' in their orientation, with the emphasis on individual pupils building up cognitive structures (Carpenter *et al.* 1982; Peterson *et al.* 1984; Baroody and Ginsburg 1990; Kieran 1990; Alexander 1991). Within the acquisition metaphor of learning, a dominant view of the role of the *social* is that it acts as the means through which individuals acquire or construct concepts and/or understandings. Primacy in learning is given to the individual, with the social acting as the 'container' for learning, shaping but not constituting the learning. The individual has a disembodied mind that acquires (or constructs) knowledge.

Learning as participation

In contrast with the view of 'learning as acquisition', many theorists are turning to a view of 'learning as participation', and developing theories that attend to the sociocultural contexts within which learners can take part (Brown *et al.*

1989; Rogoff 1990; Lave and Wenger 1991). Theories of 'learning as participation', or *situated cognition* do not accept that there is a distinction between the learner and the context within which learning takes place. Learning is not regarded as being put into practice, nor is social practice seen as simply the mechanism through which learning is brought about.

> In our view, learning is not merely situated in practice – as if it were some independently reifiable process that just happened to be located somewhere; learning is an integral part of generative social practice in the lived-in world.
>
> (Lave and Wenger 1991: 35)

Lave contrasts the image of the disembodied individual – who internalizes knowledge or constructs ideas – with 'relatedness' and the situated nature of learning:

> The claim that the person is socially constituted conflicts with the conventional view in its most fundamental form, with the venerable division of mind from body. For to view mind as easily and appropriately excised from its social milieu for purposes of study denies the fundamental priority of relatedness among person and setting and activity.
>
> (Lave 1988: 180)

Within the paradigm of situated learning, classrooms comprise 'communities of practice', and learning within a particular classroom means learning to become a 'full participant in a socio-cultural practice' (Lave and Wenger 1991: 29). Such a perspective presents particular challenges for developmental research, raising questions such as:

- Is it possible to develop curriculum in isolation from actual classrooms?
- How can curriculum materials be developed in such a way as to be usable by other teachers; if 'transfer' is a myth within mathematics learning, then 'transfer' of teaching approaches must also be a myth with teacher education?

While some writers argue the need for a paradigm shift away from (or even rejecting) acquisition perspectives in favour of participation, I agree with Sfard (1998) in the suggestion that the metaphors are not alternatives, but that both are necessary and each provides different insights into the nature of teaching and learning. However, I do suggest that participation in some sense precedes acquisition. Pupils' learning can be examined through analysis of their 'participation in socio-cultural activities' (Rogoff 1995) and learning is regarded as occurring through *changes in* and *transformation of* such participation.

Thus the focus of attention within the classroom is the nature and content of the sociocultural activities, as determined by the provisions made by the teacher, the interactions of teacher and pupils within the lessons, and the prior understandings of the participants. Analysing classroom practices within a framework of 'transformation of participation' (Rogoff 1995) may provide a discourse that examines the sociocultural activities in which pupils have the opportunity to participate.

An example is given by the representation in Figure 10.1. If you ask teachers or primary school pupils what fraction is represented, most will say three-fifths (or two-fifths, or possibly both). However, it is possible to 'read' the diagram in many other ways, including it representing one and two-thirds, two and one-half, one and one-half or two-thirds. I suggest the reason that it is almost universally read as three-fifths is not to do with the diagram per se, nor to do with pupils' ability to perceive the fraction within the diagram. Three-fifths is taken as the common reading because this is a well established common practice; everyone else from textbook, to teachers, to parents, 'reads' the diagram as three-fifths. A social practice is at the heart of reading the diagram.

Difficulties for pupils

A view of social practice as being at the heart of mathematics may help raise awareness of why some pupils experience difficulties in mathematics. A test for 10-year-olds had a question about moving around a coordinate grid. Set in the context of a ship sailing, there are many facets of knowledge about ships that pupils have to suppress in order to engage with the task as a mathematical one (as opposed to real world: ships do not travel along grid lines, they do not turn through right angles, and so forth). But in being asked 'What must you say to the ship to move it from B to C?' children have to engage in the practice of treating this 'ship' as sentient. So is it unreasonable for a child to answer, 'Ready, steady, go?', as one I came across did.

In such circumstances who is to 'blame' for the child's inappropriate answer: the test writer, the teacher, the child? I would argue that trying to locate the 'blame' for failure within any particular agent is not possible as each displays some lack of awareness of the conventions and social practices within which such test items are located. Any responsibility for an individual's inappropriate response has to be distributed across all participants (including those physically absent).

What does it mean 'to teach'?

If participation precedes acquisition, then what are the implications for teaching? Unlike our Continental neighbours, in England the term 'teach' is used very much as a catch-all term. Descriptions of how children are grouped

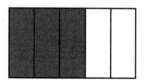

Figure 10.1 Fraction diagram

within a classroom, what texts are used, how teachers interact with individuals, would all be appropriate responses to the question, 'How do you teach?'

Within the current rhetoric about teaching, and particularly the National Numeracy Strategy, much store is placed in the form of lessons. In the introduction to the *Framework for Teaching Mathematics from Reception to Year 6* (DfEE 1999a) four key principles are identified as the recommended approach to 'teaching' mathematics:

- dedicated mathematics lessons every day;
- direct teaching and interactive oral work with the whole class and groups;
- an emphasis on mental calculation;
- controlled differentiation, with all pupils engaged in mathematics relating to a common theme.

Apart from the content reference to mental calculation, the emphasis is on the organization for teaching. This is reinforced later in the document where teachers are encouraged to have a clear, three-part structure to their lessons. This begins with 10 minutes of oral and mental activity, goes on to a main teaching part and finishes with a whole class 'plenary' drawing out the key ideas of the lesson. In other words, what I shall refer to as the 'pedagogy' of teaching is given explicit emphasis.

Effective teaching of numeracy

A research project based at King's College, considering effective teaching of numeracy, looked at teachers' pedagogic practices (Askew *et al.* 1997b). For the sample of teachers involved, no consistent association between styles of classroom organization and levels of pupil attainment was found. Teachers judged to be highly effective – in terms of pupil gains on a specially designed test of numeracy – displayed variety in how they organized their classes for mathematics teaching. Some preferred to work with the whole class, some with groups, and some adopted an individualized approach. Equally, such differing styles were found amongst the group of teachers deemed to be least effective on the basis of pupil performance.

Rather than concentrate on the form of lessons, I would argue that developmental research in England needs to attend more to the 'didactics' of teaching. By this I mean the moment to moment interactions with pupils, and the teaching tools that are available to teachers and that they draw upon to support pupils' participation in mathematical activity. From a theoretical position of learning mathematics as referring to change in participation, then developmental research needs to attend to the actual events in which pupils have the opportunity to engage. Building on Saxe's (1989) four-parameter model for examining emergent goals, I suggest that the following four parameters provide a framework for examining the key elements of mathematical (or numeracy) events (see Figure 10.2).

Each of these four parameters raise some initial questions.

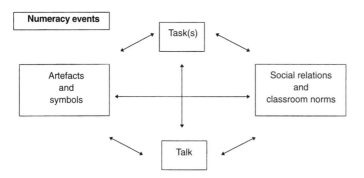

Figure 10.2 The four parameters of numeracy events

Tasks
- What tasks are offered to the pupils?
- Do the tasks have the potential to challenge pupils to think mathematically?
- Do the tasks make mathematical sense and have the potential to develop significant aspects of mathematics?
- Do the tasks engage pupils' interest?

Social interactions and classroom norms
- What behaviours are exhibited in terms of teacher–pupil and pupil–pupil interactions?
- Are interactions directed towards encouraging all pupils to participate?
- Do the interactions have a primary focus on participating in mathematics (as opposed to behaviour or simply completing tasks)?
- Are pupils' contributions valued?

Artefacts and symbols
- What 'texts' are available to support children's learning in terms of physical objects, diagrams, symbolic number representations (number lines, cards, etc.), books, and so on?
- What conventions are adopted in the classroom with respect to ways of working, recording and so on?
- Are the texts and conventions appropriate to the task?
- Do they provide the opportunity for movement from 'models of' to 'models for' a situation?

Talk
- How is mathematical ambiguity dealt with?
- To what extent does the teacher build on pupils' everyday discourse in developing lessons?
- How does discourse encourage a focus on meaning and reasoning?

Mathematical events and mathematical orientations

There is a danger, however, as Street (1999) points out, that such accounts remain at the level of the descriptive. In discussing literacy, Street distinguishes between literacy events and literacy practices, the former being descriptive accounts of happenings, the latter being the frameworks of meaning-making that participants bring to events and through which they make sense of them. In line with this distinction, I want to separate out mathematics events from mathematics orientations. Like literacy events, numeracy events are accounts of particular actions. Numeracy events can be of different orders of magnitude ranging from, say, a pupil working on her own to answer a single calculation, to a whole lesson. Events may be directly observed by a researcher, or they may be accounts from others, for example, teachers' descriptions of lessons.

Numeracy events thus form the corpus of data, while numeracy orientations are theoretical accounts for how, and why, mathematics events proceed in the way they do. This distinction is similar to that made by Brown and Dowling (1998) in discussing data indicators and concepts. Four further parameters can be examined for the questions raised about mathematics orientations (see Figure 10.3).

Self
- How do the subjects appear to perceive their roles in the classroom?
- What perceptions do the subjects appear to have of themselves as learners?

Others
- What does the behaviour of subjects towards others in the class suggest about their expectations of others?
- How does the subject relate to others in the class?

Mathematics
- What prior understandings of mathematics does the subject appear to have?
- How congruent are teachers' perceptions of pupils' prior understandings with the understandings the pupils display?
- What image of mathematics does the subject appear to have?

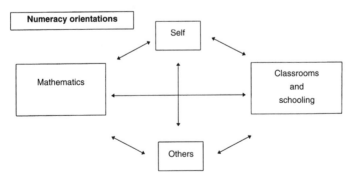

Figure 10.3   The four parameters of numeracy orientations

Classrooms and schooling
- What orientation does the subject have towards the way classrooms should be constituted?
- What orientation does the subject have towards the role and purpose of schooling?

This attending to mathematics events and mathematics orientations relates to the identification of teachers' orientations towards teaching mathematics as discussed in a previous study (Askew *et al.* 1997b). Three distinct orientations to teaching primary mathematics were identified: *transmission, discovery* and *connectionist*. In all three cases, teachers and pupils formed 'communities of practice' (Lave 1991). The mathematics events of these communities of practice influenced pupil and teacher mathematics orientations.

A *transmission* orientation, for example, placed emphasis on the role of the teacher as the main source of mathematical knowledge, with pupils in a subordinate position and practices that attended to mathematics as a discrete set of rules and procedures.

The *discovery* orientation, in contrast, placed the pupil at the centre of the learning process through an emphasis on pupils being able to construct or discover mathematical ideas for themselves. In this orientation, the role of the teacher was primarily as a provider of activities and resources, and a source of encouragement and motivation. Thus, discovery orientated lessons resulted in pupils and teachers engaging in a qualitatively different type of event, and consequently developing a different perspective on the practice of mathematics.

The third, *connectionist* orientation placed emphasis on working with the complexity of mathematics with teachers and pupils explicitly sharing the practices of doing mathematics. Such an orientation might be thought of as being closest to the 'apprenticeship' model of learning that more normally occurs outside the classroom (Rogoff and Lave 1984) although there are differences in dealing with large groups. The data collected by the Leverhulme research project at King's College suggested that such an orientation was more effective in terms of learning outcomes in relation to a test of mathematics.

Pupils' perspectives

Current research at King's is moving the focus of attention away from the teacher towards pupils' orientations in mathematics lessons. A five year longitudinal study (Leverhulme Numeracy Research Programme) is tracking some 1600 5-year-olds and 1600 8-year-olds across five years of schooling. The following example from data in the project illustrates different pupil perspectives on participation, drawing on data from one lesson where two pupils in a group adopted different strategies to complete the task set.

A lesson began with a whole-class introduction by the teacher recapping some work on fractions done previously. The main part of the lesson comprised the pupils completing worksheets of various fraction calculations.

There were worksheets set at different levels of difficulty but each had a common structure in terms of the types of calculations to be done.

One section of the worksheet required the pupils to find unitary fractions of whole numbers. In order to explain how to do this, the teacher re-cast the task into two different forms. First she explained that finding one-fourth of 36 is the same as dividing 36 by four, she then went on to remind the class that to divide 36 by four they could use the four times table and find where 36 was in that table. Two examples were worked on the board.

Sonia and Graham were both in the middle ability group and were sitting in the same group with a third girl. Table 10.1 summarizes their different approaches to this part of the worksheet. Sonia's approach to the task was consistent throughout her work on finding the fractions. She took from the teacher's introduction that the calculations to be done were divisions, and brought to the lesson a procedural method for carrying these out (a method which, in interview, the teacher explained she had previously taught). Thus Sonia would appear to have an orientation towards mathematics as meaning following set routines and treating each calculation independently from any others.

In order to understand Graham's orientation, some further details of the problem solving in which he engaged are needed. There were 12 calculations to carry out. The fifth required one-third of 21 to be found. This Graham did, as with the others, by counting on in threes, holding up a finger for each three counted, and writing down seven. Question number seven required him to find one-third of 30, and he announced that he was going to 'cheat'. Looking back at his answer to one-third of 21 he immediately held up seven fingers, counted on in threes from 21 to 30 and wrote down 10.

A later calculation asked pupils to find one-tenth of 20 for which Graham immediately wrote 10. Asked why, he explained that 'you have to find which table the number is in. Twenty is in the tens table, so the answer is 10'. Similarly, he wrote down 10 as the answer to one-eighth of 40 but quickly self corrected this to four, explaining 'I got it wrong. It's not which table it is in, but where in the table'. On this basis one-half of 50 got the answer five, and then Graham spontaneously went back and changed his answer to one-third of 30 from 10 to three and one-tenth of 20 from 10 to two!

It would seem that Graham had an orientation towards mathematics lessons as being involved with pattern spotting and looking for short-cut methods to help him figure things out quickly. Unfortunately, this led to him getting a number of the questions wrong (as well as at least one right but for the wrong reasons). The teacher's response was simply to ask him to do the corrections.

Within any mathematics lesson there are certain aspects where the teacher can determine the extent of locus of control as balanced between herself and the pupils. In particular:

- in determining the type of calculation;
- in generating examples;
- in methods of solution.

Table 10.1   Different pupils' approaches to the worksheet

	Sonia (Year 4)	*Graham (Year 4)*
Task(s)	Worksheet of fraction calculations to complete, including finding fractions of small numbers.	Worksheet of fraction calculations to complete, including finding fractions of small numbers.
Social relations and classroom norms	Limited interaction with other members of group, none initiated by Sonia herself.	Paid some attention to behaviours of other members of group
Talk	No talk about task with other members of group.	Told Sonia that she ought to be using her tables and fingers to do the calculations.
Artefacts and symbols	Worksheet set out form of recording. Used scrap paper to work each calculation out: drew lines to create columns to share amongst. For example, if trying to find 1/4 of 36, drew up four columns, and 'shared' 36 circles across the columns, drawing and counting on, counting up nine circles in each column as the answer.	Worksheet set out form of recording. Initially used tallies to calculate: to find 1/4 of 36 wrote out sets of four tallies under each other, counting on until reaching 36, then going back and counting the number of rows of tallies (nine). Quickly moved to counting on using fingers.

To a certain extent, decisions about these aspects could be made based on the purpose of the lesson. Other decisions about who has control appear to be more rooted in teachers' beliefs about the role of the different participants in mathematics lessons. We do not suggest, however, that control over activity in lessons rests solely in the hands of the teachers. As Graham's response indicates, even where there is quite tight teacher direction, the pupils' perceptions of what constitutes numeracy practices have to be taken into account in understanding their participation.

Thus our current research represents something of a shift of focus. Previously we attended to the lesson from the perspective of the teacher and the impact that this appeared to have on pupils' learning at the class level. While we are still examining class effects within the Leverhulme Numeracy Research Programme, we are also examining lessons at the level of the individual pupil. At a time when focus at the policy level is on the 'daily mathematics lessons', as though this were an objective event providing the same experience for all pupils, Sonia's and Graham's behaviours demonstrate this is not the case.

Through further detailed examination of pupils' perspectives on numeracy lessons, we aim to further our understanding of the impact of particular practices as they are interpreted by particular pupils, and to consider the implications for teachers in their attempts to reconcile working with whole classes with responding to individuals. Ultimately we hope this will help us better understand dialectical interplay between teacher and pupil orientations, and the consequent impact on learning.

11

Fostering a dialectic relation between theory and practice

Koeno Gravemeijer

Introduction

Today, the need for alternatives to the traditional 'transmission' approaches in mathematics education is internationally acknowledged. A catalyst for this awareness has been the rise of 'constructivism', which appears to be rather popular with mathematics educators and researchers of mathematics education. This popularity goes together with a broad variety of interpretations. However, if one sticks to a strict interpretation of constructivism, one cannot speak of a 'constructivist pedagogy'. Constructivism is basically an epistemological theory, which can be interpreted as a theory about learning, but it is not an instruction theory. Nevertheless, constructivist research has highlighted the shortcomings of traditional mathematics education, and partly as a consequence, the need for reform has arisen. Although constructivism does not imply a certain pedagogy, it does ask for a consideration of what mathematics education is about, or as Cobb (1994: 4) puts it: 'The critical issue is not whether students are constructing, but the *nature* or *quality* of those socially and culturally situated constructions' (italics in the original).

In general, a choice is made for mathematics education that gives more autonomy to the students. Crudely put, reform in mathematics education aims at shifting away from 'teaching by telling', and replacing it by 'students constructing', or 'inventing'. This represents a shift in emphasis from what *teachers* do, to what *students* do. Then the problem arises of how to direct this learning process, or 'how can we make students invent what we want them to invent?'

Developing a theory for realistic mathematics education

It is exactly this question that researchers at the Freudenthal Institute, and its predecessors, have been trying to answer for over two decades (see van den

Heuvel-Panhuizen, this volume). What is striven for is to develop mathematics education that corresponds to Freudenthal's ideal of 'mathematics as an human activity' (Freudenthal 1973, 1991). According to Freudenthal, students should be given the opportunity to reinvent mathematics by mathematizing, mathematizing subject matter from reality and mathematizing mathematical subject matter. In both cases, the subject matter that is to be mathematized should be experientially real for the students. That is why this approach is named Realistic Mathematics Education (RME). One of the core principles of RME is that, *mathematics can, and should be, learned on one's own authority, through one's own mental activities.*

Within the RME research community, by experimenting with mathematics education in practice and by reflecting on this experimental practice, one tries to answer the question of what mathematics education that would fulfil the above educational philosophy should look like. This reflection leads to the development of an educational theory, and this theory feeds back into new experiments (see Figure 11.1). This implies that the resulting theory, which we call a 'domain-specific instruction theory for realistic mathematics education', is always under construction.

Developing a research method

The research approach that is being followed in the Netherlands is a form of 'transformational research' (NCTM Research Advisory Committee 1988) which we call 'developmental research'. Developmental research consists of a mixture of curriculum development and educational research, in which the development of instructional activities is used as a means to explicate, elaborate, test, adjust, refine, and expand an instructional theory (for a practical application in the classroom see Menne, this volume). What is meant here is not the kind of symbiosis between research and development in which the research takes the shape of formative or summative evaluation in service to curriculum development. Instead, developmental research is seen as a form of basic research that informs practitioners such as curriculum developers,

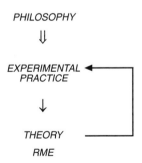

Figure 11.1   Cyclic process of theory development

teacher trainers and teachers. It is an integration of development and research that can be described both as developing-by-researching and as researching-by-developing.

This research methodology emerges from a similar cyclic process as the RME instructional theory (see Figure 11.2). As a consequence, the research methodology has a similar tentative character. Moreover, it is not always possible to adhere to all aspects that are considered important from the perspective of the research methodology, due to time and other constraints in the everyday practice of carrying out developmental research projects.

A 'constructivist teacher' as a paradigm

The approach to instructional design that is part of the developmental research differs significantly from traditional instructional design models. Traditional instructional design models concentrate on learning objectives. They focus on learning outcomes, while the process that leads to these learning outcomes is actually treated as a black box; there is no consideration of the mental activities that provide the transition from not having mastered a certain learning objective to having mastered the same learning objective. This even holds for the more refined task-analytic approaches that seem closely tied to the learning process, but actually produce learning hierarchies that describe learning steps in terms of observable objectives. In developmental research, on the contrary, the teaching–learning process and especially the mental processes of the students are central.

What is key in this type of consideration can be elucidated by Simon's (1995) analysis of the teacher's task of selecting and presenting instructional activities. His point of departure is in the observation that the planning of instruction based on a constructivist view of learning faces an inherent tension. The teacher has to integrate his or her goals and direction for learning with the trajectory of students' mathematical thinking and learning (Ball 1993). To find an answer to the question of how to deal with this tension,

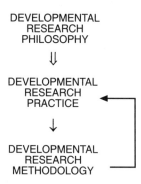

Figure 11.2 Cyclic process of the emergence of the research methodology

Simon analyses his own role as a teacher in a small classroom teaching experiment in terms of a process of decision making about content and task. His analysis shows Simon as a teacher who is constantly thinking about what the students might be thinking and how he could influence their thinking in an indirect manner. He tries to imagine the mental activities of the students as they work with the problems he might pose to them, and he tries to anticipate how their thinking might help them to develop the insights he wants them to develop.

To describe this role of the teacher, Simon (1995: 133) introduces the notion of a 'hypothetical learning trajectory' (HLT): 'The consideration of the learning goal, the learning activities, and the thinking and learning in which the students might engage make up the hypothetical learning trajectory.' Simon calls the learning trajectory 'hypothetical' because the actual learning trajectory is not knowable in advance. Nevertheless, although individual learning trajectories may vary, learning often proceeds along similar paths. The teacher, therefore, can construe an HLT based on expectations about such paths. The actual course of the teaching–learning process in the classroom offers the teacher opportunities to find out to what extent the actual learning trajectories of the students correspond with the hypothesized ones. This will lead to new understandings of the students' conceptions. These new insights, and the experience with the instructional activities will form the basis for the constitution of a modified HLT for the subsequent lessons. Simon (1995) describes this process as a 'mathematics teaching cycle' (Figure 11.3). In developing and adapting these learning trajectories, the teacher relies on all sorts of professional knowledge (see Figure 11.4).

Developmental research

This image of a 'constructivist teacher' can be seen as a paradigm for the way a developmental researcher works. Like the teacher, the developmental researcher may take ideas from various sources to construe an instructional sequence. The sources may be curricula, texts on mathematics education, research reports and the like, but note that adopting often means adapting an activity in such a manner that the instructional activities are being detached from their original context. The way this is done is determined by the researcher's overall vision of mathematics education.

This way of working may be described as 'theory-guided bricolage' (Gravemeijer 1994a, b), since it resembles the manner of working which the French call a 'bricoleur'. A bricoleur is an experienced handyman who uses, as much as possible, those materials that happen to be available and to do so, many materials will have to be adapted. Moreover, the bricoleur may have to invent new applications that differ from those for which the materials were designed. The developmental researcher follows a similar approach, as the way in which selections and adaptations are made will be guided by a theory; in our case, the theory of realistic mathematics education.

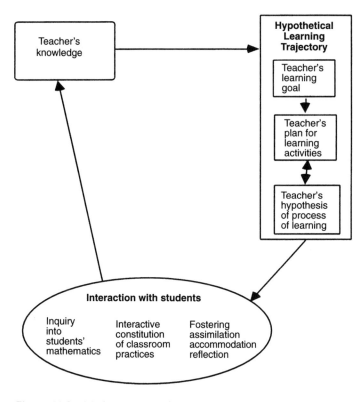

Figure 11.3   Mathematics teaching cycle
Source: Simon (1995: 135)

In the beginning, this theory was more a global philosophy on mathematics education than a theory. Gradually, however, a domain-specific instruction theory evolved. In each developmental research project, the general research question, 'What constitutes mathematics education that is consonant with the basic principles of realistic mathematics education?' is answered locally, primarily on a concrete level. That is to say, the answer is sought for a specific topic, namely by developing a prototypical course for that topic. Broadly speaking, the researcher construes a provisional set of instructional activities, which is worked out in an iterative process of (re)designing and testing. The backbone of this method of developmental research is formed by a cyclic process of thought experiments and instruction experiments (Freudenthal 1991) (see Figure 11.5).

The process that governs this research process is very similar to that of the mathematical teaching cycles as described by Simon (1995). There are, however, important differences which concern the scope and the intent of these activities.

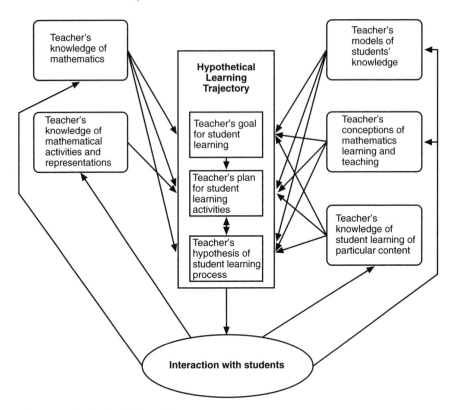

Figure 11.4   Teacher's knowledge
Source: Simon (1995: 136)

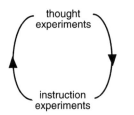

Figure 11.5   Cyclical process of thought experiments and instruction experiments

Scope

Where a teacher may focus on a time span of one or two lessons, developmental researchers direct their attention to developing instructional sequences. The developmental researcher has a long-term learning process in mind and in this long-term process, the subsequent cycles of thought and instruction experiments are connected (see Figure 11.6).

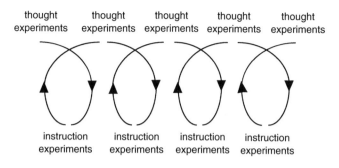

Figure 11.6   Developmental research, a cumulative cyclic process

Intent

The goal of the researcher is not to solve an immediate problem, but to constitute a well-considered, and empirically-grounded instruction theory. The
instruction theory that is developed in a given research project is a local instruction theory that gives an answer to the general research question for one given
topic. In the research project, the mathematical teaching cycles inform the
development of the local instruction theory. In fact, there is a reflexive relation
between the thought and instruction experiments, and the local instruction
theory that is being developed. On one hand, the conjectured local instruction
theory guides the thought and instruction experiments, and on the other hand,
the microinstruction experiments shape the local instruction theory (Figure
11.7).

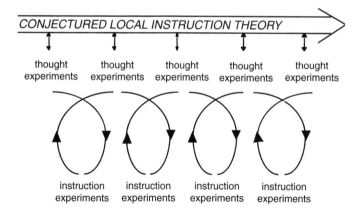

Figure 11.7   Reflexive relation between theory and experiments

Since the subsequent instruction experiments are carried out with the same students, every following instruction experiment starts with the residue of the preceding ones. Because of the cumulative interaction between the design and the assembled empirical data, the intertwinement between the two has to be unravelled to pull out the optimal instructional sequence in the end. It does not make sense to include activities that did not match their expectations, but the fact that these activities were in the sequence will have affected the students. Adaptations will, therefore, have to be made when the non-functional, or less-functional activities are left out.

The instructional sequence will consequently be put together as a reconstruction of instructional activities that are thought to constitute the most effective elements of the sequence, which will be based on the deliberations and the observations of the developmental researchers. In this manner, the result of a developmental-research experiment will be well-considered and empirically-grounded. The theory that underlies the sequence can be seen as the result of the learning process the researchers and the teacher went through during the series of thought and instruction experiments. Thus it is this learning process that has to justify the local instruction theory (see also Freudenthal 1991).

In ethnographic research this methodological norm is labelled 'trackability'; the outsider should be able to retrace the learning process of the researcher. Trackability is not only important from a methodological perspective, it is also essential for the teachers who want to use the instructional sequence developed in this process. How methodological norms can be worked out is discussed in Gravemeijer (1994a, 1994b). Here the emphasis will be on justification in the wider perspective of the acceptance by a community of researchers and practitioners. This issue will be addressed at the end of this chapter and relates to the way teachers are informed about the results of developmental research.

If the norm of trackability is truly fulfilled, the teachers can appropriate the experiences and considerations of the researcher. Then they will have at their disposal a sound basis on which to make their own assessments, and their own adaptations. That is to say, although the teacher may rely on theory and tasks developed by others, there is still room, and a need, for the teachers to construe their own hypothetical learning trajectories. Tasks will have to be trimmed to the specific situation of individual teachers with their own goals, with their students, at a particular moment in time. To make such decisions, the teacher has to construe hypothetical learning trajectories, although, when construing these HLTs, the local instruction theory can be used as a framework of reference. The theory can be seen as a travel plan, while the teacher, and the students, make the journey, to borrow Simon's (1995) journey metaphor.

Like a journey, a long-term teaching–learning process can be planned in advance, and in a similar manner; the actual teaching–learning process has to be constituted in interaction with the conditions and developments one encounters. In this sense, an externally designed instructional sequence can function as a 'travel plan' for the teacher, or better, the rationale, or the local instruction theory behind the instructional sequence, informs the teacher's travel plan, and the availability of exemplary instructional activities enables the teacher to carry out this plan. Like a traveller, the teacher will have to adjust this plan continuously by construing HLTs that fit personal interpretations of, and choices in, the actual situation.

Realistic Mathematics Education (RME) theory

In numerous developmental-research projects, Freudenthal's philosophy, or global theory, is elaborated in many prototypes that represent local theories (e.g. local instruction theories on fractions, addition and subtraction, written algorithms, matrices, differentiating, and exponential functions). In other words, the global theory is made concrete in local theories. Vice versa, the more general theory can be reconstructed by analysing local theories. Like the local instruction theories, the more general instruction theory, which we call a 'domain-specific' instruction theory for Realistic Mathematics Education, combines descriptive characteristics with elements of a rationale. At the same time, the developmental research concept brings with it that the instruction theory is also, in part, a design theory. In fact, in light of its function as a guiding theory for future developmental research projects, it may be useful to cast the theory in terms of heuristics for instructional design. From this perspective, we may distinguish three central heuristics: *guided reinvention through progressive mathematization, didactical phenomenological analysis,* and *emergent models.*

Guided reinvention through progressive mathematizing

According to the reinvention model (Freudenthal 1973) the students should be given the opportunity to experience a similar process to that by which a given piece of mathematics was invented. Thus a route has to be mapped out that allows the students to invent the intended mathematics by themselves and to do so, the researchers start with imagining a route by which they could have arrived at this outcome independently. Here, knowledge of the history of mathematics can be used as a heuristic device, for knowing how certain knowledge developed may help the developers to lay out the intermediate steps by which the intended mathematics could be reinvented.

The reinvention model can also be inspired by informal solution procedures that can often be interpreted as anticipating more formal procedures. In this case, mathematizing such solution procedures creates opportunities for a reinvention process. In a general way, one needs to find contextual problems that allow for a wide variety of solution procedures, preferably those which considered together already indicate a possible learning route through a process of progressive mathematization. Note that the reinvention process implies long-term learning processes. Unlike learning sequences, where the learning path is chopped up in separate learning steps that can be mastered independently, the reinvention process evolves as a process of gradual changes. Intermediate steps have to be viewed in a long-term perspective, and not as goals in themselves.

Didactical phenomenology

According to the didactical phenomenology (Freudenthal 1983), situations where a given mathematical topic is applied are to be investigated for two reasons: first, to reveal the kind of applications that have to be anticipated in instruction; second, to consider their suitability as points of impact for a process of progressive mathematization. If we see mathematics as historically evolved from solving practical problems, it is reasonable to expect to find the problems that gave rise to this process in present day applications. We can imagine that formal mathematics came into being next, in a process of generalizing and formalizing situation-specific problem-solving procedures and concepts about a variety of situations. It will therefore be the goal of a phenomenological investigation to find problem situations that may give rise to situation-specific solution procedures that can function as (paradigmatic) solution procedures to be taken as the basis for vertical mathematization.

The didactical phenomenological analysis may orient the researchers/developers towards applied problems that can be presented to students who do not know the mathematics in question yet. The spontaneous solutions of the students may show strategies, notations, and insights that can be used in the sequel of the learning process (Streefland 1991).

Emergent models

The third heuristic is found in the role that emergent models play in progressing from informal knowledge to more formal mathematics. Whereas manipulatives are presented as pre-existing models in product-oriented mathematics education, models emerge from the activities of the students themselves in Realistic Mathematics Education. This means a model comes to the fore first as one that is a *model of* acting in a situation that is familiar to the student. Next, by a process of generalizing and formalizing, the model then becomes an entity on its own. Only after this transition, does it become possible to use this as a *model for* mathematical reasoning (Streefland 1985; Treffers 1991a; Gravemeijer 1994a, b). (Note that the term model should not be taken too literally. It can also concern a model situation, or a model procedure.) Key to this transition is that the models first derive their meaning, for the students, from their reference to acting in experientially real situations, and that subsequently a shift takes place, where a mathematical focus on strategies begins to dominate the reference to the context, and the character of the model changes.

Initially, the models come to the fore as context-specific models. They refer to concrete or paradigmatic situations which are experientially real for the students. On this level the model should allow for informal strategies that correspond with situated solution strategies, at the level of the situation that is defined in the contextual problem. From then on, the role of the model begins to change. As the student gathers more experience with similar problems, the model gets a more general character, and the process of acting with the model gets objectified. In this sense, the model becomes an object in and of its own right. It now derives its meaning from a mathematical framework – a framework that, by the way, is formed by acting with the model. This objectified model then can become a model for mathematical reasoning.

Social and cognitive perspectives

It may be noted that the aforementioned heuristics focus on cognitive development, and in this sense it may be argued that describing the RME theory by these heuristics does not do justice to the theory as a whole, although, admittedly, in most Dutch developmental research projects, the emphasis has been on cognitive aspects with the classroom culture taken for granted in most cases. More recently, the classroom culture has become an explicit topic of attention in a number of projects (e.g. Elbers and Streefland 1997). Furthermore, both a social and a cognitive perspective form a dual focus of attention in the developmental research projects that are carried out in collaboration with Paul Cobb and his colleagues (Cobb *et al.* 1997). In relation to this, Yackel and Cobb's (1995) 'emergent' perspective should be mentioned.

This emergent perspective tries to enhance our understanding of mathematical learning by emphasizing that it is a process of both individual construction, and of enculturation to the mathematical practices of particular communities. In this view, the class is seen as a community that develops its own mathematics. The classroom community develops its own 'taken-as-shared meanings, interpretations and practices' (Cobb 1991). Together, one tries to constitute mathematical knowledge, while preserving everyone's individual responsibility. The goal is intersubjective agreement, or as Cobb (1991) puts it, 'mathematical truths are interactively constituted'. To put it differently, 'true' is that which is established as a truth by the classroom community. This, of course, asks for a certain manner of working. To some extent, the students are expected to behave like mathematicians. They have the obligation to explain and justify their own ideas and solutions, and they have the obligation to try to understand the ideas and solutions of others, and to ask for clarification and/or to challenge them if necessary. In relation to this Cobb speaks of 'social norms' (Cobb 1991). In a similar fashion, Brousseau (1990) speaks of a 'didactical contract'.

To analyse this type of instruction, Yackel and Cobb (1995) developed the interpretative framework shown in Figure 11.8. This conceptual framework incorporates a social and a psychological perspective. The psychological perspective looks at the individual from a constructivist point of view, the social perspective looks at the classroom as a social community. According to Yackel and Cobb, these two perspectives complement each other. The corresponding components, they argue, are reflexively related. The 'class-room social norms', for instance, will influence the beliefs of the individual students; at the same time, the classroom norms can be characterized as shared knowledge. The social norms exist at the mercy of a good harmony between the individual beliefs and the classroom norms. Thus, in short, the total of the individual beliefs constitutes the classroom norms, but at the same time, the individual beliefs are shaped by the classroom norms.

The 'sociomathematical norms' (Yackel and Cobb 1995) show a similar reflexivity. Sociomathematical norms deal with issues such as: what counts as a (different) solution, what counts as an insightful, or efficient solution, and what counts as an adequate explanation. Sociomathematical norms can only be established in a reflexive process. Students will use the reactions of the teacher to figure out what counts as an adequate explanation, or what counts as an efficient solution, but then there will have to be students that present explanations, or solutions that can be reacted upon by the teacher.

Classroom mathematics practices too have this two-sidedness. On one hand, there is the mathematical practice that is accepted as a 'taken-as-shared' practice at a certain moment in time. On the other hand, there are the individual insights, knowledge and abilities that lead to the constitution and acceptance of this practice. Again, the students actively contribute to the emerging practice, and at the same time the shared classroom mathematics practices influence the individual insights, knowledge and dispositions. These classroom practices then can be seen as the counterpart of the local instruction theory.

Justification and negotiation

In practice, a thorough analysis adhering to the above methodology is not always possible. How developmental research projects are carried out depends largely on the conditions set by the funding. Many projects at the Freudenthal Institute are externally financed projects in which the commissioner is more concerned with the product than with the scientific yield. Nevertheless, it can

Social Perspective	Psychological Perspective
Classroom social norms	Beliefs about own role, other's roles, and the general nature of mathematical activity in school
Socio-mathematical norms	Mathematical beliefs and values
Classroom mathematical practices	Mathematical conceptions

Figure 11.8 Interpretative framework for analysing the classroom microculture

be argued that projects that primarily have an objective of instructional design or educational development can also contribute to theory development. Key elements in this respect are the learning process of the researchers/developers, and the involvement of a larger community of practitioners and researchers.

Ongoing scientific discourse

In regard to the learning process of the researchers/developers, Freudenthal (1991: 161) speaks of 'reporting on it so candidly that the product justifies itself, and that this experience can be transmitted to others to become like their own experience'. This justification is empirical in the sense that it is rooted in the observations of the researchers and others during the experiment, but the justification is also highly argumentative. Empirical data are not blindly accepted, but are interpreted within a given interpretative framework. The justification of the conclusions will therefore always consist of a combination of empirical findings and theoretical considerations. This implies that these results are open for discussion. The same 'data' can be interpreted differently, leading to other conclusions. Furthermore, people may choose other goals or other criteria for success than the developers/researchers. Finally, the iterative character of developmental research brings with it that research outcomes never get the status of absolute facts. The results of a developmental research project should therefore be primarily seen as a contribution to an ongoing scientific discourse. This notion of scientific knowledge is also consistent with a *socioconstructivist* concept of sharing knowledge; direct transfer of knowledge is not possible, instead, sharing knowledge is only possible in a process of 'negotiation of meaning'. In this sense, the empiricist concept of objectivity is replaced by objectivity as intersubjectivity. Within the discourse in which intersubjectivity is striven for, results of all sorts of developmental research projects may play a role, as long as the empirical trackability of each result is weighed in the discussion.

Development in interaction with practitioners

The enterprise of developing instructional sequences and (local) instruction theories is primarily aimed at the community of mathematics educators. The instructional sequences are meant as prototypes that can inform and inspire textbook authors, teacher trainers, school counsellors, and last but not least, teachers. The accompanying (local) theories are meant to help these mathematics educators to understand and evaluate the intent and rationale underlying these prototypes. After all, what is hoped for is that the prototypes are adopted (and adapted!) on the basis of the underlying ideas. One cannot, however, expect practitioners to share ideas if there is no process of negotiation or dialogue involved.

The prototypical sequences play a central role in this process. The prototypes and the underlying theories are made available via journals, conferences and project publications. A forward line of mathematics educators will take the opportunity to experiment with the prototypes, and all will adapt the prototypes to their own insights, and to the setting in which they are working. These experiences will be the basis for feedback to the researchers including statements about the experienced usefulness, information on what adaptations were made, and why, and how that worked out. Furthermore, the feedback will also consist of argumentation on how the prototypical sequences fit with practice theories on one hand, and with the overall educational philosophy of RME on the other hand. This interactive process serves not only to disseminate the ideas of the researchers, it also works the other way around. It prevents the researchers from coming up with innovative activities that are out of touch with the reality of everyday classroom practice.

Conclusion

In conclusion, we might reflect upon the way to justify the new curriculum that is constituted by elaborations of prototypical sequences in textbook series. Traditionally, curriculum innovation was justified by evaluation research which showed that the new curricula were more effective than their competitors. In the RME approach, the justification does not lie in quantitative data on the performance of the students. Instead, the justification is in grounded conjectures about how students learn and how the suggested instructional activities support this learning process. This RME approach fits with the general shift in the norms of justification that is observed by the National Council for Teachers of Mathematics (NCTM) Research Advisory Committee (1996). In comparison to traditional research, they argue, norms of justification have shifted from assembling facts that prove one curriculum better than another, to providing well substantiated theories about *how* these curricula work. This fundamentally changes the position of the teachers. With the traditional justifications, the teachers would not have a way to know how to adapt curricula that were proven effective to their own situations. Crudely put, the only thing they knew was that it worked elsewhere. With the new norms, the teachers have some informative theories that they can take as a point of departure. They can take the theories of the researchers as conjectures, which they can test and modify in their own classroom. In this manner, the teachers can produce their own contribution to the development of those theories instead of being passive consumers of knowledge produced by others.

It should be noted, however, that in the Dutch situation, this is still something to be striven for. Until now, the practitioners involved in the dialogue with the researchers are mainly textbook authors, teacher trainers, and school counsellors. The participation of classroom teachers in this process is still rather limited. This frames the big challenge for the near future.

Acknowledgement

The analysis reported in this paper was supported by the National Science Foundation under grant No. REC 9604982 and by the Office of Educational Research and Improvement under the grant number R305A60007. The opinions expressed do not necessarily reflect the view of either the Foundation or OERI.

⊖ Part V

Towards a new numeracy

This section differs from any of the previous sections with a single contributor from Britain and no 'paired' contribution from the Netherlands. As Marja van den Heuvel-Panhuizen noted in Chapter 4 of this volume, although 'insightful use of calculators' is incorporated in the Key Goals of the Dutch curriculum, this has not yet been implemented in present classroom practice and research on calculator use has not been a priority. In the UK, pioneering research was established in the 1980s by Hilary Shuard and the PrIME team who developed innovative approaches that were much acclaimed by those classroom teachers who were associated with the project but this work was never validated through rigorous research. What is left is a legacy of anecdotal evidence and an enthusiasm in parts of the mathematics education community that will be evident in this section.

Kenneth Ruthven is a Reader in Mathematics Education in the University of Cambridge School of Education and a key researcher who has been involved in establishing research evidence on the implications of calculator use in the classroom. In this section he proposes arguments for the use of a calculator as a 'cognitive tool' to develop mathematical thinking but warns that the design of a calculator-aware number curriculum calls for more thoroughgoing analysis, both of content and progression. The opening sections of this chapter outline the origins and rationale of the pioneering Calculator-Aware Number (CAN) project, review the influence of the project's approach on the design of the National Curriculum, and consider the impact of the new curriculum framework and assessment measures in England on classroom practice, notably in schools from the CAN project. The central part of the chapter provides a more detailed analysis, drawing primarily on a Cambridge study that examined the experience of pupils who entered CAN project schools in 1989, when the new National Curriculum was implemented (see Brown, in this volume). Important emergent issues of pedagogy are identified within the CAN approach, and these are related to findings regarding pupil progress in general. Pupils' strategies incorporating calculator use are examined, and linked to characteristics of the curriculum framework.

Using vignettes from a research study, he shows how calculator use can make demands of pupils' understanding that are not accounted for in a hierarchical programme of study and that this involves challenging the idea that such procedures are, necessarily, mechanical. He suggests that calculation *procedures* may serve important pedagogical, as well as computational, functions; that is, they may act as means to wider mathematical learning, as well as ends of learning valued in themselves. Using research evidence from schools with contrasting attitudes and practices in calculator use, he notes that pupils' preference for mental over machine calculation is a more positive trend in schools in which calculators have an established role in pupils' learning. More strikingly, pupils in these schools were significantly more positive in using *mental calculation as a support for number learning,* being not only more prone to calculate mentally, but also more liable to adopt relatively powerful and efficient strategies for so doing.

The concluding parts of this chapter point a way forward for school arithmetic, considering how the calculator might play a part in forging stronger connections between the concepts of number, for example between fraction, decimal and division. In recognizing the dual computational and pedagogical functions of calculation procedures and schemes, he proposes the crafting of a new capstone for a calculator-aware primary mathematics curriculum, and confronting the challenges that will be a consequence of such a systematic design. He does, however, note that no matter how well designed such a curriculum may be, its successful implementation is likely to depend on it being treated as part of a coherent and committed process of school development – and ultimately of systemic reform – rather than as the isolated responsibility of individual teachers.

⊖ 12

The English experience of a calculator-aware number curriculum

Kenneth Ruthven

Introduction

In England, the idea of developing a 'calculator-aware' number curriculum has been pursued over a lengthy period. Speculative discussion amongst mathematics educators prepared the ground for practical exploration within a government-supported curriculum development project in the 1980s, and this in turn proved a significant influence on the design of a national curriculum for mathematics. Hence, the English experience provides an unusual case in which the attempt to frame and implement a calculator-aware number curriculum has moved beyond untried speculation and localized innovation to an attempt at national institutionalization.

Forging a calculator-aware number curriculum

As calculators were making their first tentative entries into English school classrooms, Girling (1977: 4–5) proposed that basic numeracy should be redefined as 'the ability to use a four-function electronic calculator *sensibly*', noting that 'if this definition is accepted it is obviously necessary to re-examine our objectives in the teaching of calculation in mathematics, particularly where it is related to the paper and pencil algorithms which form the core of this work in primary schools'. He argued that sensible use of a calculator involved being able to check a result in appropriate ways, and that this depended critically on an understanding of the relative size of numbers, and on the capacity to carry out corresponding mental calculations. He drew back, however, from suggesting that pencil and paper methods should not be taught, proposing instead that 'they should *only* be taught as part of the armoury of techniques that we have to help in an understanding of number *and not because they are useful*' (emphases in the original). Nevertheless, he saw this as having the 'dramatic consequences' of concentrating attention on understanding the process involved, of encouraging study of different algorithms, and of there being 'no need for anyone to be stopped in their progress in mathematics through being unable to perform the useless algorithms we now require'.

Algorithms versus calculators

Reviewing the place of standard written algorithms in school arithmetic, Plunkett (1979) noted advantages accruing from their being written, so creating a permanent and reviewable record of calculation; from their being standardized, so making this record more readily interpretable; and from their being contracted, efficient, automatic and general in their applicability. Nevertheless, he pointed to the important disadvantages of such algorithms not being easily grasped by pupils because of their lack of correspondence with informal methods; and of their encouragement of what he termed *cognitive passivity* and *suspended understanding*. Taking issue with Girling in this one important respect, he drew the radical conclusion that:

> The advent of calculators has provided us with a great opportunity. We are freed from the necessity to provide every citizen with methods for dealing with calculations of indefinite complexity. So we can abandon the standard written algorithms, of general applicability and limited intelligibility, in favour of methods more suited to the minds and purposes of the users . . . Children should be helped to acquire sensible methods for calculating, and for the majority of calculations met in everyday use these will be mental methods . . . More importantly children will acquire a better understanding of number from using their own mental algorithms than from the repeated application of standard algorithms they do not comprehend. With mental methods occupying their proper place as the principal means for doing simple calculations, the position of calculators is clear. They are the sensible tool for difficult calculations, the ideal complement to mental arithmetic.
>
> (Plunkett 1979: 5)

Studies of workplace mathematics, commissioned to inform the Cockcroft Report (DES 1982: 19–20), found that that the use of calculators was already widespread in many types of employment, and that where pencil and paper methods of calculation were used, these were rarely those methods traditionally taught in school. A follow-up study (Fitzgerald 1985: 38–9) found that even the use of calculators had been reduced by the spread of computerized systems; that elsewhere, use of calculators was almost ubiquitous; and that it had become very rare indeed to find an employee using written methods. Cockcroft anticipated accordingly that one of the principal effects of increasing automation would be to reduce the use of arithmetical calculation in employment. Noting the modest development work already taking place, Cockcroft (DES 1982: 113–14) recommended that 'more is needed both to consider the use of calculators as an aid to teaching and learning . . . and also the extent to which the arithmetical aspects of the curriculum may need to be modified'.

As an aid to teaching and learning, specific suggestions pointed to the value of calculators in encouraging investigation of number representations and operations. On the curriculum, the report proposed that the availability of calculators 'should influence the complexity of the calculations which pupils are expected to carry out with pencil and paper and also the time spent in practising such calculations'; in particular, that 'it is not profitable for pupils to spend time practising the traditional method of setting out long division on paper, but that they should normally use a calculator' (DES 1982: 114).

The CAN project

Echoes of all these early discussions can be found in the Calculator-Aware Number (CAN) project (Shuard *et al.* 1991), a major component of the ensuing Primary Initiatives in Mathematics Education (PrIME) programme, sponsored by the government curriculum agency. Between 1986 and 1989, the project team worked collaboratively with several clusters of primary schools and their teachers throughout England and with some in Wales. Before recruiting the clusters, the project team formulated a set of basic working principles:

- classroom activities would be practical and investigational, emphasizing language and ranging across the whole curriculum;
- exploring and investigating 'how numbers work' would be encouraged;
- children would always have a calculator available; the choice as to whether to use it would be the child's not the teacher's;
- the importance of mental calculation would be emphasized; children would be encouraged to share their methods with others;
- traditional pencil and paper methods of column addition, subtraction, multiplication and division would not be taught; children would use a calculator for those calculations which they could not do mentally.

The tangible outcomes of the project were these curriculum principles that were made concrete in a range of classroom activities and accounts, but not in a structured curriculum plan. This reflected the pedagogical style developed within the project; and in particular, an important scepticism about the very idea of a curriculum progression.

> The teachers began to develop an exploratory and investigative style of working, which allowed the children freedom to take responsibility for their own learning. Topics for exploration took the place of practice exercises as the prevailing classroom activities. Because the number sections of the mathematics schemes used in the schools had been discarded, the teachers were able to move towards a different style of working. No longer did they have to 'cover' set topics in a set order. They began to notice that children's mathematics learning did not seem to progress in the ordered linear way in which it was traditionally structured. Individual children seemed to be putting together the network of mathematical concepts in their own individual ways.
>
> (Shuard *et al.* 1991: 44)

Framing a national curriculum in mathematics

When, in 1987, the decision was made to introduce a national curriculum (see Brown, this volume), it was not surprising that the CAN project and its personnel should influence the proposals of the working group charged with devising the programme of study in mathematics.

> The universal availability of electronic calculators is changing our views about the kinds of facility in computation which are needed of pupils . . . Along with the ability to use and interpret the results obtained from calculators there is general agreement that a greater facility in mental arithmetic should be encouraged.
>
> (National Curriculum Mathematics Working Group 1987: 8)

The rejoinder of the then Minister of Education was that, 'It must be important that pupils themselves understand and are proficient in the various mathematical operations that can now be done electronically' (DES 1988: 100). Later, he asked still more pointedly, 'Is it justifiable to exclude the pencil and paper methods for long division and long multiplication from the attainment targets for mathematics, as the mathematics working group have recommended?' (NCC 1988: 92).

The final programmes of study for the National Curriculum achieved a superficial resolution of this conflict through the deliberate ambiguity of its references to 'non-calculator' methods of computation. A more explicit account of the approach favoured by the working group (confined to the pedagogical guidance accompanying the statutory orders) suggested that:

> For most practical purposes, pupils will use mental methods or a calculator to tackle problems involving calculations. Thus the heavy emphasis placed on teaching standard written methods for calculations in the past needs to be re-examined. Mental methods have assumed a greater importance through the introduction of calculators, and the use of mental methods as a first resort in tackling calculations should be encouraged. Work should be based in a firm understanding of number operations, applied to problems in a variety of contexts, and encourage pupils to select from different methods with confidence depending on the nature of the problem and the suitability of the method.
>
> (NCC 1989: E6)

Discussing the new National Curriculum, the CAN project team wrote:

> The CAN project has been very fortunate that National Curriculum mathematics is much in line with the thinking the project has developed. Teachers who work in the project have welcomed the emphasis in the National Curriculum on a broad curriculum in mathematics, on using and applying mathematics, on the encouragement for children to use their own methods of calculation, and on the possibility of using calculators for much of the work. Teachers in project schools have commented on a

number of occasions that they need to make many fewer changes to their curriculum than other teachers.

(Shuard *et al.* 1991: 71)

References to calculators

The curriculum was designed within a levelled framework intended to pre-scribe progression within teaching programmes, and to describe the resulting development of pupil capabilities. The expectation was that pupils in the lower primary (infant) phase (known as Key Stage 1) would cover the material of levels 1 to 3, and that by the end of that phase (at age 7), the great major-ity would be assessed as attaining a level between 1 and 3, with the average pupil at level 2. Similarly, during the upper primary (junior) phase (known as Key Stage 2), it was anticipated that, by the close of the phase (at age 11), the great majority of pupils would achieve a level between 3 and 5, with the typi-cal pupil at level 4, having covered the programme of study to level 5; level 6 was 'intended for only the most able children performing significantly above the normal range' (SCAA 1995).

Table 12.1 abstracts, from the mathematics programme of study, the refer-ences to calculators relevant to the primary school. This is certainly a cur-riculum that acknowledges the calculator but to what extent is it a calculator-aware curriculum? References to 'using a calculator' start warily. At levels 2 and 3, this is to be for checking or 'where necessary'. Half of the examples concern money calculations. At levels 4 and 5, cautiously affirma-tive references to 'using a calculator where necessary', working 'with the aid of a calculator' and 'check[ing] using a calculator' are easily outnumbered by prohibitive references to working 'without a calculator' or 'using non-calcu-lator methods'. A product of the fudged compromise over the relative empha-sis to be given to mental and written, standard and non-standard methods, although calculator use is integrated, the negative phraseology appears to be subversive. While there is an emphasis on interpreting results 'on a calcula-tor' and 'reading calculator displays', there is only one reference to the need to 'translate the problem . . . in order to use a calculator'. There is, however, one important innovation, in the form of 'trial and improvement' as a solu-tion strategy. Clearly dependent on calculator availability, although avoiding reference to it, this is in recognition of the possibility of distinctive calculator methods.

As the first pupils completed each key stage, a national programme of assess-ment was introduced, incorporating external testing and this testing appears to acknowledge the place of calculators. In the 1995 Key Stage 2 mathematics tests (for 11-year-olds), for example, opening instructions explained that icons indicated where the use of a calculator was allowed or prohibited. Of the 40 items across the two test papers, 14 prohibited use of a calculator. A number of these items took the form of missing digit problems presented in the verti-cal format of standard written methods, rather than in a, more methodically

Table 12.1 Calculator references in the National Curriculum programme of study in mathematics (1989 and 1991)

Level	Programme of Study	Example
1	(no references)	(no references)
2	Describe current work, record findings and check results (U&A).	Devise stories for adding and subtracting numbers up to 10 and *check with calculator* or apparatus (1989).
3	Solving problems involving multiplication or division of whole numbers or money, *using a calculator where necessary.*	Find the cost of four calculators at £2.45 each (1989, 1991).
	Using decimal notation in recording money.	Know that three £1 coins plus six 1p coins is written as £3.06, and that 3.6 *on a calculator* means £3.60 in the context of money (1989, 1991).
	Appreciating the meaning of negative whole numbers in familiar contexts.	Understand a negative output *on a calculator* (1989, 1991).
4	Adding and subtracting two 3-digit numbers, *without a calculator.* Multiplying and dividing 2-digit numbers by a single-digit number, *without a calculator.*	Work out *without a calculator* how much longer 834 mm is than 688 mm (1989).
	Solving addition and subtraction problems using numbers with no more than two decimal places, and multiplication and division problems starting with whole numbers.	Work out how many chocolate bars can be bought for £5 if each costs 19p, and how much change there will be *without the aid of a calculator* (1989, 1991). Find out how many 47-seater coaches will be needed for a school trip for a party of 352, *with the aid of a calculator, interpreting the display* (1991).
	Reading calculator displays to the nearest whole number and knowing how to interpret results which have rounding errors.	Interpret $7 \div 3 \times 3 = 6.9999999$ if it occurs *on a calculator* (1989).
	Recording findings and presenting them in oral, written or visual form (U&A).	Translate the problem of finding the number of 28p packets of crisps that can be bought for £5 into $500 \div 28 =$ in order to *use a calculator*; record the result as 17.857142 and thus decide that the result is 17 (1991).

Table 12.1   continued

Level	Programme of Study	Example
5	Understanding and *using non-calculator methods* by which a 3-digit number is multiplied/divided by a 2-digit number.	Use any pencil-and-paper method to find the number of coaches needed to take 165 Year 7 on an outing if each coach has 42 seats.
	Calculating fractions and per cent of quantities *using a calculator where necessary.*	Calculate 15% of 320; 3/5 of 170 m; 37% of £234; 1/10 of 2 m (1989).
	Using 'trial and improvement' methods and refining.	Estimate the square root of 10 and refine to 3 decimal places (1991).
	Approximating, using significant figures or decimal places.	*Read a calculator display,* approximating to 3 significant figures (1989).
	Make and test simple statements (U&A).	Explore the results of multiplying together the house numbers of adjacent houses, make a statement about the results, and *check using a calculator* (1989).
6	(no references)	(no references)

neutral, horizontal format. Such presentational features, combined with concern about the acceptability of non-standard approaches when meeting requirements that pupils should show their working, led many teachers to conclude that the testing process entailed a preference towards standard written methods. Use of a calculator was stipulated on only one item within the two test papers. Only one further item might be regarded as calculator affirmative, posing a problem in terms of unknown numbers keyed into a calculator, and permitting use of the machine. Beneath the veneer of calculator recognition, then, both national curriculum and national testing emerged as more 'calculator-beware' in spirit than 'calculator-aware'.

Impact of national reforms on professional practice

An official evaluation of the implementation of the National Curriculum reforms, across schools at large, found that teachers made little reference to the non-statutory guidance and were already confident of their teaching of number (Askew *et al.* 1993). Combine these factors with the tone of the programme of study, and it is not startling to find that school inspections reported a largely unchanged pattern of professional practice with regard to calculator use:

> In all the schools visited the teachers placed a strong emphasis on the written practice of the basic operations of addition, subtraction, multiplication and division. This dominated the work in half the schools . . . For

many schools there was an imbalance between the written practice of basic number skills and mental, oral and practical work involving number . . . The skills of using a calculator were neglected in a high percentage of the schools; in only a tenth of the lessons seen were calculators used.

(Ofsted 1993: 9–11)

However, a picture of contrasting practice emerged from the group of former CAN schools involved in a Cambridge study (Ruthven *et al.* 1997). When teachers in these schools were asked to look back on the impact of the national reforms on the experience of the pupils completing Key Stage 2 in 1996, the general tenor of their accounts was of seeking to retain the valued principles and activities from CAN; to establish the legitimacy of these principles and activities within the new order; and to tighten aspects of their implementation. Richard and Stephanie comment:

It's made very little difference in the way I taught maths personally. Very little. The other thing it had done in this school – it would have happened without the National Curriculum anyway – it refocused people's ideas on the structure that was needed right through the year groups.

(Richard)

I don't think the delivery has done anything except become a little clearer. It's forced me to sharpen up my act. I think if we want to hold on to this we've got to really be able to . . . justify it. We've got to show that it can be done in this way . . . It's not that we're being subversive. It's there in the National Curriculum. It's that it's not terribly common what we do. I feel we have to justify it.

(Stephanie)

Impact on calculator-aware practices

The substantive influence of external pressures on a calculator-aware approach had been threefold. First, some of the expansiveness of investigative work had gone, with a stronger tendency to structure and foreclose an activity than in the past.

I think what's altered is that pre National Curriculum I would have had a much broader, less clear picture of what I wanted to get out of a session, and therefore I would have been more open to other things that came up, and would have been able to pick up on those other things and delve a bit deeper with the children. I think what it's forced me to do is to keep on a much narrower pathway.

(Stephanie)

I would probably (have done) more longer investigations. Now, I do a lot more shorter activities, to get the coverage in a year.

(Tracy)

Second, although calculators continued to be readily available in the classroom, there were occasions when their use was challenged or proscribed.

> The policy is that they are there all the time, but [sometimes we say] 'Actually for this activity I don't want you to use a calculator'.
>
> (Tracy)

> There might be some negative reference: 'How are you going to do that, to use the calculator?' . . . So there might be some kind of sideways swipe at it.
>
> (Stephanie)

Third, standard written methods of recording and calculating were now taught. At Key Stage 1, teachers felt obliged to introduce pupils to vertical methods of recording, and to 'sums' presented in this way. At Key Stage 2, standard written methods were more prominent, although the expectations of secondary schools were often cited as the direct reason for this.

> [Tests] brought back more formal work. Having been through the first maths test – it was formal sums set out, which the children were not used to seeing. That's when we decided that we were going to have to introduce formal sums set out ready for them. They'd set them out any way they wanted.
>
> (Rachel)

> Conceptually they had a pretty good insight of number, but on paper, when they were presented with any kind of traditional sum on paper, which they would be at the high school, the children were worried and the parents were worried. We just felt we had to teach it them.
>
> (Richard)

Emergent tensions within the CAN approach

An important effect, then, of the reforms was to press the CAN schools towards systematic coverage of material in the national programme of study, and towards compliance with the perceived requirements of national testing. Pressure had also come from tensions experienced in developing and maintaining the CAN approach within the schools and the 'refocusing on structure' and 'sharpening up of act' reported by teachers were shaped by these tensions as well as by the national reforms.

One salient theme was the lack of calculator focus in school textbooks and the uncertainty and effort arising from abandoning a conventional mathematics scheme, with limited alternative means of support.

> We more or less abandoned schemes and went in at the deep end with CAN. Two members of staff in particular were heavily involved with it and went to meetings and then fed back to staff. But, as I remember, you were

left floating about a bit and not knowing what was right or what was wrong to do. I remember thinking if I just give them investigations and problems and help them to solve them, that's how I'll survive this. You felt as though there was nothing to support you . . . When you have a scheme, you don't use it rigidly but you know it is there as a support for you if you need it . . . The two who went to the meetings seemed to be more capable at it. You needed to go to the meetings. They got the ideas from the meetings. We just got the 'trickle down'.

(Tricia)

I came to this school having a fairly sketchy knowledge of CAN, having seen it in operation, but having a sketchy knowledge about how to proceed, and finding no resources. The resources there were photocopiable resources and packs. There would be one copy so you had to have copies made. It was incredibly hard work preparing lessons each day.

(Richard)

In such circumstances, it was difficult to plan for continuity and progression in children's learning, both from lesson to lesson and from year to year.

In CAN it was difficult to know how to progress. After an exciting lesson you thought 'Where do I go now? Where do I take them next?' You'd be rooting around for ideas.

(Tricia)

There was no structure through the school . . . I noticed in my first year that teachers were photocopying an investigation for Year 3 children and the same one was being used for Year 6 children, and nobody knowing what the children had covered at all.

(Richard)

While positive features of a high degree of self-regulation by pupils and the resulting differentiation of experience were identified, there were also some concerns as to whether benefits were shared by all.

One of the things that keeps me working in this way is that low ability children don't get so complexed about it . . . I think the weak ones do benefit from a lot of talk and being involved in things. They are not excluded because they didn't manage to get quite as much done. And for the high flyers, I think it is a brilliant way of working because they can go as far as they want; there is no ceiling on them. They can take off and go a long way with things and the talk is good for them at that end.

(Stella)

You always thought, 'Do children really understand – particularly the less able children? Do they really understand what it is they are doing?' I think it showed up with more able children, if they got an answer which was clearly wrong, they knew it was wrong. But that estimating thing was not there with less able. You'd have outrageous answers and they wouldn't have a clue it was not right . . . I didn't ensure that, like I do now, that children could add up quickly, mentally in their head . . . Looking back I think I should have done that. That would have helped the less able with their estimating . . . Some children struggled, but the children who had a gift for maths did very well. If they had a good understanding of the structure of numbers and estimating skills, then they went quite far.

(Tricia)

Correspondingly, teachers had come to recognize the complexities of supporting pupils' development. For example, in relation to methods of calculation, they were conscious of having to manage an important tension between personal insight and authenticity on the one hand, and accuracy and efficiency on the other.

We've built on what the children have actually used . . . try out the different methods and encourage them to find the one they feel most happy with . . . There is one child I did change . . . because he was not accurate, and he was slow. His methods were so long-winded . . . It is important that children do have quick accurate methods. One of the things which is really important is . . . that the children have conceptual awareness of what's happening with the numbers. If they know that then they are secure. But some of the children are going through the motions with methods they don't understand.

(Richard)

We put [pupils' strategies] very high up [but] the older a child is the more likely I am to say 'That's fine but it takes twice as long as this one' . . . There is kind of a seductiveness in working investigatively . . . and they forget that there can be a directness that is important as well.

(Stephanie)

Influence of CAN on attainment and attitude of pupils

Although the evaluation of the original CAN development reported very positive findings, the project team were conscious of the unusually favourable circumstances under which project teachers and pupils were working (Shuard *et al.* 1991: 55). The later Cambridge study provided an opportunity to compare the progress of a subsequent cohort of pupils in the post-project schools with that of their peers in non-project schools under equable conditions (Ruthven *et al.* 1997). Marked contrasts were found between the number curricula of the two groups of schools while these pupils were in the early years. In the non-project schools, there was a common emphasis on a highly structured development of written column methods of calculation, supported by the use of place-value apparatus, with calculators used of the order of 'several times a term'. In the post-project schools, the emphasis was on calculation arising within investigative or problem-solving tasks. This calculation was both mental, with acknowledgement of pupils' own methods of computation and modes of recording, and by machine. Although place-value apparatus was in use, it appears to have played a minor part. Calculators were readily available, and used on the order of 'most days'. Over the junior years, however, there was an important degree of convergence, as the non-project schools started to take greater account both of the problem-solving and investigative requirements of the National Curriculum, and of its greater emphasis on mental calculation and the use of calculators, and as practice in the post-project schools was rethought so as to meet the demands of national testing.

Results of the Cambridge study

National assessment levels awarded at the end of Key Stage 1 (age 7) and Key Stage 2 (age 11) were analysed (after taking account of the general scholastic attainment of pupils) to determine whether the odds of high or low attainment in mathematics differed between the two groups of schools. At Key Stage 1, the odds of high mathematics attainment (level 3) were found to be significantly greater in the post-project schools, and so too were the odds of low mathematics attainment (level 1). In the 'calculator-aware' post-project schools, then, pupils were more likely to be found at either extreme of the attainment distribution. However, this pattern did not persist through to the Key Stage 2 results. Bearing in mind the more sharply contrasted experience of pupils over Key Stage 1, and taking account of the challenging issues of differentiation and intervention identified by teachers in the post-CAN schools, a plausible conjecture unfolds. It is that the stronger emphasis in the post-project schools during Key Stage 1 on self-regulated work on relatively open-ended tasks produced a greater differentiation of experience between pupils, creating higher expectations of, and greater challenges for, more successful pupils, but providing less systematic structure and support for the learning of those who were making poorer progress.

Pupils' attitudes and application

At age 11, pupils also completed an attitude questionnaire. No significant differences between schools were found on the constructs *Enjoyment of number work, Reluctance to use a calculator* and *Calculator use as a support for number learning.* However, on the construct *Preference for mental over machine calculation,* there was a discernible, but non-significant, trend for pupils in the post-project schools to be more positive. And on the construct *Mental calculation as a support for number learning,* pupils in the post-project schools were significantly more positive. A further study extended these findings (Ruthven 1998). It examined the strategies used by a structured subsample of pupils, excluding those at the extremes of attainment, in tackling a set of number problems. Pupils from post-project schools proved not only more prone to calculate mentally, but also more liable to adopt relatively powerful and efficient strategies for doing so.

These outcomes seem to reflect the contrasting numeracy cultures in the two groups of schools. In the post-project schools, pupils had been encouraged to develop and refine informal methods of mental calculation from an early age; they had been explicitly taught mental methods based on 'smashing up' or 'breaking down' numbers; and they had been expected to behave responsibly in regulating their use of calculators to complement these mental methods. In the non-project schools, daily experience of 'quickfire calculation' had offered pupils a model of mental calculation as something to be done quickly or abandoned; explicit teaching of calculation had emphasized approved written methods; and pupils had little experience of regulating their own use of calculators.

Calculator use by pupils tackling a realistic number problem

As far as calculator use itself was concerned, perhaps the most revealing evidence within the Cambridge study came from a realistic number problem, tackled by the same structured subsample of pupils: '313 people are going on a coach trip. Each coach can carry up to 42 passengers. How many coaches will be needed? How many spare places will be left on the coaches?' (Ruthven and Chaplin 1997). Pupils could work out the problem however they liked; using their head, pen and paper, or calculator, or a mixture of these. The main differences that emerged between the groups were that non-project pupils were more liable to attempt written division (none with success), whereas post-project pupils were more prone to employ mental repeated addition (only a handful with success).

However, the incidence and pattern of calculator use were similar across the two groups, with around half the pupils carrying out a direct calculator division. Many pupils appeared surprised by the result.

> Karen keyed [313][÷][42][=]7.452380952. commenting 'Whoopsie!' followed by 'I've got loads of numbers'; paused, then re-keyed [313][÷][42][=]7.452380952; paused again, then keyed [42][÷][313][=] 0.134185303.

Her initial interpretation of the string of digits displayed was that she had miskeyed; when re-keying produced the same result, she then supposed that she must have entered the numbers in the wrong order. Behind such responses lay an expectation – or perhaps an aspiration – that the result of a division should be a whole number. Certainly, the 'common sense' of this problem points in this direction – 'You can't split a coach up' as another pupil commented – but other factors are also in play. In their experience of mental and written calculation these pupils had encountered division as a process yielding whole numbers as quotient and remainder. By contrast, the calculator provides a (not necessarily whole) ratio. Karen did not recognize the string of digits as incorporating a decimal resulting from a division. Yet recent testing indicated that she was capable of working successfully with the one- and two-digit decimals specified by the curriculum.

Other pupils recognized the display as the interpretable result of a division, but confused decimal part with remainder:

Damon keyed [313][÷][42][=]7.452380952, interpreting this as 'About seven coaches' and 'I think it's four [spare places] because it's seven point four'.

None of the pupils attempting this calculator division interpreted the calculator result as implying eight coaches, although some carried forward an estimate of seven into a further strategy. In this respect, Vera showed how the calculator itself could be deployed to help make sense of the result.

Vera keyed [313][÷][42][=]7.452380952; paused, then keyed [313][÷] [14][=]22.35714285; paused, then keyed [42][÷][10][=]4.2, commenting 'Four point two'; paused again, then keyed [42][x][7][=]294.

Vera gave little away about her thinking, and any interpretation of her intermediate moves must be speculative. One conjecture is that they enabled her to build a bridge between incongruous digits and familiar decimals. The division of 313 by another number resembling 42 confirmed the 'appropriateness' of the original result. By then dividing 42 by 10, Vera produced a simple decimal, completing the process of anchoring the unexpected result in a familiar category, and supporting the idea of carrying forward seven to the next move. In this interpretation, then, her moves can be seen as transitional ones of sense making.

Other less direct strategies were also used to tackle the problem. Joanne adopted trial multiplication:

Joanne keyed [42][x][12][=]504, commenting 'Forty-two times any number, but it was a bit too high'; then keyed [42][x][10][=]420, 'Forty-two times ten, that's too high so'; keyed [42][x][8][=]336, paused, 'They'd need eight coaches, and they'd have [pause] 23 places left over'.

Note Joanne's use of the calculator to multiply 42 by 10. By using the machine to carry out computations in a predictably routine way, she freed her attention to monitor her strategy and to interpret her results. She was very capable of doing such a calculation mentally; a few minutes earlier she had rapidly multiplied 24 by 10 in her head.

Some pupils used the calculator to support repeated addition or subtraction. Liam's experience was typical: 'So you need to add up how many forty-twos go into. I'll do that. I'm sure you could do it a quicker way but, well':

Liam keyed [42][+] [42][+] [42][+] [42][+] [42][+] [42][+] monitoring intermediate totals; keyed [252][+], 'Oh no!'

The calculator leaves no trace of intermediate results, making any extended calculation incorporating a parallel mental computation extremely vulnerable to failure through miskeying and/or breakdown in strategic monitoring or management. In the Cambridge study all pupils' calculator attempts of this type failed in this way; pupils who computed wholly mentally had similar difficulties of keeping track. This highlights the value of recording in supporting extended computation, whether calculator or mental.

Pupil strategies related to the National Curriculum framework

The pupils' responses to the coach problem indicate the complexity of making sense of calculator division. Many of the difficulties can be related directly to features of the progression implied by the levelled programme of study under which their primary schooling had been conducted and they point to the desirability of calculator division being embedded more centrally and comprehensively within a calculator-aware curriculum.

One issue is that of checking. Repeating the original computation, as illustrated by Karen, appeared to be the major strategy employed by pupils to check their calculations and solutions. There was no evidence, in particular, of pupils mentally calculating an approximate value for $313 \div 42$, either as a rough check on a non-calculator or calculator division, or as the basis of some further strategy. This was quite at variance with the suggestions of the pedagogical guidance.

> Whether using mental, pencil and paper or calculator methods, pupils must be able to estimate, approximate, interpret answers and check for reasonableness. The development of these skills is crucial to pupils becoming effective and confident in performing calculations, and should match the development of methods and techniques for calculating.
>
> (NCC 1989)

However, closer analysis suggests that the programme of study did not actually make provision for this close coordination. As Table 12.1 shows, 'Find out how many 47-seater coaches will be needed for a school trip for a party of 352, with the aid of a calculator, interpreting the display' is an example for the level 4 objective, 'Solving . . . multiplication and division problems starting with whole numbers'. Similarly, 'Use any pencil-and-paper method to find the number of coaches needed to take 165 Year 7 pupils on an outing if each coach has 42 seats' is an example of the level 5 objective, 'Understanding and using non-calculator methods by which a 3-digit number is multiplied/divided by a 2-digit number'. But it is not until level 6, well beyond the normal expectations of study in the primary school, that 'Estimate that $278 \div 39$ is about 7' features as an example of the objective, 'Using estimation and approximation to check that answers to multiplication and division problems involving whole numbers are of the right order'.

The priority of calculating mentally

A further issue is the assumption that such checks should be mental; indeed, the wider assertion that pupils should be encouraged to view mental methods as a first resort. Clearly, developing pupils' expertise in mental calculation is an important curricular goal, not least because components of this expertise underpin estimation in approximate calculation as well as in written methods, but an overgeneralized insistence on prioritizing mental calculation may impede pupils' thinking and inhibit their learning of other aspects of mathematics. We have already seen how, while focusing on her solution strategy, Joanne employed a calculator to execute a computation which, under other circumstances, she had shown herself perfectly capable of carrying out mentally. Equally, the reluctance of some pupils to make use of a calculator to implement a direct division led them to adopt alternative strategies based on addition, which they felt better able to compute mentally, but which often proved unreliable.

Recourse to mental calculation becomes highly problematic when the demands it makes on limited cognitive resources, such as working memory, produce overload, affecting other cognitive processes; in particular, the acquisition of new schemas (Sweller 1988). Equally, there is a vicious cycle through which such demands on working memory create anxiety, which in turn generates further demands on cognitive resources (Ashcraft 1995). As Thompson suggests (this volume) the English system may be in danger of oscillating between an inherited obsession with standard written algorithms and an uncritical enthusiasm for wholly mental calculation.

Making sense of calculations

Another issue is that of embedding constructs and procedures within broader conceptual fields. This relates to the difficulties of pupils such as Karen and Damon in making sense of the result of the calculator division. Interpreting division calculations featured in the programme of study of the National Curriculum in the form of 'understanding remainders in the context of calculation and knowing whether to round up or down' at level 3; and 'reading calculator displays to the nearest whole number' at level 4. In the examples above, however, the calculator displayed not a remainder but a decimal part, and pupils needed not so much to read it to the nearest whole number as to recognize it as lying between seven and eight.

This highlights the importance of seeing what might otherwise remain isolated constructs and procedures, as part of a wider conceptual system. In the programme of study, decimals appeared for the first time at level 3: explicitly in 'using decimal notation in recording money', and (hence) implicitly in 'solving problems involving multiplication or division of whole numbers or money, using a calculator where necessary'; then at level 4 in the form of 'using, with understanding, decimal notation to two decimal places in the context of measurement', exemplified as 'read scales marked in hundredths and numbered in tenths (1.89m)', and 'solving addition and subtraction problems using numbers with no more than two decimal places'. Gaining familiarity with these monetary and measurement contexts, and the corresponding calculation schemes, is undoubtedly important, but too literal a treatment risks encouraging a view of the decimal point as a 'separator' within a system of super- and sub-ordinate units such as pounds-and-pence or metres-and-centimetres. Not until level 6, again beyond normal curricular expectations for primary pupils, is there explicit reference to underlying relationships between division, fractions and decimals in the form of 'understanding and using equivalent fractions and equivalent ratios and relating these to decimals'. The development of stronger connections between the concepts of fraction, decimal and division would be desirable (Anghileri in press), and the example of Vera hints at how the calculator might play a part in forging such linkages.

A final issue relates to specified methods of calculation. As far as division is concerned, at level 4 of the programme of study, no *methods* as such were specified, simply 'solving division problems'. In particular, the assumption seems to have been that understanding and using calculator division could be reduced to 'interpreting the display'. At level 5, the explicit, if rather vague, development was into 'understanding and using *non-calculator* methods' for division. While several pupils did, in due course, employ some form of trial and improvement strategy, as illustrated by Joanne, I will argue the merits of explicitly recognizing and teaching a *calculator-based* method of division.

Pedagogical functions of calculation procedures

Informed by these observations, let me now extend Anghileri's suggestion (this volume) that wider mathematical knowledge and understanding can be gained through *doing* calculations, I want to suggest that calculation *procedures* may serve important pedagogical, as well as computational, functions; that is, they may act as means to wider mathematical learning, as well as ends of learning valued in themselves. This involves challenging the idea that such procedures are, necessarily, mechanical.

A fine-grained case study, involving careful analysis of the interactions between an elementary school teacher and each of the five differentiated groups of pupils in her classroom has shown persuasively how calculation procedures in action may quickly move beyond their popular characterization as routine.

> Our analysis of the actual process of instruction of the division algorithm illustrates the idea that there are processes which must properly be characterized as inter-psychological – arising from the interaction between people – which play a major role in producing cognitive changes . . . [I]n initiating the lesson, the teacher presents a precise procedural description which serves as a medium of interaction between herself and the children. In the process of the interaction, the form of the procedures which the

students learn changes from the procedural description originally presented by the teacher to alternate but equally valid procedures, including successive approximation . . . These changes lead to final versions of the procedure that differ from student to student. Yet these variations are neither spontaneous inventions by the students nor are they planned in advance by the teacher. The procedures exist and can be seen as the interaction between teacher and child. Variations in the form of the student–teacher interaction are indistinguishable from variations in the form of the long division procedure.

(Newman *et al.* 1989: 92–3)

In effect, the long division procedure has important potential (although that potential may not be widely realized) to act as a capstone for the arithmetic curriculum, drawing together ideas of place value, of the four operations, and of approximation and estimation. However, the same analysis qualifies the conventional view of this as a simple matter of the sequenced acquisition of components of progressively greater complexity.

[T]he notion of higher and lower levels may be misleading. Take . . . learning the division algorithm, a prerequisite for which, it is commonly assumed, is mastery of the multiplication facts . . . We do not want to deny that having automatized knowledge of multiplication facts helps children in learning the algorithm. We want to point out, however, that it also works the other way. Confronting the algorithm organizes and motivates the math facts. The facts and their organization are given, perhaps for the first time, a clear function.

(Newman *et al.* 1989: 154–5)

In effect, the argument is that, viewed flexibly, the division procedure is capable as much of supporting 'simplification by integration' as of being built up through 'simplification by isolation'.

The assumption of simplification by isolation [is that] in order to simplify something for inquiry, learning, or remembering, we must break it down into its separate components . . . The assumption is . . . that component skills are easier to learn when they are separated from other skills with which they are ordinarily integrated . . . A response is simple – more easily investigated, taught, understood, learned, or remembered – if it occurs in simultaneous functioning with other responses with which it is naturally integrated.

(Iran-Nejad *et al.* 1990: 509–10)

A similar idea lies at the heart of the Dutch pedagogical approach based on the progressive schematization of integrated column arithmetic (Treffers 1987a). In contrast to the American case cited above, however, it is not bare calculation that serves as the medium of negotiation between teacher and pupils, but the mathematization of context problems into column calculations. These context problems serve as a source for developing algorithms, providing meanings, motivations and supports for column calculation; building, in particular, on the informal strategies that children use when solving them.

Here, there is some resonance with CAN findings, including an emphasis on teacher and pupils discussing and appraising different strategies. However, the Dutch approach differs from CAN in important respects: teaching is explicitly guided by a 'learning trajectory' (as discussed by van den Heuvel-Panhuizen and by Gravemeijer, this volume) that charts typical steps through which informal strategies and intermediate procedures can be refined towards the ultimate ideal of a highly efficient and generic (standard written) method. The broader mathematical ideas of estimation and 'clever calculation' are linked to the processes of schematizing and abbreviating the computational procedure.

A capstone for a calculator-aware number curriculum

My argument, then, is that a calculator-aware curriculum would benefit first from an appropriate division procedure to serve as its capstone, and second, from a learning trajectory building from pupils' informal strategies towards that procedure. I will now outline such a trajectory and the procedure to which it leads. At present this is simply informed speculation; developmental research (as discussed by Askew and by Gravemeijer, this volume) is needed to test out and refine these conjectures.

The underlying representation for the procedure centres on coordinating two empty number lines (as discussed for additive situations by Beishuizen and by Menne, this volume) that can serve as a more generic spatial scheme for recording data in multiplicative situations. Taking the coach problem as our example, Figure 12.1 shows two empty number lines, with the line to the left labelled 'coaches' and the line to the right, 'passengers'. By placing the labels at the foot of the diagram, it can be extended upwards as needed. The lines are initially coordinated in additive terms, eventually in multiplicative. Their purpose is the computational one of supporting and organizing calculation involving quantities represented on the two lines, and the pedagogical one of supporting and organizing major shifts in the type

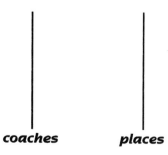

coaches   *places*

Figure 12.1   Coordinated empty number lines for the coach problem

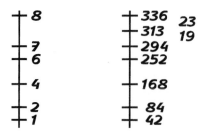

Figure 12.2   Accelerated addition on coordinated empty number lines

of mathematical reasoning guiding calculation and the computational procedures employed.

A hypothesized learning trajectory can be sketched as follows. Figure 12.2 records a 'cumulation' strategy where repeated addition of the capacity of the coach (cumulator) – here accelerated by using tactics of doubling and combining previous results – is used to build up numbers of places (cumulates) and the corresponding numbers of coaches (cumulands). By using normal 'differencing' strategies on the empty number line, the excess and deficit of places (remainders) compared with the target number of passengers are derived. A simple check is that excess and deficit (remainders) sum to the capacity of the coach (cumulator).

Next, Figure 12.3 shows an 'estimation' strategy where trial multiplication by the capacity of the coach (multiplier) is used to translate estimated numbers of coaches (multiplicands) into corresponding numbers of places (multiples). The transition from 'cumulation' to 'estimation' strategies depends on a shift from coordinating additive relationships *within* each delineated quantity, to recognizing, and focusing on, the multiplicative relationship *between* the delineated quantities (cumulator becomes multiplier; cumulands become multiplicands; cumulates become multiples). This also requires a capacity for the corresponding direct computations (which may be provided by a calculator). Hybrid strategies between the two are particularly likely to arise when pupils fall back on mental cumulation in order to generate multiples.

Figure 12.4 shows a 'precision' strategy where ratio-division of the number

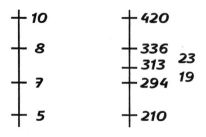

Figure 12.3   Trial multiplication on coordinated empty number lines

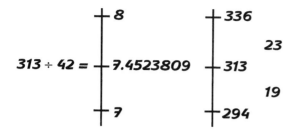

Figure 12.4   Direct division on coordinated empty number lines

of passengers (dividend) by the capacity of the coach (divisor) gives a 'precise' number of coaches (ratio quotient) which is then 'sandwiched' to generate realistic upper and lower (whole) numbers of coaches (rounded quotients). The three (delineated) values to the left (ratio quotient, sandwiched between rounded quotients) are than translated, as in the 'estimation' strategy, into the corresponding (delineated) values to the right (ratio multiple sandwiched between rounded multiples), and the differences corresponding to excess and deficit of places (remainders) are derived, as previously. Again, there is a notable shift between 'estimation' and 'precision' strategies, calling for con-ceptualization of the situation in dual terms of multiplication and division (the multiplier in a left-to-right translation becomes the divisor in a reversed right-to-left translation, and so on); and for extension of number concepts to allow the 'precise' results of calculator division (involving decimal parts) to be integrated with wholes (on the line to the left), and ideally .4523809 on the left (decimal) to be related to 19/42 (fraction) derived from the right. In terms of computational demand, the initial division computation depends on use of a calculator, but there is scope for flexibility in carrying out other computa-tions depending on fluency of mental computation.

As well as serving pedagogical functions, this representation and the refined procedure offer important computational advantages. First, the coordinated empty number lines provide a powerful generic scheme for recording and organizing data arising within multiplicative relationships. Second, the redun-dancy built into the final procedure incorporates several checks: one arises from the reversal of the original division (so that the ratio multiple on the line to the right can be checked against the original dividend); and others, prefig-ured in earlier versions of the procedure, involving the values on the line to the right (which can be checked for increasing size), and the sum of the two remainders they generate (which can be checked against the divisor). These computational advantages are particularly relevant as a means of redressing the limited use of recording and checking noted in the earlier discussion of pupils' work. Equally, the learning trajectory sketched above, with the new cal-culator-based division procedure as capstone, fits a developmental arithmetic curriculum aiming to develop and draw together key mathematical ideas: addition and multiplication; multiplication and division; division, decimals and fractions; order and place-value properties; estimation and approximation.

Challenges of systematic design and systemic reform

Such an approach offers a promising synthesis of key elements of the English calculator-aware and the Dutch realistic approaches. As van den Heuvel-Panhuizen suggests (this volume), the constructivist turn in mathematics education has encouraged too singular a concentration on microdidactic issues and too ready a rejection of macrodidactic frameworks. In particular, the idea of a learning trajectory provides an important element linking the micro- and macrodidactic levels, something apparently lost in the reflex rejection of curricular hierarchies within the original CAN project, and not adequately developed within the levelled programme of objectives provided by the National Curriculum.

The earlier discussion of the treatment of calculators within the National Curriculum provides a further illustration of Brown's observation (this volume) that the formulation of national frameworks for teaching and learning mathematics in England has tended to be highly pragmatic, with the emphasis more on political negotiation and compromise than on didactical analysis and design. The resulting lesson might be baldly stated as 'plans need principles', but the experience of the highly principled case of CAN suggest an important corollary: 'principles need plans'.

The design of a calculator-aware number curriculum calls for more thoroughgoing analysis, both of content and progression, than it has had to date. This emerges both from the accounts of the teachers involved and from the analysis of pupils' responses to the coach problem in relation to the National Curriculum framework. Renewed attention should be given to developing a systematic design for a calculator-aware curriculum and an appropriate pedagogy of calculator use (Ruthven 1999a).

However well designed such a curriculum, its successful implementation is likely to depend on it being treated as part of a coherent and committed process of school development, and ultimately of systemic reform, rather than as the isolated responsibility of individual teachers. This can be seen both in the problems of coordination that emerged within the CAN schools and in the limited impact of the National Curriculum reforms on the teaching of number across the system. These organizational issues are often neglected by mathematics educators but they emerge as critical to successful institutionalization.

Some of these lessons have been learned in England. A government-supported numeracy project has piloted and refined a more systematically planned programme of study in mathematics for the primary school and its implementation is being treated as an aspect of school improvement, calling for sustained commitment and support from school managers, as well as the involvement and professional development of all teachers. This now forms the basis of an ongoing National Numeracy Strategy (DfEE 1998a). And the missing elements? The new English programme of study for primary mathematics needs to be more developmentally-researched and calculator-aware. One can hardly reproach the designers for this, caught between a paucity of relevant research and renewed moral panic and political pressure. In particular, the calculator has now been cast as scapegoat for low standards of numeracy in English primary schools, despite evidence that it was little used, and that, where it was used, this was not to the detriment of pupils' achievement (SCAA 1997a, 1997b).

The policy emphasis remains that 'children's first strategy in the classroom should be to use mental calculation skills whenever possible'; but now, 'for each operation at least one standard written method of calculation should be taught', on the basis that 'these are methods that will be needed throughout their lives'. Use of the calculator is largely confined to the last two years of primary education, treated as a relatively isolated element of the number curriculum, concerned with teaching children 'when it is, and is not, appropriate to use a calculator' and 'the technical skills needed to use it constructively and efficiently'. Used well, however, the document suggests, 'calculators can be an effective tool for learning about numbers and the number system . . . perhaps with the teacher using an overhead projector calculator to demonstrate to the whole class'; and 'calculators can also play an important part in subjects such as science, geography or history, by allowing children to use real data gathered in experiments or research, which will often combine numbers that make calculations more difficult' (DfEE 1998: 52–3). These principles are understandable within a short-term strategy aimed at stabilizing a system in difficulties. Use of technology is grafted onto an essentially pre-technological curriculum. Its potential as a computational device and teaching aid is recognized, but it is not recognized as a cognitive tool. A longer term need remains: for developmental research into new forms of mathematical thinking, augmented by cognitive tools such as the calculator and cognitive supports such as the empty number line, with the aim of integrating technology use with broader mathematical development to create a 'new numeracy'.

Acknowledgements

This article draws on work supported by the Economic and Social and Research Council (award number R000221465), and by the School Curriculum and Assessment Authority. As research assistant to the ESRC project, Di Chaplin made a most important contribution, conducting the teacher and pupil interviews discussed in this chapter, and transcribing them.

Ideas and drafts for sections of this chapter were presented and discussed (at a distance) at an international conference on The Future of Computation, organized by the Australian Institute for Research in Primary Mathematics Education at Edith Cowan University in September 1998; and (in person) at the international conference on The Teaching of Arithmetic in England and the Netherlands, held at Homerton College

Cambridge in March 1999; and the 23rd Annual Conference of the International Group for the Psychology of Mathematics Education, held at the Technion – Israel Institute of Technology – in July 1999 (Ruthven 1999b). I am grateful for the invitations to participate in these meetings, and for the many helpful ideas and suggestions gleaned.

References

Alexander, P. A. (1991) A cognitive perspective on mathematics: issues of perception, instruction and assessment, in *NATO Advanced Research Workshop: Information Technologies and Mathematical Problem Solving Research*, Oporto, Portugal.

Anghileri, J. (1995a) *Children's Mathematical Thinking in the Primary Years: Perspectives on Children's Learning*. London: Cassell.

Anghileri, J. (1995b) Language, arithmetic and the negotiation of meaning. *For the Learning of Mathematics*, 21(3): 10–14.

Anghileri, J. (1996) Language and strategies in children's solution of division problems. Proceedings of the BSRLM Conference, Sheffield, 24 February.

Anghileri, J. (1997) Using counting in multiplication and division, in I. Thompson (ed.) *Teaching and Learning Early Number*. Buckingham: Open University Press.

Anghileri, J. (1998) A discussion of different approaches to arithmetic teaching. Proceedings of the 22nd Conference on Psychology of Mathematics Education (PME22), Stellenbosch, South Africa, 12–19 July.

Anghileri, J. (in press) Development of division strategies for Year 5 pupils in ten English schools. *British Education Research Journal*.

Anghileri, J. and Beishuizen, M. (1998) Counting, chunking and the division algorithm. *Mathematics in School*, 27(1): 519–38.

Anghileri, J., Beishuizen, M., Van Putten, K. and Snijders, P. (1999) A comparison of English and Dutch Year 5 pupils' calculation strategies for division. Paper presented at the British Education Research Association (BERA) conference, University of Sussex, 2–5 September.

Ashcraft, M. (1995) Cognitive psychology and simple arithmetic: a review and summary of new directions. *Mathematical Cognition*, 1(1): 3–34.

Askew, M., Bibby, T. and Brown, M. (1997a) *Raising Attainment in Numeracy: Final Report*. London: King's College, University of London.

Askew, M., Brown, M., Rhodes, V., Wiliam, D. and Johnson, D. (1997b) *Effective Teachers of Numeracy: Report of a Study Carried out for the Teacher Training Agency*. London: King's College, University of London.

Askew, M., Brown, M., Johnson, D.C., Millett, A. and Walsh, A. (1993) *Evaluation of the Implementation of National Curriculum Mathematics at Key Stages 1, 2 and 3, Volume 1: Report; Volume 2: Appendix*. London: School Curriculum and Assessment Authority.

Askew, M. and Wiliam, D. (1995) *Recent Research in Mathematics Education*. London: HMSO.

Atkinson, S. (1992) *Mathematics with Reason*. London: Hodder & Stoughton.

Ball, D. (1993) With an eye on the mathematical horizon: dilemmas of teaching elementary school mathematics. *Elementary School Journal*, 93: 373–97.

Ball, D. L. (1991) What's all this talk about 'discourse'? *Arithmetic Teacher*, 39(3): 44–8.

Baroody, A. and Ginsburg, H. P. (1986) The relationship between initial meaningful and mechanical knowledge of arithmetic, in J. Hiebert (ed.) *Conceptual and Procedural Knowledge: the Case of Mathematics*. Hillsdale, NJ: Lawrence Erlbaum Associates.

Baroody, A. J. and Ginsburg, H. P. (1990) Children's mathematical learning: a cognitive view, in R. B. Davis, C. A. Maher and N. Noddings (eds) *Constructivist Views on the Teaching and Learning of Mathematics*. Reston, VA: NCTM.

Becker, J. and Selter, C. (1996) Elementary school practices, in C. Bishop, C. Laborde and K. Keitel (eds) *International Handbook on Mathematics Education*. Dordrecht: Kluwer.

Beishuizen, M. (1997) Mental arithmetic: mental recall or mental strategies? *Mathematics Teaching*, 160: 16–19.

Beishuizen, M. (1999) The empty number line as a new model, in I. Thompson (ed.) *Issues in Teaching Numeracy in Primary Schools*. Buckingham: Open University Press.

Beishuizen, M. and Anghileri, J. (1998) Which mental strategies in the early number curriculum? A comparison of British ideas and Dutch views. *British Educational Research Journal*, 24(5): 519–38.

Beishuizen, M., Felix, E. and Beishuizen, J.J. (1990) A genetic model for tutoring addition and subtraction skills in an adaptive computer program, in J.M. Pieters, K. Breuer and P.R.J. Simons (eds) *Learning Environments – Contributions from Dutch and German Research*. New-York/Heidelberg: Springer Verlag.

Beishuizen, M., Gravemeijer, K.P.E. and Van Lieshout, E.C.D.M. (eds) (1997a) *The Role of Contexts and Models in the Development of Mathematical Strategies and Procedures*. Utrecht: Freudenthal Institute.

Beishuizen, M., Van Putten, C.M. and Van Mulken, F. (1997b) Mental arithmetic and strategy use with indirect number problems up to one hundred. *Learning and Instruction*, 7 (1): 87–106.

Bell, A. (1986) Outcomes of the diagnostic teaching project, in *Proceedings of the Tenth International Conference on the Psychology of Mathematics Education Conference*. London: University of London, Institute of Education.

Bell, A.J. (1993) Some experiments in diagnostic teaching. *Educational Studies in Mathematics*, 24(1), 115–37.

Bierhoff, H. (1996) *Laying the Foundation of Numeracy: a Comparison of Primary School Textbooks in Britain, Germany and Switzerland*. London: National Institute of Economic and Social Research.

Black, P. and Wiliam, D. (1998) *Inside the Black Box: Raising Standards Through Classroom Assessment*. London: King's College, University of London.

Board of Education (1931) *Report of the Consultative Committee on the Primary School*, (Hadow Report). London: HMSO.

Bowers, J. (1995) Designing computer learning environments based on the theory of realistic mathematics education, in L. Miera and D. Carraher (eds) *Proceedings of the Nineteenth Conference of the International Group for the Psychology of Mathematics Education*. Recife, Brazil: PME.

Bramald, R. (1998) Why does 'mental' have to mean 'no fingers, no paper'? *Equals* 4(1): 5–7.

Brousseau, G. (1990) Le contrat didactique: le milieu. *Recherches en Didactique de Mathé-matiques*, 9(3): 308–36.

Brown, A. and Dowling, P. (1998) *Doing Research/Reading Research: a Mode of Interrogation for Education*. London: Falmer Press.

Brown, J. S., Collins, A. and Duguid, P. (1989) Situated cognition and the culture of learning. *Educational Researcher*, 18: 32–42.

Brown, M. (1989) Graded assessment and learning hierarchies in mathematics – an alternative view. *British Educational Research Journal*, 15(2): 121–8.

Buys, K., Boswinkel, M., Meeuwisse, T., Moerlands, F. and Tijhuis, T. (1999) *Wis en Reken*, textbook series for primary school mathematics education. The Netherlands: Baarn.

Carpenter, T. P. (1997) Models for reform of mathematics teaching, in M. Beishuizen, K. P. E. Gravemeijer and E. C. D. M. Van Lieshout (eds) *The Role of Contexts and Models in the Development of Mathematical Strategies and Procedures*. Utrecht: Freudenthal Institute.

Carpenter, T. P. and Fennema, E. (1992) Cognitively guided instruction: building on the knowledge of students and teachers. *International Journal of Research in Education*, 17: 457–70.

Carpenter, T. P., Fennema, E. and Franke, M. L. (1996) Cognitively guided instruction: a knowledge base for reform in primary mathematics instruction. *Elementary School Journal*, 97: 3–20.

Carpenter, T. P., Franke, M. L, Jacobs, V. R., Fennema, E. and Empson, S. B. (1998) A longitudinal study of invention and understanding in children's multidigit addition and subtraction. *Journal for Research in Mathematics Education*, 29(1): 3–20.

Carpenter, T. P. and Moser, J. M. (1983) The acquisition of addition and subtraction concepts, in R. Lesh and M. Landau (eds) *Acquisition of Mathematical Concepts and Processes*. New York: Academic Press.

Carpenter, T. P., Moser, J. M. and Romberg, T. A. (1982) *Addition and Subtraction: a Cognitive Perspective*. Hillsdale, NJ: Lawrence Erlbaum Associates.

Case, R. and Bereiter, C. (1984) From behaviourism to cognitive behaviourism to cognitive development: steps in the evolution of instructional design. *Instructional Science*, 13: 141–58.

Central Advisory Council for Education (CACE) (1967) *Children and their Primary Schools* (Plowden Report). London: HMSO.

Cobb, P. (1991) Reconstructing elementary school mathematics. *Focus on Learning Problems in Mathematics*, 13(2): 3–22.

Cobb, P. (1994) Constructivism in mathematics and science education. *Educational Researcher*, 23(7): 4.

Cobb, P. (1997) Instructional design and reform: a plea for developmental research in context, in M. Beishuizen, K.P.E. Gravemeijer and E.C.D.M. Van Lieshout (eds) *The Role of Contexts and Models in the Development of Mathematical Strategies and Procedures*. Utrecht: Freudenthal Institute.

Cobb, P. and Bauersfeld, H. (1995) *The Emergence of Mathematical Meaning: Interaction in Classroom Cultures*. Hillsdale, NJ: Erlbaum.

Cobb, P. and Merkel, G. (1989) Thinking strategies as an example of teaching arithmetic through problem solving, in P. Trafton (ed.) *New Directions for Elementary School Mathematics*. Reston, VA: National Council of Teachers of Mathematics.

Cobb, P. and Yackel, E. (1996) Constructivist, emergent, and sociocultural perspectives in the context of developmental research. *Educational Psychologist*, 31: 175–90.

Cobb, P., Gravemeijer, K., Yackel, E., McClain, K. and Whitenack, J. (1997) Mathematizing and symbolizing: the emergence of chains of signification in one first-grade classroom, in D. Kirschner, and J. A. Whitson (eds) *Situated Cognition Theory: Social, Semiotic, and Neurological Perspectives*. Hillsdale, NJ: Erlbaum.

Cobb, P., Wood, T., Yackel, E. and McNeal, B. (1992) Characteristics of classroom mathematics traditions: an interactional analysis. *American Educational Research Journal*, 29: 573–604.

Crowther (1959) *A Report of the Central Advisory Council for Education*. London: HMSO.

Dantzig, T. (1954) *Number: the Language of Science*. New York: The Free Press.

De Goeij, E., Nelissen, J. and Van den Heuvel-Panhuizen, M. (1998) TAL *Tussendoelen Annex Leerlijnen. Consultatienota* (TAL Intermediate goals Annex Learning/teaching trajectories. Consultancy report). Utrecht: Freudenthal Institute.

De Jong, R. (1986) *Wiskobas in Methoden* (Wiskobas in textbooks). Utrecht: OW&OC, Utrecht University.

De Wit, C. N. M. (1997) *Over Tussendoelen Gesproken. Tussendoelen als Component van Leerlijnen* (Talking about intermediate goals. Intermediate goals as a component of teaching/learning trajectories). 's-Hertogenbosch: KPC Onderwijs Innovatie Centrum.

Department of Education and Science (DES)/Her Majesty's Inspectors (HMI) (1979) *Mathematics 5–11: A Handbook of Suggestions*. London: HMSO.

Department of Education and Science (DES) (1982) *Inquiry into the Teaching of Mathematics in Schools, Mathematics Counts: Inquiry into the Teaching of Mathematics in Schools* (Cockcroft Report). London: HMSO.

Department of Education and Science (DES) (1985) *Better Schools*. London: HMSO.

Department of Education and Science (DES) (1988) *Mathematics for Ages 5 to 16*. London: DES.

Department of Education and Science (DES) (1989) *Mathematics in the National Curriculum*. London: HMSO.

Department of Education and Science (DES) (1991) *Mathematics in the National Curriculum (1991)*. London: HMSO.

Department for Education (DfE) (1995) *Mathematics in the National Curriculum*. London: HMSO.

Department for Education and Employment (DfEE) (1998a) *The Implementation of the National Numeracy Strategy: the Final Report of the Numeracy Task Force*. London: DfEE.

Department for Education and Employment (DfEE) (1998b) *Teaching: High Status, High Standards. Requirements for Courses of Initial Teacher Training*. London: DfEE.

Department for Education and Employment (DfEE) (1999a) *Framework for Teaching Mathematics from Reception to Year 6*. London: DfEE.

Department for Education and Employment (DfEE) (1999b) *The National Curriculum: Handbook for Primary Teachers in England*. London: QCA.

Department for Education and Employment (DfEE) (1999c) Press release 10/99 (11/1/99) Times table key in £55 million numeracy drive. London: DfEE.

Desforges, C. and Cockburn, A. (1987) *Understanding the Mathematics Teacher – A Study of Practice in First Schools*. London: Falmer.

Elbers, E. and Streefland, L. (1997) De klas als onderzoeksgemeenschap (The classroom as a research community), in C. van den Boer and M. Dolk (eds) *Naar een Balans in de Reken-wiskundeles; Interactie, Oefenen, Uitleggen en Zelfstandig Werken*. Utrecht: Panama/Freudenthal Institut.

Ernest, P. (1985) The number line as a teaching aid. *Educational Studies in Mathematics*, 16: 411–24.

Felix, E. J. H. M. (1992) Learner-based versus expert-based tutoring of arithmetic skills. PhD dissertation, Free University, Amsterdam, the Netherlands.

Fischbein, E., Deri, M., Nello, M. and Marino, M. (1985) The role of implicit models in solving verbal problems in multiplication and division. *Journal for Research in Mathematics Education,* 16: 3–17.

Fitzgerald, A. (1985) *New Technology and Mathematics in Employment.* Birmingham: University of Birmingham Faculty of Education.

Foxman, D. and Beishuizen, M. (1999) Untaught mental calculation methods used by 11-year-olds: some evidence from the APU Survey in 1987. *Mathematics in School,* November.

Foxman, D., Ruddock, G., McCallum, I. and Schagen, I. (1991) *APU Mathematics Monitoring – Phase 2.* London: School Examinations and Assessment Council.

Freudenthal, H. (1968) Why to teach mathematics so as to be useful. *Educational Studies in Mathematics,* 1: 3–8.

Freudenthal, H. (1971) Geometry between the devil and the deep sea. *Educational Studies in Mathematics,* 3: 413–35.

Freudenthal, H. (1973) *Mathematics as an Educational Task.* Dordrecht: Reidel Publishing Company.

Freudenthal, H. (1977) Antwoord door Prof. Dr H. Freudenthal na het verlenen van het eredoctoraat (Answer by Prof. Dr H. Freudenthal upon being granted an honorary doctorate). *Euclides,* 52: 336–8.

Freudenthal, H. (1979) Structuur der wiskunde en wiskundige structuren; een onderwijskundige analyse (Structure of mathematics and mathematical structures; an educational analysis). *Pedagogische Studiën,* 56(2): 51–60.

Freudenthal, H. (1983) *Didactical Phenomenology of Mathematical Structures.* Dordrecht: Reidel.

Freudenthal, H. (1991) *Revisiting Mathematics Education.* Dordrecht: Kluwer Academic Publishers.

Fuson, K.C., Smith, S.T. and Cicero, A.M.L. (1997) Supporting Latino first graders' ten-structured thinking in urban classrooms. *Journal for Research in Mathematics Education,* 28: 738–66.

Fuson, K.C., Wearne, D., Hiebert, J. *et al.* (1997) Children's conceptual structures for multidigit numbers and methods of multidigit addition and subtraction. *Journal for Research in Mathematics Education,* 28(2): 130–62.

Gee, J.P. (1996) *Social Linguistics and Literacies: Ideology in Discourses,* 2nd edn. London: Falmer Press.

Girling, M. (1977) Towards a definition of basic numeracy. *Mathematics Teaching,* 81: 4–5.

Gravemeijer, K. (1994a) Educational development and educational research in mathematics education. *Journal for Research in Mathematics Education,* 25(5): 443–71.

Gravemeijer, K. (1994b) *Developing Realistic Mathematics Education.* Utrecht: CD-ß Press / Freudenthal Institute.

Gravemeijer, K. (1997a) Instructional design for reform in mathematics education, in M. Beishuizen, K.P.E. Gravemeijer and E.C.D.M. Van Lieshout (eds) *The Role of Contexts and Models in the Development of Mathematical Strategies and Procedures.* Utrecht: Freudenthal Institute.

Gravemeijer, K. (1997b) Mediating between concrete and abstract, in T. Nunes and P. Bryant (eds) *Learning and Teaching Mathematics – An International Perspective.* Hove, East Sussex: Psychology Press Ltd.

Gravemeijer, K., Cobb, P., Bowers, J. and Whitenack, J. (2000) Symbolizing, modeling, and instructional design, in P. Cobb, E. Yackel and K. McClain (eds) *Communicating and Symbolizing in Mathematics: Perspectives on Discourse, Tools, and Instructional Design.* Mahwah, NJ: Lawrence Erlbaum Associates.

Gravemeijer, K., Van den Heuvel-Panhuizen, M., Van Donselaar, G. *et al.* (1993) *Methoden in het Reken-wiskundeonderwijs, een Rijke Context voor Vergelijkend Onderzoek* (Textbook series in mathematics education, a rich context for comparative research). Utrecht: CD-ß Press/Freudenthal Institute, Utrecht University.

Gregg, J. (1992) Instructional activity design and theory. Unpublished manuscript, Purdue University, West Lafayette, IN.

Groot, W. (1999) *Draagvlak voor Tussendoelen* (Support for Intermediate Goals). Den Haag: OC&W.

Harries, T. and Sutherland, R. (1999) Primary school mathematics textbooks: an international comparison, in I. Thompson (ed.) *Issues in Teaching Numeracy in Primary Schools*. Buckingham: Open University Press.

Hart, K. (ed.) (1981) *Children's Understanding of Mathematics: 11–16*. London: John Murray.

Hart, K. M. (1984) *Ratio: Children's Strategies and Errors. A Report of the Strategies and Errors in Secondary Mathematics Project*. Windsor: NFER-Nelson.

Hart, K. (1989) Place value: subtraction, in D.C. Johnson (ed.) *Children's Mathematical Frameworks 8–13*. Windsor: NFER-Nelson.

Hart, K., Johnson, D.C., Brown, M., Dickson, L. and Clarkson, R. (1989) *Children's Mathematical Frameworks 8–13: a Study of Classroom Teaching*. Windsor: NFER-Nelson.

Hart, K., Brown, M., Kerslake, D., Kuchemann, D. and Ruddock, G. (1985) *Cheslea Diagnostic Mathematics Tests*. London: NFER-Nelson.

Heibert, J., Carpenter, T. P., Fennema, E. *et al.* (1997) *Making Sense: Teaching and Learning Mathematics with Understanding*. Portsmouth, NH: Heinemann.

Holt, J. (1982) *How Children Fail*, revised edn. New York: Dell Publishing Co.

Hope, J. A. and Sherrill, J.M. (1987) Characteristics of unskilled and skilled mental calculators. *Journal for Research in Mathematics Education,* 18(2): 98–111.

Howson, A. G. (1982) *A History of Mathematics Education in England*. Cambridge: Cambridge University Press.

Ifrah, G. (1987) *From One to Zero. A Universal History of Numbers*. New York: Penguin Books.

Iran-Nejad, A., McKeachie, W. J. and Berliner, D. C. (1990) The multisource nature of learning. *Review of Educational Research,* 60(4): 509–15.

Janssen, J., Bokhove, J. and Kraemer, J-M. (1992) *Leerlingvolgsysteem Rekenen-Wiskunde 1* (System for following students, Arithmetic Mathematics 1). Arnhem: CITO.

Kieran, C. (1990) Cognitive processes involved in learning school algebra, in P. Nesher and J. Kilpatrick (eds) *Mathematics and Cognition: a Research Synthesis by the International Group for the Psychology of Mathematics Education* (ICMI Study Series). Cambridge: Cambridge University Press.

Klein, A. S., Beishuizen, M. and Treffers, A. (1998) The empty number line in Dutch second grades: realistic versus gradual programme design. *Journal for Research in Mathematics Education,* 29 (4): 443–64.

Krummheuer, G. (1995) The ethnography of argumentation, in P. Cobb and H. Bauersfeld (eds) *The Emergence of Mathematical Meaning: Interaction in Classroom Cultures*. Hillsdale, NJ: Erlbaum.

Lampert, M. (1990) When the problem is not the question and the solution is not the answer: mathematical knowing and teaching. *American Educational Research Journal,* 27: 29–63.

Lave, J. (1990) The culture of acquisition and the practice of understanding, in J. W. Stigler, R. A. Shweder and G. Herdt (eds) *Cultural Psychology*. Cambridge: Cambridge University Press.

Lave, J. (1988) *Cognition in Practice: Mind, Mathematics and Culture in Everyday Life*. Cambridge: Cambridge University Press.

Lave, J. (1991) Situating learning in communities of practice, in L. B. Resnick, J. M. Levine and S. D. Teasley (eds) *Perspectives on Socially Shared Cognition*. Washington DC: American Psychological Association.

Lave, J. and Wenger, E. (1991*) Situated Learning: Legitimate Peripheral Participation*. Cambridge: Cambridge University Press.

Lindquist, M. M. (1997) Forword, in J. Heibert, T. P. Carpenter, E. Fennema *et al*. *Making Sense: Teaching and Learning Mathematics with Understanding*. Portsmouth, NH: Heinemann.

McIntosh, A. (1981) When will they ever learn? (article reprinted from *Forum*, 19(3)), in A. Floyd (ed.) *Developing Mathematical Thinking*. London: Addison-Wesley, for The Open University.

Menne, J. (1996/1997/1998) *Oefenen in de Rekenkring* (Practising in the arithmetic circle), (internal publication). Utrecht: Freudenthal Institute.

Menne, J. (1997) Op Waku-waku kun je rekenen (You can count on Waku-waku). *Willem Bartjens*, 16(5): 12–15.

Menne, J. and Veenman, I. (1997) (Re)productief oefenen in de rekenkring ((Re)productive practice in the arithmetic circle), in C. van den Boer and M. Dolk (eds) *Naar een Balans in de Reken-wiskundeles: Interactie, Oefenen, Uitleggen en Zelfstandig Werken* (To a balance in the arithmetic mathematics class: interaction, practice, explanation and working independent). Utrecht: Freudenthal Institute.

Merttens, R., Kirkby, D. and Lumb, D. (1996) *Abacus*. Aylesbury: Ginn.

Millett, A. and Johnson, D. C. (1996) Solving teachers' problems? The role of the commercial mathematics scheme, in D.C. Johnson and A. Millett (eds) *Implementing the Mathematics National Curriculum*. London: Paul Chapman.

Mulligan, J. and Mitchelmore, M. (1997) Young children's intuitive models of multiplication and division. *Journal for Research in Mathematics Education,* 28(3): 309–30.

Mullis, I.V.S., Martin, M.O., Beaton, A.E. *et al*. (1997) *Mathematics Achievement in the Primary School Years: IEA's Third International Mathematics and Science Study (TIMSS)*. Chestnut Hill, MA: Boston College.

Murray, H., Olivier, A. and Human, P. (1991) Young children's division strategies, in F. Furinghetti (ed.) *Proceedings of the Fifteenth International Conference for the Psychology of Mathematics Education*, Vol. 3, Assissi.

National Council of Teachers of Mathematics (1989) *Curriculum and Evaluation Standards for School Mathematics*. Reston, VA: NCTM.

National Council of Teachers of Mathematics (1999) *Standards 2000* (draft version). Reston, VA: NCTM.

National Curriculum Council (NCC) (1988) *Mathematics in the National Curriculum*. York: NCC.

National Curriculum Council (NCC) (1989) *Mathematics Non-Statutory Guidance*. York: NCC.

National Curriculum Mathematics Working Group (1987) *Interim Report*. London: DES.

NCTM Research Advisory Committee (1988) NCTM Curriculum and evaluation standards for school mathematics: responses from the research community. *Journal for Research in Mathematics Education,* 19: 338–44.

NCTM Research Advisory Committee (1996) Justification and reform. *Journal for Research in Mathematics Education,* 27(5): 516–20.

Newman, D., Griffin, P. and Cole, M. (1989) *The Construction Zone: Working for Cognitive Change in School*. Cambridge: Cambridge University Press.

Newman, J. R. (1956) *Men and Numbers* (The World of Mathematics, Vol. 1), New York: Simon and Schuster.

Nuffield Mathematics Project/British Council (1978a) *Mathematics: from Primary to Secondary*. Edinburgh: Chambers/Murray/Wiley.

Nuffield Mathematics Project/British Council (1978b) *Mathematics: the First 3 Years*. Edinburgh: Chambers/Murray.

Nuffield Mathematics Project/British Council (1978c) *Mathematics: the Later Primary Years*. Edinburgh: Chambers/Murray/Wiley.

Office for Standards in Education (Ofsted) (1993) *The Teaching and Learning of Number in Primary Schools*. London: HMSO.

Office for Standards in Education (Ofsted) (1998) *Educational Research – A Critique*. London: Ofsted.

Peterson, P. L., Swing, S. R., Stark, K. D. and Waas, G. A. (1984) Students' cognitions and time on task during mathematics instruction. *American Educational Research Journal*, 21: 487–515.

Plunkett, S. (1979) Decomposition and all that rot. *Mathematics in School*, 8(3): 2–5.

Qualifications and Curriculum Authority (QCA) (1999a) *Teaching Mental Calculation Strategies*. London: QCA.

Qualifications and Curriculum Authority (QCA) (1999b) *Standards in Mathematics: Exemplification of Key Learning Objectives from Reception to Year 6*. London: QCA.

Reynolds, D. and Farrell, S. (1996) *Worlds Apart? A Review of International Surveys of Educational Achievement Involving England*. London: HMSO.

Reys, R., Reys, B., Nohda, N. and Emiro, H. (1995) Mental computation performance and strategy use of Japanese students in grades 2, 4, 6 and 8. *Journal for Research in Mathematics Education*, 26(4): 304–26.

Richards, J. (1991) Mathematical discussions, in E. von Glasersfeld (ed.) *Radical Constructivism in Mathematics Education*. Dordrecht: Kluwer.

Robitaille, D. F. and Garden, R. A. (1989) *The IEA Study of Mathematics II: Contexts and Outcomes of School Mathematics*. Oxford: Pergamon Press.

Rogoff, B. (1990) *Apprenticeship in Thinking: Cognitive Development in Social Context*. New York: Oxford University Press.

Rogoff, B. (1995) Evaluating development in the process of participation: theory, methods, and practice building on each other, in E. Amsel and A. Renninger (eds) *Change and Development: Issues of Theory, Application and Method*. Hillsdale, NJ: Lawrence Erlbaum.

Rogoff, B. and Lave, J. (eds) (1984) *Everyday Cognition: Its Development in Social Context*. Cambridge, MA: Harvard University Press.

Rousham, L. (1997) Jumping on an empty number line. *Primary Mathematics and Science Questions*, 2: 6–8.

Ruthven, K. (1998) The use of mental, written and calculator strategies of numerical computation by upper-primary pupils within a 'calculator-aware' number curriculum. *British Educational Research Journal*, 24(1): 21–42.

Ruthven, K. (1999a) The pedagogy of calculator use, in I. Thompson (ed.) *Issues in Teaching Numeracy in Primary Schools*. Buckingham: Open University Press.

Ruthven, K. (1999b) Constructing a calculator-aware number curriculum: the challenges of systematic design and systemic reform, in O. Zaslavsky (ed.) *Proceedings of the 23rd Conference of the International Group for the Psychology of Mathematics Education*. Haifa: Technion.

Ruthven, K. and Chaplin, D. (1997) The calculator as a cognitive tool: upper-primary pupils tackling a realistic number problem. *International Journal of Computers for Mathematical Learning*, 2(2): 93–124.

Ruthven, K., Rousham, L. and Chaplin, D. (1997) The long-term influence of a 'calcula-tor-aware' number curriculum on pupils' mathematical attainments and attitudes in the primary phase. *Research Papers in Education*, 12(3): 249–82.

Saxe, G. B. (1989) Transfer of learning across cultural practice. *Cognition and Instruction*, 6(4): 331–66.

Saxe, G. B. (1991) *Culture and Cognitive Development: Studies in Mathematical Understanding*. Hillsdale, NJ: Lawrence Erlbaum Associates.

School Curriculum and Assessment Authority (SCAA) (1995) *Report on the 1995 Key Stage 2 Tests and Assessment Tasks in English Mathematics and Science*. London: SCAA.

School Curriculum and Assessment Authority (SCAA) (1997a) *The Use of Calculators at Key Stages 1–3*. London: SCAA.

School Curriculum and Assessment Authority (SCAA) (1997b) *The Use of Calculators at Key Stage 1*. Unpublished report to the Secretary of State for Education and Employment.

School Curriculum and Assessment Authority (SCAA) (1997c) *The Teaching and Assessment of Number at Key Stages 1–3*. Discussion Paper No. 10. London: SCAA, Ma/97/762.

Sfard, A. (1998) On two metaphors for learning and the dangers of choosing just one. *Educational Researcher*, 27: 4–13.

Shuard, H. (1986a) *Primary Mathematics Today and Tomorrow*. York: Longman for SCDC.

Shuard, H. (1986b) *PrIME Newsletter 2*, Cambridge, Homerton College.

Shuard, H., Walsh, A., Goodwin, J. and Worcester, V. (1991) *Calculators, Children and Mathematics: the Calculator-Aware Number Curriculum*. Hemel Hempstead: Simon & Schuster, for the NCC.

Silver, E., Shapiro, L. J. and Deutch, A. (1993) Sense making and the solution of division problems involving remainders: an examination of middle school students' solution processes and their interpretation of solutions. *Journal for Research in Mathematics Education*, 24: 159–66.

Simon, M. A. (1995) Reconstructing mathematics pedagogy from a constructivist perspective. *Journal for Research in Mathematics Education*, 26: 114–45.

Skemp, R. (1976) Relational understanding and instrumental understanding. *Arithmetic Teacher*, 77: 20–6.

Slavenburg, A. and Krooneman, P.J. (1999) *Leerlijnen en Tussendoelen in het Reken-wiskundeonderwijs Gepeild* (Learning/teaching trajectories and intermediate goals gauged). Amsterdam: Regioplan.

Steffe, L. P. (1994) Children's multiplying schemes, in G. Harel and J. Confrey (eds) *The Development of Multiplicative Reasoning in the Learning of Mathematics*. Albany, NY: State University of New York Press.

Steffe, L. P., Cobb, P. and von Glasersfeld, E. (1988) *Young Children's Construction of Arithmetical Meanings and Strategies*. New York: Springer-Verlag.

Steffe, L. P. and Kieren, T. (1994) Radical constructivism and mathematics education. *Journal for Research in Mathematics Education*, 25: 711–33.

Steffe, L. P., von Glasersfeld, E., Richards, J. and Cobb, P. (1983) *Children's Counting Types: Philosophy, Theory and Application*. New York: Praeger Scientific.

Steinberg, R. M. (1985) Instruction on derived facts/strategies in addition and subtraction. *Journal for Research in Mathematics Education*, 16(5): 337–55.

Stephan, M. L. (1998) Supporting the development of one first-grade classroom's conceptions of measurement: analyzing students' learning in social context. Unpublished doctoral dissertation, Vanderbilt University, Nashville, TN.

Stephan, M., Cobb, P., Gravemeijer, K. and McClain, K. (1998) Reconceptualizing measurement investigations: supporting students' learning in social context. Paper presented at the annual meeting of the American Educational Research Association, San Diego, CA, April.

Straker, A. (1996) The National Numeracy Project, *Equals*, 2: 14–15.

Straker, A. (1999a) The National Numeracy Project: 1996–99, in I. Thompson (ed.) *Issues in Teaching Numeracy in Primary Schools*. Buckingham: Open University Press.

Straker, A. (1999b) Written methods: The National Numeracy Strategy's approach. Notes accompanying talks to mathematics educators, London, May.

Streefland, L. (1985) Wiskunde als activiteit en de realiteit als bron (Mathematics as an activity and the reality as a source). *Tijdschrift voor Nederlands Wiskundeonderwijs (Nieuwe Wiskrant)*, 5 (1): 60–7.

Streefland, L. (1991) *Fractions in Realistic Mathematics Education. A Paradigm of Developmental Research*. Dordrecht: Kluwer Academic Publishers.

Streefland, L. (1996) Learning from history for teaching in the future. Lecture held at ICME-8, Sevilla, Spain, July.

Street, B. (1999) Literacy 'events' and literacy 'practices': theory and practice in the 'New Literacy Studies', in K. Jones and M. Martin-Jones (eds) *Multilingual Literacies: Comparative Perspectives on Research and Practice*. Amsterdam: John Benjamin.

Swan, M. (1990) Becoming numerate: developing conceptual structures, in S. Willis (ed.) *Being Numerate: What Counts?* Victoria, Australia: Australian Council for Educational Research.

Sweller, J. (1988) Cognitive load during problem solving: effects on learning. *Cognitive Science*, 12: 257–85.

TAL Team (1998) *Tussendoelen Annex Leerlijnen. Hele Getallen. Onderbouw Basisschool* (Intermediate goals annex learning/teaching trajectories. Whole number. Lower grades in primary school). Utrecht: Freudenthal Institute in collaboration with SLO and CED.

Tate, T. (1854) *The Philosophy of Education*. London.

Thompson, I. (1994) Young children's idiosyncratic written algorithms for addition. *Educational Studies in Mathematics*, 26 (4): 323–45.

Thompson, I. (1997a) The early years number curriculum today, in I. Thompson (ed.) *Teaching and Learning Early Number*. Buckingham: Open University Press.

Thompson, I. (1997b) Mental and written algorithms: can the gap be bridged?, in I. Thompson (ed.) *Teaching and Learning Early Number*. Buckingham: Open University Press.

Thompson, I. (1999a) Prop or tool? *Times Educational Supplement*, 22 March.

Thompson, I. (1999b) Written methods of calculation, in I. Thompson (ed.) *Issues in Teaching Numeracy in Primary Schools*. Buckingham: Open University Press.

Thompson, I. and Smith, F. (1999) *Mental Calculation Strategies for the Addition and Subtraction of 2-Digit Numbers – Final Report March 1999*. University of Newcastle: Department of Education.

Treffers, A. (1978) *Wiskobas doelgericht* (Wiskobas goal-directed). Utrecht: IOWO.

Treffers, A. (1987a) Integrated column arithmetic according to progressive schematisation. *Educational Studies in Mathematics*, 18(2): 125–45.

Treffers, A. (1987b) *Three Dimensions. A Model of Goal and Theory Description in Mathematics Instruction – The Wiskobas Project*. Dordrecht: Reidel Publishing Company.

Treffers, A. (1991a) Didactical background of a mathematics program for primary education, in L. Streefland (ed.) *Realistic Mathematics Education in Primary School*. Utrecht: Cd-ß Press.

Treffers, A. (1991b) Realistic mathematics education in the Netherlands 1980–1990, in L. Streefland (ed.) *Realistic Mathematics Education in Primary School*. Utrecht: CD-ß Press/Freudenthal Institute, Utrecht University.

Treffers, A. (1997) *Rekenonderwijs naar Menselijke Maat: Gedifferentieerd en Klassikaal: een Onjuiste Tegenstelling* (Arithmetic education to human measurement / proportion: Differentiated and group teaching: a mistaken antithesis). *Willem Bartjens*, 17(1): 5–8.

Treffers, A. (1998) *Tussendoelen Annex Leerlijnen: Hele Getallen Onderbouw Basisschool* (Intermediate Goals Annex Learning/Teaching Trajectories: Whole Number Lower Grades in Primary School). Utrecht: Freudenthal, SLO and CED.

Treffers, A. and Beishuizen, M. (1999) Realistic mathematics education in the Netherlands, in I. Thompson (ed.) *Issues in Teaching Numeracy in Primary Schools*. Buckingham: Open University Press.

Treffers, A., De Moor, E. and Feijs, E. (1989) *Proeve van een Nationaal Programma voor het Reken-wiskundeonderwijs op de Basisschool. Deel I. Overzicht Einddoelen* (Design of a national curriculum for mathematics education at primary school. Part I. Overview of goals). Tilburg: Zwijsen.

Treffers, A. and De Moor, E. (1990) *Proeve van een Nationaal Programma voor het Reken-Wiskunde-onderwijs op de Basisschool. Deel 2: Basisvaardigheden en Cijferen* (Specimen of a national programme for primary mathematics teaching. Part 2: Basic mental skills and written algorithms). Tilburg, the Netherlands: Zwijsen.

Treffers, A., Streefland, L. and De Moor, E. (1996) *Proeve van een Nationaal Programma voor het Reken-wiskundeonderwijs op de Basisschool. Deel 3B. Kommagetallen* (Design of a national curriculum for mathematics education at primary school. Part 3B. Decimal numbers). Tilburg: Zwijsen.

Treffers, A., van den Heuvel-Panhuizen, M. and Buys, K. (eds) (1999) *Jonge Kinderen Leven Rekenen. Tussendoelen Annex Leerlijnen. Hele Getallen Onderbouw Basisschool* (Young children learning/teaching arithmetic. Intermediate goals annex learning/teaching trajectories. Whole number. Lower grades in primary school). Groningen: Wolters-Noordhoff.

Van den Boer, C. (1997) Allochtone leerlingen in het wiskundeonderwijs (Immigrants' children in mathematics education). *Tijdschrift voor Nascholing en Onderzoek van het Reken-wiskundeonderwijs*, 15(4): 27–34.

Van den Brink, J.F. (1989) *Realistisch Rekenonderwijs aan Jonge Kinderen* (Realistic arithmetic education to young children). Utrecht: OW&OC, Utrecht University.

Van den Heuvel-Panhuizen, M. (1995) A representational model in a long term learning process — the didactical use of models in Realistic Mathematics Education. Paper presented at the 1995 American Educational Research Association, San Francisco, CA, April.

Van den Heuvel-Panhuizen, M. (1996) *Assessment and Realistic Mathematics Education*. Utrecht: CD-ß Press/Freudenthal Institute, Utrecht University.

Van den Heuvel-Panhuizen, M. (1998) Realistic Mathematics Education: work in progress, in T. Breiteig and G. Brekke (eds) *Theory into Practice in Mathematics Education*. Kristiansand, Norway: Faculty of Mathematics and Sciences.

Van den Heuvel-Panhuizen, M. and Vermeer, H. (1999) *Verschillen Tussen Meisjes en Jongens Bij het vak Rekenen-wiskunde op de Basisschool* (Differences between boys and girls in primary schools mathematics). Utrecht: CD-ß Press/Freudenthal Institute, Utrecht University.

Webber, B. and Haigh, J. (1999) *How to be Brilliant at Mental Arithmetic*. Dunstable: Brilliant Publications.

Whitney, H. (1973) Are we off the track in teaching mathematical concepts?, in A. G. Howson (ed.) *Developments in Mathematical Education*. Cambridge: Cambridge University Press.

Wigley, A. (1997) Approaching number through language, in I. Thompson (ed.) *Teaching and Learning Early Number*. Buckingham: Open University Press.

Yackel, E. (1992) The evolution of second grade children's understanding of what constitutes an explanation in a mathematics class. Paper presented at the Seventh International Congress of Mathematics Education, Quebec City, August.

Yackel, E. (1995a) Children's talk in inquiry mathematics classrooms, in P. Cobb and H. Bauersfeld (eds) *The Emergence of Mathematical Meaning: Interaction in Classroom Cultures*. Hilldsale, NJ: Erlbaum.

Yackel, E. (1995b) The classroom teaching experiment. Unpublished manuscript, Purdue University, West Lafayette, IN.

Yackel, E. (1997) Explanation as an interactive accomplishment: a case study of one second-grade mathematics classroom. Paper presented at the annual meeting of the American Educational Research Association, Chicago, IL, April.

Yackel, E. and Cobb, P. (1996) Sociomathematical norms, argumentation, and autonomy in mathematics. *Journal for Research in Mathematics Education*, 27: 458–77.

Yackel, E. and Cobb, P. (1995) Classroom socio-mathematical norms and intellectual autonomy, in L. Meira and D. Carraher (eds) *Proceedings of the Nineteenth International Conference for the Psychology of Mathematics Education*. Recife, Brazil: Program Committee of the 19th PME Conference. Volume 3: 264–71.

Zaslovsky, C. (1984) How Africa counts, in D.M. Campbell and J.C. Higgins (eds) *Africa Counts*. Belmont: Wadsworth.

Name index

Subject index

ISSUES IN TEACHING NUMERACY IN PRIMARY SCHOOLS
Ian Thompson (ed.)

This timely book provides a detailed and comprehensive overview of the teaching and learning of numeracy in primary schools. It will be particularly helpful to teachers, mathematics co-ordinators and numeracy consultants involved in the implementation of the National Numeracy Strategy. It presents an accessible guide to current British and Dutch research into numeracy teaching. Leading researchers describe their findings and discuss implications for practising teachers. The projects include studies of effective teachers of numeracy and ICT and numeracy, an evaluation of international primary textbooks, assessment, using and applying mathematics, and family numeracy. The book also includes chapters on pedagogy, focusing on the teaching of mental calculation; the transition from mental to written algorithms; the place of the empty number line; and the use of the calculator as a teaching aid. Most chapters include practical suggestions for helping teachers develop aspects of their numeracy teaching skills.

Contents
Section 1: Numeracy: issues past and present – Swings of the pendulum – Numeracy matters: contemporary policy issues in the teaching of mathematics – Realistic mathematics education in the Netherlands – The National Numeracy Project: 1996–99 – Section 2: Curriculum and research project issues – Primary school mathematics textbooks: an international comparison – Using and applying mathematics at Key Stage 1 – Family numeracy – It ain't (just) what you do: effective teachers of numeracy – ICT and numeracy in primary schools – Section 3: Assessment issues – Choosing a good test question – Context problems and assessment: ideas from the Netherlands – Section 4: Pedagogical issues – Getting your head around mental calculation – The empty number line as a new model – Written methods of calculation – Issues in teaching multiplication and division – The pedagogy of calculator use – Index.

Contributors
Julia Anghileri, Mike Askew, Meindert Beishuizen, Margaret Brown, Gill Close, Charles Desforges, Tony Harries, Marja van den Heuvel-Panhuizen, Steven Higgins, Martin Hughes, Ruth Merttens, Christine Mitchell, Daniel Muijs, David Reynolds, Kenneth Ruthven, Anita Straker, Rosamund Sutherlands, Ian Thompson, Adrian Treffers.

224 pp   0 335 20324 8 (Paperback)   0 335 20325 6 (Hardback)

TEACHING AND LEARNING EARLY NUMBER

Ian Thompson (ed.)

. . . the book includes plenty of clear suggestions for practical action in the classroom . . . Don't be fooled by the comfortable familiarity of the title. This is a radical and influential book, that ought to be read and acted upon, and that will continue to be quoted and discussed for some time to come.

Times Educational Supplement

. . . a well-produced and effectively edited examination of a wide range of issues concerned with children's acquisition of the fundamental concepts of number.

Mathematics in School

- Is it time to question the traditional approach to the teaching of early number?
- What does research tell us about how young children acquire number concepts?
- What can teachers do to facilitate the development of number understanding?

This book presents an accessible guide to current research into the teaching and learning of early number concepts. The beliefs and number understanding of nursery and reception children are examined, and the book provides a detailed account of the role of counting in the acquisition of number understanding and in the development of derived fact strategies for addition, subtraction and multiplication. Practical activities are described to help teachers develop various aspects of number understanding.

Contents

Prologue: The early years number curriculum today – Section 1: The numerical understanding and beliefs of pre-school children – Children's beliefs about counting – Children's early learning of number in school and out – Section 2: The place of counting in number development – The importance of counting – Uses of counting in multiplication and division – The role of counting in derived fact strategies – Compressing the counting process: developing a flexible interpretation of symbols – Section 3: Written number work – 'When should they start doing sums?' A critical consideration of the 'emergent mathematics' approach – Writing and number – Mental and written algorithms: can the gap be bridged? – Section 4: Perspectives on teaching number – Approaching number through language – Developing young children's counting skills – The role of calculators – Teaching for strategies – Epilogues: The early years number curriculum tomorrow – Index.

Contributors

Julie Anghileri, Carol Aubrey, Janet Duffin, Sue Gifford, Eddie Gray, Effie Maclellan, Penny Munn, Ian Sugarman, Ian Thompson, Alan Wigley.

176 pp   0 335 19851 1 (Paperback)   0 335 19852 X (Hardback)

NUMERACY AND BEYOND

Martin Hughes, Charles Desforges and Christine Mitchell with Clive Carré

One of the fundamental problems in education is that of applying skills and knowledge that learners have gained in one context to problems they encounter in another. This is particularly so in mathematics, where the problems encountered by learners in applying mathematical knowledge are well documented.

Using and applying mathematics has been a central component of the National Curriculum in mathematics. However, the National Numeracy Strategy has adopted a new approach, in which 'using and applying' is integrated throughout the mathematics curriculum. This book aims to help teachers develop their understanding and practice in this crucial area. It is based on the findings of a major research study, funded by the Nuffield Foundation, in which a group of primary teachers worked closely with the research team to develop their thinking and practice. The book provides a clear conceptual analysis of the problem of application, together with extensive examples of ways in which teachers can address it in their classrooms at Key Stages 1 and 2. A novel feature of the book is that it includes first-hand accounts of practice in Japanese classrooms, and outlines what teachers in the UK and elsewhere may learn from Japanese methods.

Contents
Introduction – The problem of application – Application in the mathematics curriculum – Teachers' ideas about application – Teaching for application at Key Stage 1 – Teaching for application at Key Stage 2 – Teaching for application in Japan – Application in theory and practice – References – Index.

136 pp   0 335 20129 6 (Paperback)   0 335 20130 X (Hardback)